MERIDIAN

Crossing Aesthetics

Werner Hamacher

Editor

*Stanford
University
Press*

———

*Stanford
California*
2001

SPEECH ACTS IN LITERATURE

J. Hillis Miller

Stanford University Press
Stanford, California

© 2001 by the Board of Trustees of the
Leland Stanford Junior University

Printed in the United States of America
on acid-free, archival-quality paper.

Library of Congress Cataloging-in-Publication Data

Miller, J. Hillis
    Speech acts in literature / J. Hillis Miller.
    p.   cm. — (Meridian, crossing aesthetics)
    Includes bibliographical references and index.
    ISBN 0-8047-4215-4 (alk. paper)—
    ISBN 0-8047-4216-2 (pbk. : alk. paper)
      1. Criticism—History—20th century.
2. Speech acts (Linguistics) I. Title.
II. Meridian (Stanford, Calif.)
PN68 .M55   2001
801'.95'0904—dc21   2001020687

Original printing 2001

Last figure below indicates year of this printing:
10   09   08   07   06   05   04   03   02   01

Typeset by James P. Brommer
in 10.9/13 Garamond and Lithos display

Contents

Preface   *ix*

Introduction   1

§ 1   J. L. Austin   6

§ 2   Jacques Derrida   63

§ 3   Paul de Man   140

§ 4   Passion Performative: Derrida,
      Wittgenstein, Austin   155

§ 5   Marcel Proust   177

      Coda: Allegory as Speech Act   214

      Notes   219

      Index   233

Preface

This book began as what I imagined would be a brief introductory chapter to a book I have been writing, "Speech Acts in Henry James." It seemed necessary to begin with a short introduction to speech-act theory in its relation to literature. I chose Austin, Derrida, and de Man as examples of important speech-act theorists that differ quite a bit from one another. As I might have expected, my attempt to read their work carefully from this perspective and to explain what they say about speech acts to myself and to potential readers of my book on James got longer and longer and more and more absorbing. Ultimately, that brief introductory chapter became a book on its own, this very one here you are now holding in your hands. I have taken great pleasure in writing this book. This pleasure has been not purely intellectual or "theoretical." Austin's *How to Do Things with Words*, Derrida's *Limited Inc*, de Man's various essays on speech acts, Austin's essays "Other Minds" and "Pretending," Wittgenstein's *Blue and Brown Books*, and the three episodes in Proust's *A la recherche du temps perdu* I have chosen to read as exempla of speech-act "theory" are wonderful texts. They are often powerfully ironic and funny while being deeply serious (who could doubt it?). I hope my readers enjoy my report on these writings as much as I enjoyed my adventures in exploring and explaining them, following a somewhat sinuous track from page to page. I warmly thank all those who listened to early versions of this material in lectures and seminars at the University of California at Irvine and at other universities here and there around the world. My listeners can in no way be blamed for what I say here, but that saying is the better for their comments and responses.

J. Hillis Miller
Irvine, California
November 20, 1999

SPEECH ACTS
IN LITERATURE

Introduction

How to "Bog, by Logical Stages, Down"

What are speech acts? What is their role "in literature"? The phrase "speech acts in literature" has at least three possible and by no means necessarily compatible meanings. All meaningful utterances are in a sense acts, though just what is meant by "act" in this case is by no means transparent. I am using the term "speech acts" to mean speech that acts, that does something with words. How problematic that is I shall, with Austin's help and then with Derrida's and de Man's, proceed to show. That is a promise.

"Speech acts in literature" can mean speech acts that are uttered within literary works, for example promises, lies, excuses, declarations, imprecations, requests for forgiveness, apologies, pardons, and the like said or written by the characters or by the narrator in a novel. It can also mean a possible performative dimension of a literary work taken as a whole. Writing a novel may be a way of doing things with words. The title of Anthony Trollope's *Can You Forgive Her?* asks not only whether Plantagenet Palliser can forgive his wife's near adultery and John Gray can forgive Alice Vavasor (inside the novel) but also whether we as readers can forgive the two women (appraising the novel from outside), just as the media drama of President Clinton's impeachment turned on whether Clinton's wife, his political associates, and the "American people" could or could not forgive him for his "scandalous affair." Private forgiveness or pardon in both cases becomes a question of public forgiveness.

I

More obscurely, however, and less idiomatically, the "in literature" in "speech acts in literature" might be taken as parallel to "in
drag" or "in costume" or "incognito" or Andrew Marvell's "anti-
podes in shoes," his witty term for the Australians who "shod their
heads in their canoes." A "normal" or "standard" speech act may
disguise itself as literature, and vice versa. How would you know
when you had a "normal" speech act in hand? Finally, how would
you know whether a given speech act is "felicitous" or not, that is,
whether uttering it in the given circumstances is, or is not, an efficacious way of doing things with words?

I shall approach these questions through a discussion of what
J. L. Austin, Jacques Derrida, and Paul de Man say about speech
acts, especially about speech acts in literature.[1] First, however, a
preliminary example. Suppose I write, as I have just done, or suppose I say, or inscribe on a blackboard at the beginning of a seminar, the words "How to 'Bog, by Logical Stages, Down.'" What
can one say about this locution? Is it constative, that is, a statement
of fact to be judged by its truth or falsity? Or is it a performative
utterance, that is, a speech act in which the saying or writing of the
words in some way or other does what the words say? That is the
basic definition of a speech act. The words of a speech act do what
they say. They are speech that acts, rather than describes. In the
case of a speech act, as Austin puts it, "to say something is to do
something, or in saying something we do something, or even *by*
saying something we do something."[2]

On the one hand, the words "How to 'Bog, by Logical Stages,
Down'" appear to be constative. They are a title, one that describes
the essay or seminar that is expected to follow them. The essay or
seminar either will do what the words say or will not, and therefore
they will be proved either true or false as a descriptive label. On the
other hand, the words "How to 'Bog, by Logical Stages, Down'" are
a promise. They promise that the essay will teach the reader or auditor how to do that, how to bog, by logical stages, down, whatever
that means. A promise is an elementary example of a speech act. It
commits its utterer to do what the words say. The one who promises
is made different by uttering the words. He or she is bound by what

has been said and henceforth must be measured by whether or not the promise is fulfilled, whether or not he or she commits a breach of promise (often by another performative). The locution in my subtitle seems to be either constative or performative, depending on how you take it.

A further complication, however, is that the words are a citation from Austin's *How to Do Things with Words* (*HT*, 13). That is how Austin, at one point, defines what is happening or is going to happen to his argument. That argument is centered on getting a clear and infallible way to distinguish performative from constative locutions. That enterprise is bogging down. It is bogging down by logical stages. I take it this means the attempt to follow out the logic of his initial premises, rigorously, stage by stage, never missing a step in the sequence, is just what leads to the bogging down. In using Austin's figure of bogging by logical stages down, I have done no more than cite Austin. A citation, it would appear, is denatured, "etiolated," to use another of Austin's figures. It is "mention," not "use." This means it can never be a felicitous way of doing things with words, whatever it may have been when Austin first "used" it. To cite an utterance is to suspend it, as with the clothespins of the quotation marks I have used. Citation turns an utterance, in a manner of speaking, into literature, into fiction.

That seems clear enough. It is clear, that is, until one remembers that many paradigmatically felicitous speech acts proffered by Austin are citations, for example the "I do's" in a wedding ceremony. The couple are happily married because a certain form of words that has been used millions of times before is recited in the appropriate circumstances. "There must," says Austin, "exist an accepted conventional procedure having a certain conventional effect, that procedure to include the uttering of certain words by certain persons in certain circumstances" (*HT*, 14). Citation, or repetition, seems both necessary to a felicitous speech act and at the same time capable of vitiating it.

My introduction's subtitle is a description, and, at the same time, a promise. It promises that I will show you how to bog, by logical stages, down (whatever *that* means). By what authority do I state this fact or make this promise? Am I the right person in the right place at the right time to do this? Is what I am saying under the aegis of truth? Or is it a "performative"? Could it be "literature"? How can one speak other than literarily about literature? Certainly I hope what I say is true and not false, since, as we all know, bad things happened to Socrates for being a false teacher. The vague threat of the hemlock hangs over all teachers, even in a free country like the United States. What I say may also have a performative aspect, and, if so, of course I hope it will be a felicitous speech act. How would one know? Felicity depends, Austin tells us, on the context, among other things; on the circumstances. It is "the total speech-act in the total speech-situation" that must be elucidated, says Austin (*HT,* 148).

The context of the English seminar room at the University of California at Irvine, where my subtitle words were originally written on the blackboard and then read aloud, is certainly a highly determinate or even overdetermined one. It is expected that I will speak in English there. When I spoke these words there, I had been authorized in complex ways to give a particular seminar (by being "appointed," by being given "tenure," by having my seminar description approved beforehand, by a yearly review of my competence, and so on). If someone, "some low type," to borrow Austin's phrase for the man who mischristens the British warship and calls it the *Generalissimo Stalin,*[3] were to come in off the street, enter the seminar room, and utter exactly the same words I said in exactly the same tone as I said them, all would agree that he was out of order, that he was not "giving a seminar," nor authorized to give one. This would be analogous to Austin's example of the quack dentist: "But suppose there is a quack dentist. We can say 'In inserting the plate he was practising dentistry'" (*HT,* 128). How would I know for sure that I have not been "practicing seminar-giving" all these years, that I am not a low type, too?

I can easily imagine someone, perhaps an analytical philosopher jealous of his or her turf, saying that since I am not trained in philosophy I have no right to be claiming to speak authoritatively of a text presumed to belong to philosophy, that is, Austin's *How to Do*

Things with Words. The idea that philosophy can be read rightly only by a secret guild of philosophers is an absurd or even pernicious idea, destructive of philosophy's proper social role. Austin himself was willing to fulfill that social responsibility, for example by giving a talk on the BBC about speech-act theory. I hope my competence as a reader of Austin is demonstrated in my chapter about his work. I approach Austin from the perspective of the great utility his work has for literary study. In any case, the student's or reader's complicity (your complicity, dear reader) is required. If you are not willing to grant me the authority to speak as a professor giving a seminar or writing an essay, then the whole scene collapses. It can easily come to appear as farcical playacting, in which I play the role of the authoritative professor laying down the law about speech-act theory and you play the role of students or readers obediently attending to what I say. These social roles are extremely fragile, however solid their support appears to be, however much we seem to be the proper people doing the proper thing at the proper time, scrupulously following all the rules and codes.

What is the difference between me and the "low type"? All teachers are, or ought to be, haunted by the possibility that they may not be authorized. That is one reason such a fuss is made nowadays about threats to academic tenure. Nevertheless, a lot of leeway is granted to the teacher, though there are always limits, different in each country and even in each institution. How does one determine the limits, as when we say, "What he (or she) said in the classroom was beyond the pale"? Is asking such questions perhaps beyond the pale, since the smooth working of a graduate seminar or of a chapter in a book depends on taking many things for granted and not putting them in question? Is what I am now writing serious, or is it literature, hollow and void "in a peculiar way," as Austin says of poetry or soliloquy (*HT*, 22)? Such questions will remain hovering over this whole book.

§ 1 J. L. Austin

The Title

Let me begin at the beginning, with Austin's title: *How to Do Things with Words*. Both my title for the introduction and the title of Austin's book are labels from a familiar genre, the "how-to" book. The bookstores are full of such books: *How to Grow Prize Vegetable Marrows in a Window Box, How to Win Friends and Influence People, How to Make Beer, How to Speak Cat* (a real example), *How to Make a Powerful Bomb with Materials Available in Any Hardware Store and Garden Center.*[1] I have already shown how my own subtitle vibrates, like a Gestaltist duck/rabbit, between being constative and being performative, depending on how you look at it. The same thing is clearly true of Austin's title. It both describes and promises. Just how does that doubleness or duplicity function in Austin's case?

Austin himself, in *How to Do Things with Words*, discusses the vexed nature of "how." Does it have a performative valence or a constative one? This is one place (there are many) where Austin is covertly talking about his own text, that is, about what is problematic in it. He has been talking about the difference between saying "by" and saying "in" in descriptions of performatives. An example would be the difference between saying "By saying 'I promise' I promise" and saying "In saying 'I promise' I promise." "Finally," asserts Austin, "we have said there is another whole range of questions about 'how we are using language' or 'what we are doing in saying something' which we have said may be, and intuitively seem to be, entirely different—further matters we are not trenching upon," and later, in the same chapter or lecture: "But none the less, 'by' and 'in' deserve scrutiny every bit as much as, say, the now-becoming-notorious 'how.'"[2] "How" has now, I think, lost its notoriety. Few people stay awake nights thinking about it, though as soon as you think about it, you might become sleepless.

As the dictionary indicates, "how" hovers between being, usually, an adverb and being, sometimes, a noun. As an adverb it hovers again, this time between descriptive, constative uses ("in what manner or way"; "to what degree or extent, number or amount"; "in what state or condition," etc.) and performative uses, for example in an invitation ("How about a game of tennis?").[3] The latter locution is not constative. It does not describe. It does something with words, namely, invites someone to play tennis. "How" can be used performatively as an integral part of an utterance. In this case, the locution puts its recipient in the situation of having been invited to play tennis. She must say yes or no. This is parallel to one of Austin's examples, though in this case "how" is not used: "Do have another whack of ice-cream" (*HT*, 125). This could be rephrased as "How about another whack of ice-cream?" But while the status of "how" as performative or constative in such epitomes is clear enough, in some uses of "how," the attempt to decide whether it is constative or performative leaves the other possibility hovering uneasily as a shadow in the background. This is certainly the case with the "how" in *How to Do Things with Words*.

"To do things," the next part of Austin's title, seems idiomatic enough and transparent enough in meaning, until one begins to think about it. I shall think about it, according to Austin's practice, by inventing or finding situations in which the phrase is used. I might say to a colleague, "Can we have lunch on Thursday," and he or she might answer: "I'm not sure I'll be free. I have to do a lot of things that day." That's odd. What does it mean to *do things*? What is the force of "do" and "things" here? "Do" as in "do up," "do in," or "do over"? "Things" here certainly does not mean, or usually does not mean, *res,* in the sense of inanimate objects. The meaning of "things" in "to do things" is more like *res* in *res publica*: public affairs. The word "thing" originally meant, in various Germanic languages, including Old English, an assembly, for example a judicial or legislative assembly gathering together the elders of a tribe or nation. "Thing" in the now-everyday primary sense of an inanimate object ("What thing is that?" "A stone is a thing") has a meaning much derived and narrowed from the Anglo-Saxon "thing," though Heidegger, notoriously, in "Das Ding" wants to associate modern German *Ding* ("thing") with the older sense of gathering.[4] Following that line would take me a long way out of the way, though I suppose when I say, "I have a thing or two to do," or "I'll teach him a thing or two," the word "thing" does not mean a single object but a whole gathered assembly of features and circumstances, as the idiomatic adding of "or two" suggests. Things in these senses never come in ones. The more primitive or "original" meaning is still latent in current idiomatic usage.

Two examples from literature will indicate the richness inherent in Austin's apparently transparent putting together of "things" and "do." King Lear, in his incoherent rage at his daughters Goneril and Regan, says:

> I will have such revenges on you both
> That all the world shall—I will do such things—
> What they are, yet I know not; but they shall be
> The terrors of the earth.
> (Shakespeare, *King Lear* II.iv.276–79)

Lear's rage and his impotence, his impotent rage, are all carried in that "I will do such things— / What they are, yet I know not." "Do things" is always somehow a little vague or evasive. If Lear knew what terrors of the earth he was going to perform, he might to his advantage be more specific, but of course the whole point is that he has not the slightest idea what things he is going to do, and has in any case no power left to do anything, unless one could say that his speech is itself a way to do things with words. The evasive vagueness in "do things" is also present when I say, uttering an excuse (another cardinal example of a speech act): "I'm sorry. I can't play tennis today. I have a lot of things to do." The person to whom I say that would be justified in suspecting that what I say is "just an excuse," that I simply do not want to play tennis today, or at least not with the person who has invited me. The difficulty of deciding whether anything is done when a performative phrase is uttered, and just what that thing is, is admirably carried by the slightly ominous "to do things" in Austin's title, with its possible echo of *King Lear*. That this is an echo will not seem so unlikely when we discover that *How to Do Things with Words* is inhabited by a multitude of Shakespearean echoes.

Another, quite different use of "do things" is to be found in the noble peroration of Henry James's preface to the New York Edition of *The Golden Bowl*. This paragraph is the conclusion of the admirable series of prefaces to the 24 original volumes of the New York Edition. The peroration is not just noble but even suspiciously noble when one thinks about what sort of thing James did when he wrote *The Golden Bowl*. Here is what James says just toward the end of the preface:

> The whole conduct of life [This is Emerson's phrase, the title of one of his last books; so what James says here is put under the aegis of Emersonian high-minded New England solemnity.—JHM] consists of things done, which do other things in their turn, just so our behaviour and its fruits are essentially one and continuous and persistent and unquenchable, so the act has its way of abiding and showing and testifying, and so, among our innumerable acts, are no arbitrary, no senseless separations. The more we are capable of acting the less gropingly we plead such differences; whereby, with any capability, we recognise that to "put" things is very exactly and responsibly and interminably to do them. Our expression of them, and the terms on which we understand that, belong as nearly to our conduct and our life as every other feature of our freedom; these things yield in fact some of its most exquisite material to the religion of doing. More than that, our literary deeds enjoy this marked advantage over many of our acts, that, though they go forth into the world and stray even in the desert, they don't to the same extent lose themselves; their attachment and reference to us, however

strained, needn't necessarily lapse—while of the tie that binds us to *them* we may make almost anything we like. We are condemned, in other words, whether we will or no, to abandon and outlive, to forget and disown and hand over to desolation, many vital or social performances—if only because the traces, records, connexions, the very memorials we would fain preserve, are practically impossible to rescue for that purpose from the general mixture. We give them up even when we wouldn't—it is not a question of choice. Not so on the other hand our really "done" things of this superior and more appreciable order [He means works of literature.—JHM]—which leave us indeed all licence of disconnexion and disavowal [That is, I assume, we can always say "I didn't mean it" or "I didn't mean to do it. It was just literature."—JHM], but positively impose on us no such necessity.[5]

James distinguishes here between two ways to "do things," the manifold ordinary social things we do in interaction with our fellows as against that curious form of doing things that involves "putting them in words." For James, it is clear, writing literary works is a way to do things with words. To "put things," that is, to transport them into words, is to "do them," as when we say, "I did that paper."

James's passage can serve as a gloss on the final words of Austin's title. His book, his title promises, will tell the reader not just how to do things, but how to do things with words as tools or levers or instruments. The many ways that putting things in words is a way of doing them is a matter for interminable speculation and dramatization in James's fictions and in its accompanying prose.

In the preface just quoted, James apparently argues against, for example, what George Eliot's narrator says in the "Finale" of *Middlemarch* about the long-lasting effect of small social deeds. George Eliot's narrator has in mind, in particular, Dorothea's hidden acts as wife and mother: "But the effect of her being on those around her was incalculably diffusive: for the growing good of the world is partly dependent on unhistoric acts; and that things are not so ill with you and me as they might have been, is half owing to the number who lived faithfully a hidden life, and rest in unvisited tombs."[6] James, on the contrary, asserts the superiority of doing by writing over social doing. The difference lies not in the way social doing, for him, is ineffective (James does not disagree with Eliot about the efficacy of social doing, its often terrible efficacy), but in the way it is forgotten, so we need not or cannot acknowledge what we have done. How can we be expected to take responsibility for what we have totally forgotten we did or were not even aware we were doing when we did it, as in the unintentional effect on another person of a gesture or a raised eyebrow, social acts that are effaced from my memory or never even entered my consciousness? Doing things by putting them in words and writing them down, on the contrary, always leaves traces behind, the words on the page, so that we may, or even must, say, "Yes, I wrote that. I own up to it. I'm glad (or sorry) I wrote it." The superiority of writing-doing over social-doing lies in the better opportunities afforded by the former for taking responsibility. "Taking responsibility" is a key concept and is given a high value in the preface to *The Golden Bowl*, as well as in the novel itself.

Well, after all this is said, what can we put in words about Austin's title? Is it true or false? Is it a felicitous performative? Only a careful reading of the book itself can tell. I turn now to that.

How to Do Things with Words is a great work of ironic philosophical speculation. It demands and repays the closest attention to its details of language. Meanwhile, on the brink of that, Austin's title hovers there on the cover or title page, faintly smiling, enigmatic, quizzical, ironical, a little like the photograph on the front cover of the paperback edition of his *Philosophical Papers*. That photograph shows Austin as the patriarch, grandfather, or *capo* of speech-act theory. Austin's title for *How to Do Things with Words* is the first joke among many jokes in this admirable joke book. One wonders if any library or bookstore has ever filed this book among the how-to books. That would no doubt have pleased Austin.

Bogging Down

Both *How to Do Things with Words* and the associated BBC talk, "Performative Utterances," are narratives of a peculiar failure. The former was given as the William James lectures at Harvard in 1955 and then published in 1962, after Austin's death (1960). Austin himself never published either the lectures or the talk. They were things he did with words, all right, but he was never willing to publish them and sign his name to them as a way of saying "I put these forward as done things." They remained tentative and incomplete. The book as we have it is Austin's voice speaking in ghostly resurrection from beyond the grave. He speaks words that he never took full responsibility for when he was alive, though not publishing them if he was not satisfied with them may have seemed to him the most responsible thing to do.

Both texts start off bravely enough with the announcement of a revolutionary (Austin's figure) new discovery, the performative utterance, that is, uses of language that are not descriptive, or as Austin says, not "constative," but do something in saying something. Austin's apparently simple and attainable goal, he tells the reader, or rather listener, is to discriminate clearly between the two kinds of utterance. He wants to identify the distinguishing marks of both, and to make a preliminary taxonomy, based on examples from ordinary language, of the different kinds of performatives.

This seemingly simple and easily fulfillable goal quickly "bogs down." It then bogs down again and again when new strategies are tried. *How to Do Things with Words*, like "Performative Utterances," is the report of an intellectual catastrophe, to some considerable degree a ruefully comic report. Austin's BBC talk, like *How to Do Things with Words*, might be titled, in echo of Alexander Pope's title,[7] "Peri Bathous, or the Art of Sinking in Philosophy." Of course wonderfully productive and provocative insights into the way language works are attained along the way, but they are attained through the process of trying to do what turns out to be impossible to do, for Austin at least. The insights are attained through the process of bogging down. This feature of Austin's work has been ignored at their peril by subsequent theoreticians who have attempted to build a solid and comprehensive theory of speech acts on the foundations Austin laid. "Poor man," they in effect say, "he was a great genius, but he died young, 'at the height of his powers,'[8] leaving us with an incomplete text and a few small problems to solve, a little clearing up to perform. By doing that we can establish a lasting philosophical legacy for him and for ourselves: a clear and unambiguous doctrine of speech acts and a complete repertoire of the different kinds." If such speech-act theorists had been slightly more careful readers of Austin, they would have seen that he had already conclusively demonstrated the impossibility of establishing a clear and complete doctrine of speech acts.

Austin's grand anticlimax of bogging down occurs in successive stages in *How to Do Things with Words*. These lectures are organized in three sections. In each section, Austin proposes a new terminology that is carried as far as it will go, until it founders. A single simple binary opposition gets more and more complex and unwieldy as Austin proceeds. He then draws himself up and proposes a new, somewhat more complex set of terms. "Performative" and "constative" are replaced by "locutionary," "illocutionary," and "perlocutionary." This second set of terms is once more followed as far as it will go, until Austin bogs down again. Finally a third, even more complex and "rebarbative" (Austin's term for them: *HT*, 151), set of terms is proposed: "behabitives," "expositives," "exercitives," "commissives," and "verdictives." This move, too, fails to establish the clear distinction between performative and constative utterances Austin wants and the clear identification of each speech act's characteristic grammatical marks. The project frays out into increasingly unmanageable complexity, the complexity of everyday usage in ordinary language.

How to Do Things with Words ends with a rueful confession of failure and with an exhortation by Austin to himself, or rather to some collective "we," presumably the community of ordinary-language philosophers at large, for which he claims throughout simply to speak, impersonally. He exhorts this "we" to start over again even further back or further down, with more elementary questions:

> I have as usual failed to leave enough time in which to say why what I have said is interesting. Just one example, then. Philosophers have long been interested in the word "good" and, quite recently, have begun to take the line of considering how we use it, what we use it to do.

It has been suggested, for example, that we use it for expressing approval, for commending, or for grading. But we shall not get really clear about this word "good" and what we use it to do until, ideally, we have a complete list of those illocutionary acts of which commending, grading &c., are isolated specimens—until we know how many such acts there are and what are their relationships and inter-connexions. (*HT*, 163–64)

At the very end of the last lecture Austin admits ruefully that he has been doing two things he does not "altogether like doing," lecturing and "producing a programme, that is, saying what ought to be done rather than doing something." This is followed by the assertion that he has not been "proclaiming an individual manifesto" but rather modestly "sorting out a bit the way things have already begun to go and are going with increasing momentum in some parts of philosophy" (*HT*, 164). These disclaimers are quite disingenuous. *How to Do Things with Words* is a radical manifesto, and it is actually a doing of something, a doing something with words. Nor does it simply swim with the stream and continue a movement already moving forward irresistibly. Rather, it forms a decisive and revolutionary break in philosophical tradition, as Austin somewhat obliquely asserts at the beginning of the first lecture. In his farewell to his audience, however, Austin wants to deny all that.

The increasing complexity—the bogging down—of his analysis takes three forms. One is the immense proliferation of details and distinctions that arises from the complexity of ordinary language, making it impossible to distinguish clearly among different forms of performative utterances. Austin is committed to honoring that complexity: "We must at all costs avoid over-simplification" (*HT*, 38). Though this avoidance is an admirable commitment to rigor and truth, it nevertheless tends to mire in a welter of detail the clear distinctions Austin seeks.

Austin begins with the notion that the paradigmatic performative utterance is a first-person singular pronoun, "I," followed by a singular present-tense indicative active verb taken from a limited and identifiable repertoire: "I promise," "I bet," "I warn," "I apologize," and the like. Austin is smart enough (he was nothing if not extremely intelligent) to recognize that this will not work, that many clearly performative locutions exist that do not take this form. An example is the single word "Bull!" uttered to warn someone that there is a bull in that field. There is not time to say, "I warn you that there is a bull in that field." You just say, "Bull!"[9] Moreover, no finite list of verbs that must be used if the performative is to be felicitous can be identified. Each verb, furthermore, generates a different species of performative utterance demanding its own separate analysis, perhaps an interminable analysis, another form of bogging down. To say "I bet" is not quite the same sort of thing as to say "I promise," or "I warn," and so on for all the others.

Moreover, a huge number of such verbs exist, too many to hold in the mind at once. The possibilities exceed the mind's grasp, in a sort of sublime excess. "Using then," says Austin, "the simple test (with caution) of the first person singular indicative active form, and going through the dictionary (a concise one should do) in a liberal spirit, we get a list of verbs of the order of the third power of ten" (*HT*, 150). A characteristically ironic and funny footnote is appended to this sentence: "Why use this expression instead of 1,000? First, it looks impressive and scientific; second, because it goes from 1,000 to 9,999—a good margin—whereas the other might be taken to mean 'about 1,000'—too narrow a margin" (*HT*, 150). That "margin" of uncertainty stretches out in all directions like the bog in which Austin is mired.

The second form Austin's bogging down takes is perhaps even more disastrous for his initial project. In this form, it becomes increasingly evident that it is impossible to say for sure that you have a pure performative in hand. All constative statements are at least a little performative, and vice versa. As Austin says at one point, "a belief in the dichotomy of performatives and constatives . . . has to be abandoned in favor of more general *families* of related and overlapping speech-acts" (*HT*, 150). This crossbreeding or cross-contamination is perhaps the chief and most valuable discovery of *How to Do Things with Words*, though it certainly does not help to fulfill the promise made in the second lecture to distinguish clearly between constative and performative. Austin's genius as a philosopher is to allow his intelligence to be led, "by logical stages," to conclusions that he does not, at least not apparently, want to reach. The other, related, mark of his genius is his ability to adduce examples that cause the most trouble for the general doctrine he is trying to prove.

Moments when the clear distinction between performative and constative utterances, the "revolutionary" discovery with which he began, breaks down punctuate *How to Do Things with Words* and "Performative Utterances" at rhythmic intervals. At the beginning of the sixth lecture of *How to Do Things with Words*, Austin says, "Very commonly the *same* sentence is used on different occasions of utterance in *both* ways, performative and constative. The thing seems hopeless from the start, if we are to leave utterances *as they stand* and seek for a criterion" (*HT*, 67). The eleventh lecture opens with a rueful question: "Whenever I 'say' anything (except perhaps a mere exclamation like 'damn' or 'ouch') I shall be performing both locutionary and illocutionary acts, and these two kinds of acts seem to be the very things which we tried to use, under the names of 'doing' and 'saying,' as a means of distinguishing performatives from constatives. If we are in general always doing both things, how can our distinction survive?" (*HT*, 133). Somewhat later, discussing "behabitives" and "expositives," Austin rather anxiously comments on the problems he is having: "Behabitives are troublesome because they seem too miscellaneous altogether: and expositives because they are enormously numerous and important, and seem both to be included in the other classes and at the same time to be unique in a way that I have not succeeded in making clear even to myself. It could well be said that all aspects are present in all my classes" (*HT*, 152). Austin had the great merit of knowing when he was confused, when he had not successfully cleared things up.

A final confession that the distinctions he is trying to make remain blurred occurs in the discussion of "expositives" as the fifth of the five classes of performatives he proposes in his third shift in terminology:

> We have said repeatedly that we [There is that "we" again. Who is this "we"?—JHM] may dispute as to whether these [expositive speech acts

involving "the expounding of views, the conducting of arguments, and the clarifying of usages and of references"] are not verdictive, exercitive, behabitive, or commissive acts as well; we may also dispute whether they are not straight descriptions of our feelings, practices, &c., especially sometimes over matters of suiting the action to the words, as when I say "I turn next to," "I quote," "I cite," "I recapitulate," "I repeat that," "I mention that." (*HT*, 161)

What use are these distinctions if they do not really serve to distinguish? What is left of the distinction between performative and constative utterances if, in the end, "we" cannot tell the difference between one and the other, if it is not a matter of some objective feature of the words themselves but a matter of how any given set of words is taken? Austin explicitly says just this at one point toward the end of *How to Do Things with Words*:

> What then finally is left of the distinction of the performative and constative utterance? Really we may say that what we had in mind here was:
>
> (*a*) With the constative utterance, we abstract from the illocutionary (let alone the perlocutionary) aspects of the speech-act, and we concentrate on the locutionary etc. . . .
>
> (*b*) With the performative utterance, we attend as much as possible to the illocutionary force of the utterance, and abstract from the dimension of correspondence with facts. (*HT*, 145–46)

On the one hand, this does not seem to give much help in spotting and interpreting performatives in literary works, if any utterance whatsoever can be taken as either constative or performative. On the other hand, it is a precious clue for the inquiring reader of literature, Henry James's work for example, since it says that all performatives are a little constative, all constatives a little performative. Usage, that is, how the locution is "taken," is everything. This invites the reader to search literary works for much more than just locutions like "I promise," if it is the performative dimension he or she is after.

The third form Austin's bogging down takes is perhaps the most disastrous of all for his project. His goal has been not only to get a clear definition of performative speech acts, so you could know for sure whether or not you have one in hand, but also to distinguish clearly the conditions that make a speech act "felicitous," that is, efficacious in doing something and doing what you want it to do, what you intend that it should do. This too turns out to be impossible. Felicity is always contaminated by infelicity, one of Austin's chief names for which is "literature." If I want to utter a felicitous speech act, "I must not be joking, for example, nor writing a poem" (*HT*, 9). "We shall not always mention," says Austin in a footnote, "but must bear in mind the possibility of 'etiolation' as it occurs when we use speech in acting, fiction and poetry, quotation and recitation" (*HT*, 92). The firm exclusions of literature echo throughout *How to Do Things with Words* with stern but slightly desperate frequency. Austin is like a man who has exorcised a ghost only to find that it keeps coming back. Literature is the ghost that haunts *How to Do Things with Words*. It keeps creeping back in and vitiating the attempt to establish the conditions of a felicitous performative and so constitutes another kind of failure.

Austin repeatedly confronts impasses in his project. And repeatedly he picks himself up, dusts himself off, and starts bravely forward again with a new set of terms, each set more elaborate and less clear than the last. His lectures end with yet further promises to try again or exhortations to "us" to try again. This comic scenario may be thought of according to two analogies that come to mind, one dyslogistic, as the rhetoricians say, the other eulogistic. The first is the scene in Dickens's *Great Expectations* in which Pip, the blacksmith's boy, unwillingly fights Herbert Pocket, the educated town boy. Pocket comes at him with a great show of pugilistic skill, is knocked down by one blow from Pip, picks himself up, comes at Pip again, only to be knocked down again, and so on, cheerfully following out to the end the rules of the game of fisticuffs. Likewise, Austin obediently follows the rules of philosophical discourse and, in so doing, gets himself in great intellectual trouble.[10]

The other, eulogistic, comparison shows how Austin belongs to a great philosophical tradition, in spite of his self-deprecatory modesty. Plato's dialogues often end at an impasse in the argument, with

Socrates, still undaunted, saying they must take up the subject again later at a still more foundational level. An example is the end of the *Protagoras*, where Socrates realizes that for all their talk, Protagoras and he have accomplished only the recognition that you cannot decide whether virtue can be taught (they have, dismayingly for the reader, changed positions on that in the course of the dialogue) until you are sure you know what virtue is. Socrates says, "For my part, Protagoras, when I see the subject in such utter confusion I feel the liveliest desire to clear it up. I should like to follow up our present talk with a determined attack on virtue itself and its essential nature. Then we could return to the question whether or not it can be taught" (361c).[11] Similarly, Austin, at the end of "Performative Utterances," says "we need to go very much farther back," and "what we need . . . is a new doctrine about all the possible forces of utterances . . . ; and then, going on from there, an investigation of the various terms of appraisal that we use in discussing speech-acts of this, that, or the other precise kind—orders, warnings, and the like" (*PP*, 251). For Austin, as for Socrates, the discussion is over, but all the work is yet to do.

Socrates is an august predecessor for Austin, but perhaps the best metaphors for Austin's situation are his own, not only the figure of bogging down but another one parallel to that, as I will discuss. Both are part of a constant series of what might be called metalanguage in the book and in the BBC lecture. Austin has a habit of commenting on what he is doing, to some degree from the outside, as though he were two persons, the one doing it and the other watching the first doing it. These comments are often wryly ironic, modest, or comic. The figure of bogging down appears both in *How to Do Things with Words* and in "Performative Utterances." In the former, Austin observes that by recognizing that not all language is descriptive we have removed a severely inhibiting prejudice. The question is where to go from there:

> So far then we have merely felt the firm ground of prejudice slide away beneath our feet. But now how, as philosophers, are we to proceed? [There is "how to" again!—JHM] One thing we might go on to do, of course, is to take it all back [I presume by saying, "I didn't really mean

it. All language *is* descriptive after all. This has all been a joke."—
JHM]; another would be to bog, by logical stages, down. But all this
must take time. (*HT,* 13)

In "Performative Utterances," the bog image returns and is
played with as Austin shows how performatives cannot, after all, be
clearly told from constatives. The words are nearly the same as in
How to, but not quite: "So far we have been going firmly ahead,
feeling the firm ground of prejudice glide away beneath our feet
which is always rather exhilarating, but what next? You will be
waiting for the bit when we bog down, the bit where we take it all
back, and sure enough that's going to come but it will take time"
(*PP,* 241). Not all that much time. Just five pages later he extends
this figure: "So far we [we!] have been going along as though there
was a quite clear difference between our performative utterances
and what we have contrasted them with, statements or reports or
descriptions. But now we begin to find that this distinction is not
as clear as it might be. It's now that we begin to sink in a little"
(*PP,* 246). If what we are sinking into is a vast bog, as ordinary language is proving to be, then a little sinking goes a long way. This is
parallel to a passage in *How to:* "I must explain again that we are
floundering here. To feel the firm ground of prejudice slipping
away is exhilarating, but brings its revenges" (*HT,* 61).

The bog image is related to another, adjacent figure, also used in
both texts. In *How to,* the alternative figure, actually a triple figure,
characteristically ironic and comic, comes twelve pages after the
bog image, and at the beginning of the third lecture, entitled "Infelicities: Misfires": "So then we may seem to have armed ourselves
with two shiny new concepts [the concept of the performative utterance and the concept of infelicity] with which to crack the crib
of Reality, or as it may be, of Confusion—two new keys in our
hands, *and* of course, simultaneously two new skids under our feet.
In philosophy, forearmed *should* be forewarned" (*HT,* 25). These
are pretty weird sentences, if you think about them. The two fun-
damental·concepts of Austin's revolutionary new doctrine, "a revolution in philosophy . . . the greatest and most salutary in its history" (*HT,* 3), are compared to a housebreaker's tools. "Crack a

crib" is British thieves' slang for "to break into a house" (see *The Oxford English Dictionary*, under "crack"). The house is "Reality" and/or "Confusion." The burglar's tools are also, more benignly, keys in his hands, though no doubt illicitly obtained, or they are, with an abrupt and total mixing of metaphors, "two new skids under our feet." In "Performative Utterances," almost the same words appear just before the figure of bogging down and indicate the secret relation between the two figures (*PP*, 241). The concepts are tools that are also keys and also at the same time skids. As skids these two revolutionary concepts, which seemed to promise so much clarity and so much beneficent understanding, turn out to be the very things that transport "us," irresistibly, by logical stages, down a slippery slope into the bog. This brings us back around to "bogging, by logical stages, down" as the best name for the splendid comic fiasco of *How to Do Things with Words.*

Is *How to Do Things with Words* Constative or Performative?

It would seem that the answer to this question should be easy to give. *How to Do Things with Words* is explicitly intended to be constative through and through. Austin wants to find out the truth about performative utterances and to tell that truth. The lecture series is firmly put under the aegis of truth or falsehood by the admirably ironic first sentence of the first lecture: "What I shall have to say here is neither difficult nor contentious; the only merit I should like to claim for it is that of being true, at least in parts" (*HT*, 1). This seems clearly enough to say that the whole book is intended to be constative, that its failure is a matter of not always reaching the truth.

Things are not so simple, however, as the reader will already have guessed. One problem with the sentence just cited is that it starts off with two lies. A lie is, at least in one of its components, a performative utterance, as Austin himself recognizes at several points in *How to Do Things with Words* (*HT*, 20, 40–41, 50). A lie is a way to do things with words if you can get people to believe the lie and act on that belief. *How to Do Things with Words* is both difficult and contentious, whatever Austin says. It is not at all easy to understand, to grasp as a whole and hold in the mind as a continuous argument. Moreover, the book has certainly given rise to contention, as in the angry exchange between John Searle and Jacques Derrida, to be discussed below. Moreover, to claim, as Austin does, that his book is "true, at least in parts," is ominously odd, though it may seem to be simply modest. How would readers tell which parts are true, which false? He claims that his book falls in the category of constative statements. Or rather he says this of his lectures, since he did not himself publish them, whatever his contractual promise to Harvard may have been. (The copyright is held by the president and fellows of Harvard College.) The lectures are true or false— "true, at least in parts," leaving the remainder presumably false, though that is uncertain. Maybe he means the other parts are performative, though that seems unlikely. Or that they are nonsense. More likely. Those are the four categories. It looks like a given piece of language must be one of the four: true, false, performative, or nonsense. In the first sentence, Austin claims that he has at least in parts spoken the truth about the distinction between performatives and constatives. He invites the reader to measure the worth of the book by its truth value and perhaps dares the reader to tell the true from the false.

It does not take anything more than a careful reading coached by Austin's own criteria, however, to show that *How to Do Things with Words*, like "Performative Utterances," has a pervasive, explicit, and nevertheless problematic performative dimension. This is easiest to see in Austin's proposals for his three sets of new terminology. In all these cases the terms are put forward in locutions that are, by Austin's own criteria, performative: "Not all true or false statements are descriptions, and for this reason I prefer to use the word 'Constative'" (*HT*, 3); "What are we to call a sentence or an utterance of this type? I propose to call it a *performative sentence* or a performative utterance, or, for short, 'a performative'" (*HT*, 6); "we shall call in general those infelicities . . . which are such that the act for the performing of which, and in the performing of which, the verbal formula in question is designed, is not achieved, by the name MISFIRES: and on the other hand we may christen those infelicities where the act *is* achieved ABUSES (do not stress the normal connotations of these names!)" (*HT*, 16); "we may reasonably christen the second sort—where the procedure does exist all right but can't be applied as purported—*Misapplications*" (*HT*, 17); "feelings and attitudes which I christen 'BEHABITIVES'" (*HT*, 81); "for example in what I call *verdictives*" (*HT*, 88); "The act of 'saying something' in this full normal sense I call, i.e. dub, the performance of a locutionary act" (*HT*, 94). "I call," "I name," "I christen," as one christens a baby, "I dub," as one dubs a knight: all these are explicit performative utterances, as Austin must have known. He calls attention in one place to the way "I call" can be used at the same time both performatively and constatively (*HT*, 64–65). Austin's use of "dub" and "christen," more ostentatious figures than "call" or "name," especially suggests that Austin was deliberately and self-consciously employing performative language. These phrases bring about the thing they say. In a christening the hitherto nameless baby is now named "Matthew" or "Dorothy." In a dubbing, the commoner becomes a knight and is henceforth to be addressed as "Sir Frank" or whatever. The hitherto nameless kind of utterance is henceforth to be dubbed a "performative."

These ostentatious performatives are, moreover, just the tip of the iceberg. Not only are there dozens of other locutions in Austin's lectures that by his own measure must be called performatives, but also *How to Do Things with Words* "as a whole," if it is a whole, may be called one vast somewhat disheveled performative utterance of a specific kind.

Just what sort of performatives are these passages where Austin says "I name," "I christen," or "I dub"? Just what sort of performative is the text as a whole? The answer is that they belong to the species "an act of foundation," in this case the foundation of a new, hitherto unheard-of doctrine. *How to Do Things with Words* is the inaugural document founding a new branch of philosophy, the theory of speech acts.

Are the performatives Austin utters felicitous or infelicitous? Do they work or do they misfire? For Austin, an ideally felicitous performative must be uttered by the right person in the right circumstances. The right words must be said, and they must be authorized by preexisting institutions with the accompanying required forms of speech. A paradigmatic example, often referred to by Austin, is a marriage ceremony. Only the captain, not the purser, may, for example, marry people on shipboard. The captain has authority to do this only on his own ship, not on land. Neither the bride nor the bridegroom may be already married, coerced, or drunk. You cannot marry a monkey, as Austin at one point says, any more than you can baptize a penguin or a dog (*HT,* 24, 31), so both persons in a marriage ceremony must be human beings. The right words must be said by everyone concerned. These words are part of an already established ritual, a highly conventionalized and legalized procedure, surrounded by all sorts of safeguards. Someone I know was told that he and his fiancée could say anything they liked at the marriage ceremony as long as a bona fide Justice of the Peace at some point uttered the magic words, "I pronounce you husband and wife." The words are "magic" because before they are uttered by the right person in the right circumstances, in the presence of witnesses, the couple is not married, and after the words echo in the air the couple is married, for better or for worse. How do Austin's performatives measure up to these criteria?

On the one hand, Austin goes to considerable lengths to establish that he is the right person at the right time in the right place to utter felicitous performatives that will install a new terminology and found a new domain of philosophy. He is, after all, White's Professor of Moral Philosophy at Oxford University, delivering the William James lectures at Harvard University. That is about as much authority as you can get in the academic world. Someone from an obscure university lecturing in another obscure university could hardly hope to accomplish so much.

Austin's claim to authority appears also in several ways in his language, for example in his casual, ironic, and self-deprecatory tone. You can afford to speak softly and make jokes if you really have authority, as in that opening sentence, already cited: "What I shall have to say here is neither difficult nor contentious; the only merit I should like to claim for it is that of being true, at least in parts" (*HT*, 1). That sentence is a way of saying that any person of intelligence and good will is certain to agree with him, for the most part. You are an idiot or a "low type" if you don't. Austin has mastery of the idiom of ordinary-language philosophers and speaks as one of them. The ubiquitous "we" that we (I!) have already noticed is a way of disclaiming responsibility for what he is saying. He speaks for a whole group that collectively has great authority: Oxford common-language philosophers as a whole. This is reinforced by the easy allusions to Kant, Cervantes, Shakespeare, Euripides, Voltaire, Donne, Whitman. By these references Austin casually establishes himself as an educated man who can hold his own at the high table of an Oxford college. The use of Greek letters rather than Roman ones to label a series of points is another such claim to authority, as is the citation he makes in Greek from Euripides. You must have had a lot of expensive education to use Greek so casually.

Moreover, Austin makes a point of claiming in the introductory remarks of the first lecture that what he is about to say is not radically inaugural. He is simply continuing in a direction "philosophy," meaning ordinary-language philosophy, has already been going in for quite a while, ever since Kant, in fact, who is twice invoked as a predecessor (*HT*, 2, 3). Austin's language is circumspect and carefully impersonal, in the passive tense. He says, "It has come to be seen . . ." or "Along these lines it has now been shown piecemeal, or at least made to look likely, that many traditional philosophical perplexities have arisen through a mistake—the mistake of taking as straightforward statements of fact utterances which are *either* (in interesting non-grammatical ways) nonsensical *or else* intended as something quite different" (*HT*, 3). He does not say who has done the seeing or the showing. Presumably it is "we" ordinary-language philosophers, certainly not Austin as a private citizen acting on his own hook. He is continuing only what others have set in motion, and he speaks only with their delegated authority.

In another quite contrary strand of language intertwined with the first, however, Austin quietly and with careful hedging defines himself as radically inaugural or initiatory, as doing something that no one has ever done before. Of the use of language to do something, he says in the second and third sentences of the first lecture: "The phenomenon to be discussed is very widespread and obvious, and it cannot fail to have been already noticed, at least here and there, by others. Yet I have not found attention paid to it specifically" (*HT*, 1). Austin did in truth do something altogether new in philosophy, something that made a clean break with previous philosophical thinking, in spite of the invocation of Kant and of some indeterminate "we" as predecessors.

By the third page, Austin is defining this novelty in the most grandiose and hyperbolic terms, in a tone quite different from the ironic modesty with which he has spoken so far. Of the distinction between constative and performative language and its associated concepts, he says: "It cannot be doubted that they are producing a revolution in philosophy. If anyone wishes to call it the greatest and most salutary in its history, this is not, if you come to think of it, a large claim" (*HT*, 3–4). This is an amazing, almost megalomaniac statement, if you come to think of it. I am too modest to call it the greatest revolution in the history of philosophy, says Austin in effect, but he does nevertheless call it that in saying that if someone else calls it that, this will not be a large claim for something so earthshaking.

Austin's presentation of the William James lectures at Harvard in 1955 was an event, no one can doubt it, in the same way that Kant's third *Critique* was, according to Paul de Man, an event, an "occurrence."[12] Those who heard the lectures were lucky to be present at something so epoch making, though from what I have heard most of them were not aware of what was happening. No attempt by Austin to blame this event on others or on some collective "we" can hide from the reader, the reader now at least, the radical nature of the event.

The name for such an event is "revolution," as Austin correctly notes. A revolution, however, is a performative event that definitely does not fit Austin's criteria for a felicitous performative. A genuine revolution, one that makes a decisive break in history, cannot depend on pre-existing conventions, laws, rights, justifications, and formulations, however much it characteristically attempts to claim that it does. A revolution is a performative act of a particular, "nonstandard" kind, namely the anomalous kind that creates the circumstances or conventions that validate it, while masking as a constative statement. A revolution is groundless, or rather, by a metaleptic future anterior, it creates the grounds that justify it. Austin wants the reader to believe that he is simply continuing a movement in philosophy that has already been under way at least since Kant. At the same time he quietly claims that he is performing the greatest and most salutary revolution in the history of philosophy, that he is doing something altogether new and hitherto unheard-of or at least unnoticed: "Yet I have not found attention paid to it specifically."

What is the instrument or tool that brings this revolution off, if it is indeed felicitous? It is the one most appropriate for a book about how to do things with words, namely the invention of a new terminology that creates new distinctions. This is a terminology of "rebarbative" (*HT*, 151) names, that is, aggressively and ostentatiously ugly words, words like thrusts of your beard into an antagonist's face (that's what "rebarbative" means). Austin has in mind the neologisms "performative," "constative," "perlocutionary," "behabitive," and the rest. It is appropriate that the most explicit performative language in Austin's own text comes at the places where he is introducing these new terms. A new language creates a new realm, a whole new world, in this case the domain of speech-act theory.

Austin himself implicitly recognized the radically initiatory aspect of his enterprise. Speaking of the supposed evolutionary development of language from primitive exclamations like "Bull!" and "Thunder!" to present-day differentiated and sophisticated syntax, language such as philosophers use, he says, rather casually, and without specific reference to his own enterprise: "Sophistication and development of social forms and procedures will necessitate clarification. But note that this clarification is as much a creative act as a discovery or description. It is as much a matter of making clear distinctions as of making already existent distinctions clear" (*HT*, 72).

To answer my question in the title of this section: *How to Do Things with Words* is a truly revolutionary philosophical event attempting to masquerade as a constative statement of fact that does no more than continue a development in thinking already long under way. Since perpetrators of failed revolutions tend to get hanged in one way or another—for example, by being called a bumbler and becoming an object of ridicule among one's peers—Austin was right to be careful. However, like those who signed the United States Declaration of Independence, Austin pulled off a successful revolution, albeit, as is usual with revolutions, with a considerable betrayal of the principles on which the revolution was founded.

Exorcising Literature

Why does Austin have it in so fiercely for literature? I have already cited his statement that for a performative to be felicitous, one must not be joking or writing a poem. He returns again and again to this topic, excluding literature again and again, like a man whose act of conjuration does not quite come off. Why is excluding literature so necessary for the doctrine Austin wants to propound, and why does he, as if by an irresistible necessity, return so often and so anxiously to this topic?

The best approach to these questions is by way of Austin's remarks about intention and sincerity. This is a crux in his argument. It is a place where, by what may be an ineluctable necessity, given his premises, he must contradict himself. He needs to have it two ways at once.

On the one hand, the performative depends on the intentions or sincerity of the one who speaks. As other commentators on speech-act theory have noted, Austin's concept of the felicitous performative is closely tied to the presupposition of the self-conscious "I," the male ego capable of speaking words like "I promise" or "I bet" or "I declare" in full possession of his senses and with sincere intentions. "It [a behabitive]," says Austin parenthetically in one place, "could of course be *insincere* always" (*HT*, 84), and that would be enough to vitiate it. In an earlier place: "The insincerity of an assertion is the same as the insincerity of a promise, since both promising and asserting are procedures intended for use by persons having certain thoughts. . . . to say 'I promise,' without intending, is parallel to saying 'it is the case' without believing" (*HT*, 50). Austin's theory belongs to the epoch of the Cartesian concept of the ego. (Why the standard performative "I" is male I shall explain later.) The first-person pronoun as well as a present indicative verb uttered by a self-conscious ego or subject is a necessary condition of the paradigmatic performative. "[If] a monkey," says Austin, "makes a noise indistinguishable from 'go' it is still not a phatic act." A phatic act is the uttering of a noise "belonging to and as belonging to, a certain vocabulary, conforming to and as conforming to a certain grammar" (*HT*, 96, 95). "Actions," says Austin, imperturbably, as if there were not enormous problems in what he is saying, "can only be performed by persons, and obviously in our cases the utterer must be the performer. . . . The 'I' who is doing the action does thus come essentially into the picture. An advantage of the original first person singular present indicative active form . . . is that this implicit feature of the speech-situation is made *explicit*" (*HT*, 60–61). In order for a performative to be felicitous, I must mean what I say, and must know what I mean and that I mean what I say, with no *arrière pensée*, no unconscious motives or reservations. A Freudian notion of the unconscious would pretty well blow Austin's theories out of the water, as Derrida observes at one point in *Limited Inc.*

On the other hand, the performative must *not* depend on the intentions or sincerity of the one who speaks. If Austin's theory is to be cogent, and if he is to attain his goal of securing law and order, the words themselves must do the work, not the secret intentions of the speaker or writer. For civil order to be maintained, we must be able to hold speakers and writers responsible for their words, whatever their intentions at the time. Austin's is a doctrine of how to do things with words, not a doctrine of how to do things by thinking about them.

The passage where Austin says this is characteristically forceful and ironically amusing. Since it is an essential crux in his concept of the performative, it must be cited and interpreted in detail. Speaking of an objection someone might raise about "some of the more awe-inspiring performatives such as 'I promise to... ,'" Austin says (I must now begin to quote the whole sequence cited in part above): "Surely the words must be spoken 'seriously' and so as to be taken 'seriously'? This is, though vague, true enough in general—it is an important commonplace in discussing the purport of any utterance whatsoever. I must not be joking, for example, nor writing a poem" (*HT*, 9). The basic objection to poetry, it can be seen from this, is that it is, like joking, "not serious." Austin goes on, however, to make a sardonic attack on what might be concluded from this apparent need for sincerity if promises or other performative utterances are to be valid or "felicitous":

> But we are apt to have a feeling that their being serious consists in their being uttered as (merely) the outward and visible sign, for convenience or other record or for information, of an inward and spiritual act: from which it is but a short step to go on to believe or to assume without realizing that for many purposes the outward utterance is a description, *true or false*, of the occurrence of the inward performance. The classic expression of this idea is to be found in the *Hippolytus* (l. 612), where Hippolytus says
>
> η γλῶσσ' ομωμοχ', η δε φρην ανωμοτο
>
> [hê glôss' omômoch', hê de phrên anômotos]
>
> i.e. "my tongue [Greek: 'glôss,' as in 'glossary'] swore to, but my heart (or mind or other backstage artiste [Greek: 'phrên,' as in 'frenzy']) did not." Thus "I promise to... " obliges me—puts on record my spiritual assumption of a spiritual shackle. (*HT*, 9–10)

The echoes of Christian language here ("outward and visible sign . . . of an inward and spiritual act") tells the reader that much is at stake. Jesus said, "Whosoever looketh on a woman to lust after her hath committed adultery with her already in his heart" (Matt. 5:28). Christian morality in general (remember that Austin was a professor of moral philosophy at a nominally Christian university) measures acts by their purity or impurity of intention. What counts most is not what you say but what you do, but the most important doing takes place invisibly or in a place visible only to God, namely in the heart, mind, or spirit. God knows our secret feelings and thoughts. Those are what matter most, whatever we say.

Austin levels a joyfully ironic dismissal at all this way of thinking. He argues that it leads straight to immorality and to the justification of immorality:

> It is gratifying to observe in this very example how excess of profundity, or rather solemnity, at once paves the way for immorality. For one who says "promising is not merely a matter of uttering words! It is an inward and spiritual act!" is apt to appear as a solid moralist standing out against a generation of superficial theorizers [Another biblical echo there, as in Jesus' "O generation of vipers, how can ye, being evil, speak good things" (Matt. 12:34)—JHM]: we see him as he sees himself, surveying the invisible depths of ethical space, with all the distinction of a specialist in the *sui generis*. Yet he provides Hippolytus with a let-out, the bigamist with an excuse for his "I do" and the welsher with a defence for his "I bet." Accuracy and morality alike are on the side of the plain saying that *our word is our bond*. (*HT*, 10)

This is a powerful argument. The smooth working of society, of "law and order," depends, it can be argued, on ignoring whatever goes on secretly in people's hearts and holding them to the rule that says our word is our bond. Suppose I were to try to get out of paying a house mortgage by saying, "Yes, I signed that mortgage note promising to pay so much every month, but I did not really mean it. My pen promised but my mind did not." That would not wash at all with the court, in which I would be sued for nonpayment and have my house repossessed. This would seem to mean, however, that what I said or wrote when I was drunk, coerced, at the point of a gun, or insane would also be held to bind me. Austin later, however, rules that out. I must be in my right mind and not coerced. That, however, is not the same thing as saying my word is my bond. It smuggles the concepts of seriousness and sincerity back in as necessary conditions of a felicitous performative. It must be uttered by a fully self-conscious ego in complete possession of its wits and its intentions. It is clear that Austin needs to have it both ways, illogically, and that "we" have identified a major crux or even aporia in his doctrine.

On the one hand, Austin is unwilling, in spite of what he says, to assert unqualifiedly that our word is our bond. This would mean that it would be difficult to discriminate between the monkey's "go" and my "I promise," since it is the sound that matters, not the intention. It would put Austin where he does not want to be, that is, with de Man, who sees language, especially performative language, as something that operates mechanically, regardless of what the speaker thinks, feels, or intends, usually against his intentions. "The 'inhuman,'" said de Man, "is not some kind of mystery, or some kind of secret; the inhuman is: linguistic structures, the play of linguistic tensions, linguistic events that occur, possibilities which are inherent in language—independently of any intent or any drive or any wish or any desire we might have."[13] This conclusion is just what Austin resists, with all his force, though it is the insight toward which his discovery of "performative utterances" was ineluctably leading him. Austin's bogs down, one might argue, because he endlessly resists recognizing that his book should not be called *How to Do Things with Words*, as if language were an instrument in human beings' full control, like a knife or a hammer, with which they may at their will "do things." Rather it should be called *How Words Do Things to You*, or *How to Be Done In by Words*, in recognition of the autonomous power of language to do unforeseen things, "independently of any intent or any drive or any wish or any desire that we might have." Among those things is the generation, as an illusion or specter, of the autonomous self, the ego or "I" that Austin presupposes and takes for granted as the necessary foundation of felicitous speech acts.

On the other hand, Austin does want to be able to say plainly, "Our word is our bond." He does want words to have an autonomous power to make something happen. Whatever we were thinking when we said it, what we say binds us. So he wavers back and forth. The potentially endless investigation of the ways (they are legion) in which performatives can go wrong or be infelicitous is to a considerable degree a consequence of this double bind. This investigation takes up most of *How to Do Things with Words*, as Austin bogs further and further down. In this case as in most others, you cannot have your cake and eat it too, though that is what Austin thought he needed to do, if law and order were to be preserved.

This need to have it both ways can be clearly seen in a curious footnote to the odd phrase about the "backstage artiste," Austin's figure for the mind or heart that did not swear when Hippolytus's tongue swore. What in the world is a "backstage artiste"? He or she sounds like some "low type," hardly respectable, furtive and probably dishonest, like all people, in Austin's view, associated with the stage and with playacting. Acting on the stage, for Austin, is as bad as joking and writing poetry, as in one of his examples where he says, plausibly enough until you begin to think about it, that no one would assume two actors married on the stage in a play are really married. The odd and obscure footnote extends the theatrical image: "But I do not mean to rule out all the offstage performers— the lights men, the stage manager, even the prompter; I am objecting only to certain officious understudies, who would duplicate the play" (*HT*, 10). This is obscure, I think, because it is an example of Austin's need to have it both ways. The lights men, stage manager, and prompter (shadowy things or forces out of sight but necessary to the play's working, like my sincerity or clarity of mind) are part, even a necessary part, of the felicitous speech act's necessary circumstances, but the real speech act is the words Hippolytus speaks on the stage. Austin just wants to rule out the idea that the real action is performed offstage, by some "backstage artiste." The alert reader will note that Hippolytus is a character speaking on the stage, a fictitious being whose utterances are firmly excluded by Austin from serious speech acts. How did this figure get in here, in spite of Austin's expulsion of literature?

The passage just discussed shows what Austin's need to have it, impossibly, both ways has to do with his need to exorcise the ghost of poetry. Literature is, for Austin, the prime example of the not-serious, the insincere. He must get it out of the way in order to make felicitous speech acts possible, that is, speech acts uncontaminated by literature. I shall now look more closely at two remarkable extended passages where Austin dismisses poetry, interspersing my citations with a running commentary in brackets as the most economical way to say what I want to say. I shall in effect be creating a kind of miniature dialogue after the fact, somewhat like the many little imaginary dialogues in *How to Do Things with Words*. In these, Austin puts objections in the mouths of invented adversaries ("You will say," he says, or the like) and then answers them. The difference is that I shall often rudely interrupt Austin, even in the middle of a sentence:

> JLA: As *utterances* our performatives are *also* heir to certain other kinds of ill which infect *all* utterances.
>
> [JHM: Note both the learned allusion to "ills the flesh is heir to" and the implications of the disease figure as such. To say poetry infects serious performatives, as Austin is about to do, is certainly not a neutral way of putting it, in spite of the irony in the tone of mock hyperbole which makes it also say, "Don't take my figure too seriously."]
>
> JLA: And these [ills] likewise, though again they might be brought into a more general account, we are deliberately at present excluding.
>
> [JHM: He implies that he could account for these ills but chooses not to do so just at present. Such an utterance has the structure of a deferred claim. It is a special kind of performative: "I could do it, believe me, but I deliberately do not do it now."]
>
> JLA: I mean, for example, the following:
>
> [JHM: Here is an example of Austin's ubiquitous locution "for example," about which I shall have more to say later.]
>
> JLA: a performative utterance will, for example [Again!—JHM], be *in a peculiar way* hollow or void
>
> [JHM: What's peculiar about it? Why does he say that and italicize it? Is there some unpeculiar way to be hollow and void? Presumably that would be cases where, for example, not all the words are said, though otherwise the circumstances are all in order. A few pages earlier, Austin had already distinguished between "hollow" and "void": "When the utterance is a misfire, the procedure which we purport to invoke . . . is void or without effect. . . . On the other hand, . . . {in cases where the proper feelings are not present} we speak of our infe-

licitous act as 'professed' or 'hollow' rather than 'purported' or 'empty,' and as not implemented or not consummated, rather than as void or without effect" (*HT*, 16).]

JLA: if said by an actor on the stage, or if introduced in a poem, or spoken in soliloquy.

[JHM: A soliloquy is like a private language. There is no point in saying "I promise you" or "I bet you" *sotto voce*. A speaker and a hearer must be present, also a third, *terstis*, testifier, unbiased witness.]

JLA: This applies in a similar manner to any and every utterance— a sea-change in special circumstances.

[JHM: That is a wonderful phrase: "a sea-change in special circumstances." I suppose what he means is that a perfectly executed performative in the special circumstances of being performed in a play or said in poetry or in soliloquy is transmuted, transformed, transmogrified into something rich and strange. The reference to Shakespeare's *The Tempest* (and possibly Eliot's *The Wasteland*) makes this count as another literary reference, like the citation from Euripides. Another Shakespearean reference is to the pound of flesh in *The Merchant of Venice* (*HT*, 34). Another is to the handkerchief motif in *Othello* (*HT*, 111). The sea-change in Ariel's song in *The Tempest* says the bones of those drowned in the storm have been turned into coral, but Ferdinand's father and the others were not really dead. It was a sea-change that did not really happen. Poetry, this would imply, is apparently dead, but not really dead, like a half-killed virus in an inoculation or like a ghostly revenant. Ariel's song is of course a lie. It is not just a false constative but also a species of felicitous performative, since it leads Ferdinand to believe his father is dead and to act on that belief. For him, for a time, his father lies drowned. Poetry, Austin's figure implies, is like a lie. (What could be a more traditional idea than that?) Like a lie, however, it is dangerous because it may have a spectral power to make something happen, to bring about some form of what it names. Therefore it must be severely kept down. Here is Ariel's song:

> Full fathom five thy father lies;
>> Of his bones are coral made;
> Those are pearls that were his eyes;
>> Nothing of him that doth fade
> But doth suffer a sea change

Into something rich and strange.
Sea nymphs hourly ring his knell.
(I.ii.399–405)]

JLA: Language in such circumstances is in special ways—intelligibly—used not seriously, but in ways *parasitic* upon its normal use—ways which fall under the doctrine of the *etiolations* of language.

[JHM: *What* doctrine? Has he not just invented it, in another of those inaugural, revolutionary acts of naming? This is the first we have heard of this "doctrine of the *etiolations* of language." Austin's use of the term "parasitic," I note in passing, may conceivably be the source of Meyer Abrams's well-known assertion that a deconstructive reading is parasitic on the "normal," commonsensical reading, to which I tried long ago to respond.][14]

JLA: All this we are *excluding* from consideration. Our performative utterances, felicitous or not, are to be understood as issued in ordinary circumstances. (*HT*, 21–22)

[JHM: "We are excluding" is of course a performative. As if "ordinary circumstances" could exclude all poetry, all etiolations, or possibilities thereof! What a melange of mixed, "poetic" metaphors Austin uses: hollow, void, sea-change, parasitic, etiolations! Each invites its commentary.

Being void is not quite the same thing as being hollow, as a passage already cited from Austin observes. We say a check is void but not hollow, in spite of the fact that void means empty, too. You void your bladder. The vast silence of empty space is "void," or used to be thought so, but you would not be likely to say that astronomical space is "hollow." Or would you?

Parasitic certainly means "dependent on," as a parasitic plant is dependent on, lives off of, its host. The word "parasitic" originally referred to a man who eats you out of house and home: the man who came to dinner and stayed. It means, etymologically, in Greek, "beside the grain," *para* ("beside") plus *sitos* ("grain"). The question is whether the parasite may not belong in the home, or come to be at home there, that is, whether literature may not after all be an essential part of the economy of speech acts. If *How to Do Things with Words* is taken as an example, that is certainly the case, since the parasitic, in the form of jokes, irony, hidden citations, dramatic examples, obscure dialogues, and so on, is essential to the working of the performative revolution Austin is trying to effect. Nevertheless, these features may at the same time undercut his project, undermine it, make it in a peculiar way hollow or void. How could someone bring about a revolution in philosophy, the greatest since Plato, by means of jokes, irony, and literary allusions? But how else could it be done, since the possibility of being nonserious, of being a joke, ironical, poetical, is always a feature of even the most apparently serious speech act? And vice versa. My intention may be to tell a joke, or to write a poem, but that does not necessarily inhibit my utterance from functioning. Or does it? A performative utterance's possibility of working, of doing something, appears to depend on its impossibility, on its being haunted by a ghost of poetry that cannot be exorcised.

"Etiolated" means artificially whitened, like asparagus grown away from sunlight, under straw, or like those white roses the gardener-playing cards are painting red in *Through the Looking Glass*. (Austin twice refers to the Alice books: *HT*, 90, 96.) White roses are an etiolated form of "normal" red ones. To call poetry "etiolated" is to use a striking and powerful figure. Adding the term "doctrine" to it only obscures its power by claiming for it logical rigor. "Etiolated" suggests something deprived of force and life, limp and pale. It is also another way of naming the secondary, derived character of poetry, jokes, soliloquies. They are just like the real thing, but they have been denatured. For Derrida, however, as I shall show in good time, the white rose comes first as the "normal" case, and the red rose is secondary, derived, a special case.]

Another passage expelling jokes, acting, and poetry from the commonwealth of reason is equally forceful but approaches literature from another angle. This new rejection of literature arises in the context of the opposition between use and mention. Austin has by this time introduced the notion of force, with its quasi-material, quasi-Nietzschean idea that language may act almost like a physical energy to make something happen. He calls this "the doctrine of 'illocutionary forces'" (*HT*, 100), another performative invention. The reader will remember that Austin has said, "Actions can only be performed by persons" (*HT*, 60). The person has to be an "I" in full self-possession; therefore animals are excluded, even if by accident they utter a sound that could be understood as a performative ("Go!" or whatever). And women? Are they capable of

"performing an action" with words? Austin does not say they are
not, but the few examples he uses in which women figure are
mostly counterexamples, such as the woman who says "I will not"
(*HT*, 37) when asked if she will take this man as her lawfully wed-
ded husband, thereby destroying the efficacy of a marriage ceremony. Here is the second passage. Again I interpolate my comments in dialogical parentheses:

> JLA: To take this further, let us be quite clear that the expression
> "use of language" can cover other matters even more diverse than the
> illocutionary and perlocutionary acts and obviously quite diverse from
> any with which we are here concerned.
> For example,
> [JHM: There is that leitmotif again.]
> JLA: we may speak of the "use of language" *for* something, e.g. for
> joking; and we may use "in" in a way different from the illocutionary
> "in," as when we say "in saying '*p*' I was joking" or "acting a part" or
> "writing poetry"; or again we may speak of "a poetical use of language"
> as distinct from "the use of language in poetry."
> [JHM: It is not immediately clear what purpose this last distinction
> serves here. The distinction is clear enough, but why bring it in at this
> point, since his example is of someone explicitly writing a poem, not
> someone who, like Austin himself, constantly makes a poetical use of
> language, for example in saying, as he does at one point, that he is
> about to let some of his cats on the table? Austin is haunted by poetry
> and wants to get rid of it, but he keeps coming back to it as to a nag-
> ging reminder of something that he cannot quite get banished but also
> cannot quite get to fit his project. Here he has to define poetry as "pe-
> culiar," as "diverse" from any use of language with which he is con-
> cerned, though he must use it all the time.]
> JLA: These references to "use of language" have nothing to do with
> the illocutionary act.
> [JHM: That is, they are "uses," but uses without force to make any-
> thing happen, whereas the illocutionary act does make something
> happen.]
> JLA: For example, if I say "Go and catch a falling star," it may be
> quite clear what both the meaning and the force of my utterance is,
> but still wholly unresolved which of these other kinds of things I may
> be doing.

[JHM: I do not quite understand this. Which other kinds of things? He has said poetry has "nothing to do with the illocutionary act." That should be the end of it. I suppose he means that using language to write a poem, as John Donne does in Austin's allusion, is to do *something*, just not ever to be uttering a felicitous performative.]

JLA: There are etiolations, parasitic uses, etc., various "not serious" and "not full normal" uses.

[JHM: They are uses, but uses that do not have force. They are useless uses. We are not supposed to go and catch a falling star, but then there are no cats on Austin's table and no bull in his field either, to cite two of his own locutions. Nevertheless, such etiolated uses of language appear to be altogether necessary for him to say what he wants to say. In that sense they are serious. There are no cats on the table, but he means by saying that he is letting his cats on the table that he is giving away his underlying motives or goal. But "giving away" is still a figure. Letting your cats out of the bag. Putting your cards on the table. To say "I am letting my cats on the table" is a witty joke, conflating two figurative idioms.

One way to define Austin's problems is to say that he remains in his analyses at the level of grammar and logic without ever going on explicitly to the tropological or rhetorical levels. He uses tropes brilliantly and commands a powerful rhetoric, but he does not generally reflect on the implications of the way his use of tropes is necessary to get said what he wants to say.]

JLA: The normal conditions of reference may be suspended, or no attempt made at a standard perlocutionary act, no attempt to make you do anything, as Walt Whitman does not seriously incite the eagle of liberty to soar. (*HT*, 104)

[JHM: Come on, J.L., surely you can't mean that. It is clear enough that that eagle of liberty is a shorthand substitute, a metaphor, for what the poem does intend to bring about, namely, political actions or feelings that Whitman defines in a figure as letting the eagle of liberty soar. If you were to apply what Austin says to his own use of figures, his whole project would be etiolated. He does not let any real cats on any real table, but that does not mean what he says is not perfectly clear and effective, forceful. The cats figure calls attention to the performative dimension of Austin's own language and is intended in a good-humored, self-mocking way to do that. Here is one example among many where Austin's inattention to rhetoric (he remains, as I have said, at the level of grammar and logic) seriously gets in his way. He is, nevertheless, brilliant at using rhetorical devices of the most sophisticated kind, taking "rhetoric" both in the sense of tropes and in the sense of persuasion; that is—to put it in his own terminology— Austin excels at making something happen through the use of words.]

So much for Austin's anathemas against poetry. He is like the sorcerer's apprentice in reverse, not wielding magic formulas by accident but trying unsuccessfully to get them to work as exorcisms. Literature keeps rising from the dead, in spite of being firmly banished, buried repeatedly with a stake through its heart: "All this we are *excluding* from consideration."

Is *How to Do Things with Words* Literature?

Having argued that *How to Do Things with Words* is primarily, though of course not exclusively, performative rather than constative, I now claim that it is permeated with literature. It is a literary work through and through, in spite of Austin's refusals to "trench upon" poetry and his strenuous attempts to keep it out. I mean by this not that he refers now and then to literary works by others— Euripides, Shakespeare, Donne, Carroll, Whitman, Eliot, nursery rhymes (see *HT*, 108, for the latter), and so on—but that his own discourse is, necessarily, by his own criteria, often literature. What do I mean by that, and what is its effect on the performative felicity of *How to Do Things with Words*?

Literature or "literariness" appears in *How to Do Things with Words* in at least three distinct ways: in the pervasive irony, in the constant introduction of imaginary examples, and in the frequent use of little fictional dialogues, often presented in indirect discourse, a basic resource of narrative fiction.

How to Do Things with Words is ironic throughout, from the title right to the end, especially in the self-mocking tone but also in the discrepancy between the solemn goal of getting performatives right and the comic or flippant examples that are constantly introduced. One example of mock apology (I have already cited some others in other connections) is what he says about the whole course of lectures just before the end of the last one: "Of course, this is bound to be a little boring and dry to listen to and digest; not nearly so much as to think and write. Moreover I leave to my readers the real fun of applying it in philosophy" (*HT,* 164). Austin, the reader may think, both means this and does not mean it. It is a double irony. Dumb readers or listeners may find the lectures boring, but those in the know will listen or read with fascinated attention, as I have. They will know that they are in the presence of a decisive event in the history of philosophy, that they are watching a revolution unfold. Moreover, it is far from the case that Austin is bored by his own work. The whole book is pervaded by a kind of savage fun in promulgating a new doctrine that he knows will seem scandalous to many, in thinking of striking and often somewhat insolent examples, and in tracing with evident ironic delight the course of his own bogging down.

As for examples of irony, they are legion. Most of Austin's examples are ironically and grotesquely funny, as well as nevertheless serious, since they constitute sharp challenges to the doctrine he is trying to promulgate. I mention only two, one the story of the "low type" who came in at the wrong time and in the wrong place and christened the great new British warship the *Joseph Stalin,* the other (from outside *How to Do Things with Words*), the central (true) story in Austin's essay "A Plea for Excuses," that of the keeper in an insane asylum who accidentally left the hot water on too long and scalded a patient to death. The question is whether the perpetrator can get away with the excuse of saying it was an accident, he didn't mean to do it. (In the historical case Austin is citing, the scalder was exonerated.)

On the one hand, this constant flavor of irony would seem to make *How to Do Things with Words* nonserious through and through. It would be "literary" in the sense that irony is a device we associate especially with literature. Therefore the lectures would be vitiated in their performative felicity. Irony comes up explicitly in one place in a list of features that may make an act of thanking or informing misfire: "it is always possible, for example, to try to thank or inform somebody yet in different ways to fail, because he doesn't

listen, or takes it as ironical, or wasn't responsible for whatever it
was, and so on" (*HT*, 106). Irony says one thing and means another. It fatally undercuts the force of whatever is said. How can we
take seriously a man, like Austin, who always is or always may be
ironically joking?

On the other hand, the reader may remember the odd assertions
at the beginning and end of de Man's "The Concept of Irony."
There de Man unexpectedly, to me at least, asserts that irony can
be performatively effective. It can even be effective in bringing
about an event, or in being an event, that is truly "historical," in
the sense of making history or of making a decisive break in history, as did *How to Do Things with Words* in the history of philosophy. "Irony," says de Man, "also very clearly [Very clearly?!—JHM]
has a performative function. Irony consoles and it promises and it
excuses. It allows us to perform all kinds of performative linguistic
functions which seem to fall out of the tropological field, but also
to be very closely connected with it."[15] The last sentence of de
Man's essay returns somewhat enigmatically to this issue: "Irony
and history seem to be curiously linked to each other. This would
be the topic to which this would lead, but this can only be tackled
when the complexities of what we could call performative rhetoric
have been more thoroughly mastered."[16]

How irony can be performatively effective is not at all clear on
the face of it. How could I be held to a promise that I make ironically, that is, by saying one thing and meaning another? How could
a locution so self-undermining as Austin's ironic self-mockery have
the power, the "Zumbah," as Harold Bloom puts it, borrowing an
African word, to constitute a historical event? How could this etiolated white rose act like a red rose? Nevertheless, if de Man is right,
it may be the irony of *How to Do Things with Words* that makes it
performatively effective. Just because irony is a force of rupture, just
because it is, as Friedrich Schlegel said irony always is, madness, ab-
surdity,[17] words as sheer material sound, it may, paradoxically, determine the felicity of a performative utterance. Irony may give a
performative the Zumbah it needs.

The imaginary examples and the fictional dialogues, my two

other categories of literariness in *How to Do Things with Words,* are devices that are closely connected, since the former often involve the latter. Nevertheless, I make them distinct categories because some dialogues are not examples but part of the give and take of Austin's interchanges with an imaginary reader.

Examples are absolutely necessary to Austin's promulgation of his revolutionary new doctrine. At the same time, like the constant introduction of "poetry," they threaten its seriousness. On the one hand, how could Austin make clear what he is trying to say if he remained at a purely abstract, conceptual level and did not give "concrete examples" of locutions that are, in the right circumstances and taken in the right way, either happy performative utterances or infelicitous ones? Moreover, "ordinary-language philosophy" is committed to reflection on what people actually say, how they actually "use" language. It is impossible to analyze ordinary-language usage without giving examples of it.

On the other hand, there are great dangers, of several sorts, in examples. No example is innocent. Of philosophers and theorists in general it can be said, "By their examples ye shall know them." The best philosophers, from Plato on down, choose examples that are memorable and that put the greatest pressure on the doctrines they are propounding. That is conspicuously the case with Austin. His examples, like the two I have mentioned above, stick in the mind, whereas John Searle's examples in his speech-act theory books, if I may dare to say so, are relatively flat and unimaginative, except perhaps when they are embarrassingly self-revealing, as when he thinks of a man who pretends to be Richard Nixon and tries to enter the White House,[18] or a man who writes notes to his neighbor during a philosophy lecture, or who writes grocery lists to himself. All these examples are analyzed by Derrida with ironic exuberance.[19]

Examples are examples of the trope called synecdoche, part for whole. Their efficacy depends on assuming that the whole is homogeneous and that the example chosen is a fair sample of the whole: "All the other cases are like that." This is conspicuously not so with Austin's examples, or indeed with examples generally. Each example tends to be *sui generis,* an incomparable special case that in the end turns out to exemplify only itself, not to be "typical" at all. Austin's examples always do more or do less than they are supposed to. They exceed their function as illustrations of conceptual points that could have been made without them. They are hyperbolic or hypobolic, and are always in one way or another askew, incongruous, ironic. For example, Austin illustrates a grand idea about passing judgment, making a verdictive, with the demeaning example of the umpire saying, "You're out" (*HT*, 153). Or again, he illustrates the way one may advise or warn or accuse tacitly with the grotesque example of asking the adulterous wife whether that was her handkerchief in X's room (*HT*, 111). In "A Plea for Excuses," he exemplifies the problematic of excuses with a little scene in which you shoot someone's donkey by mistake. "I say, old sport, I'm awfully sorry, &c., I've shot your donkey *by accident*" (*PP*, 185). Austin has a wild, comic imagination of disaster, transgression, and grotesque mishap. This does not always comport with the sober tone of his argumentation. The latter, however, is also characteristically infected with irony, as when he says, "A genuinely loose or eccentric talker is a rare specimen to be prized" (*PP*, 184).

The problematic of the example is something like the problematic of signature. On the one hand, each signature is no doubt an example of signatures in general, or of signatures by one particular individual, but what it exemplifies is that each signature is a species with one example, that each signature has its own unique nature and occasion. A residue of singularity or specificity makes each signature exceed general analysis and renders it opaque, dense with a materiality that resists conceptualization. A signature requires a proper name. On the one hand, each proper name is unique and particular. In a sense, a proper name is meaningless since it falls outside any language system. On the other hand, a signature draws its force from the fact that it repeats earlier signatures by the same hand and can be checked against them for accuracy. In that sense, it is not unique at all.[20] A proper name, moreover, as everybody knows, is almost always also a common name, as is my name "Miller," not to speak of "Hillis," which means "of the hills," or even "Joseph," which in Hebrew means, the Bible tells me,

"Adding" (Gen. 30:24), and is in any case an allusion to all those Josephs in the Bible. My proper name identifies me as male, as probably Caucasian, Anglo-Saxon, or of German extraction. (The last is the case.) Even proper names form part of a system. Even if they were truly unique and therefore meaningless their meaning is to differentiate the one who bears the name from everyone else, just as my email address works because it is different from every other one in the world, though it achieves this difference by being part of a system of email naming.

Austin's project is caught on the horns of a doubleness in examples that is like this doubleness of proper names. On the one hand, each example is unique. On the other hand, examples can be sorted in various ways, classified, if only by a rudimentary method, such as the alphabetization of proper names. If examples are like proper names, however, this helps us (us!) to understand why more and more examples are always needed, potentially an infinite number. More and more are needed if there is to be any hope of covering the whole field of the concept, for example the concept of the performative utterance. A major cause of Austin's "bogging down" is his pragmatic or empirical discovery, through the exploration of examples, that each kind of performative utterance differs from all the others. Each requires its own separate analysis. Moreover, an extremely large number of verbs is to be found, even in a concise dictionary, that might be used performatively. As a result, the number of examples needed, each adding something essential to our understanding of speech-act doctrine, is virtually limitless, particularly if we remember that each performative verb, even the most "standard," like "promise," is capable of being used in ordinary language in many different and distinct ways, each needing to be exemplified.

The more examples Austin adduces, the more he bogs down in fascinating details. Austin has a genius for thinking up wonderful examples that are memorable as problems, not as solutions. Actors married on the stage, for example, are not really married, no one can doubt that, but the marriage in a play reminds one that a "real" marriage is also dismayingly a little like a play. It is the repetition of

a script that has been performed a million times before. The bride
may be superstitiously forbidden to play her own role in the rehearsal of the marriage ceremony for fear that the marriage will already have been performed at the rehearsal. If that is the case, then
the maid of honor, who plays the bride's part as understudy in the
rehearsal, may already be married to the bridegroom, making him
a bigamist the next day, when the "real" ceremony is performed.

More than a little irony inhabits de Man's assertion at the end of
"The Concept of Irony" that "the complexities of what we could
call performative rhetoric" must "have been more thoroughly mastered" before we can begin to tackle the question of how irony and
history are related. The complexities are in the details, in the dismayingly large number of distinguishable performative utterances.
As de Man well knew when he wrote those words, *How to Do
Things with Words,* in its bogging down, not to speak of de Man's
own work with speech-act theory, had already shown that even ap-
proximate mastery of performative rhetoric appears to be an interminable task.

A final problem with examples is that they are, strictly speaking
and by Austin's own criteria, literature. This is so in the sense that
they are nonserious, etiolated, mention rather than use. No reader
is likely to think that Austin is trying to marry anyone to a monkey,
or tempt someone to have another whack of ice cream, or christen
a British warship the *Generalissimo Stalin* when he adduces these as
examples. The examples are, at least supposedly, denatured of any
performative force they might have if used in a "real situation." This
is made clear in one place where Austin refers explicitly to that basic literary device, a fundamental convention of novels as a genre,
indirect discourse. To report someone's speech in *oratio obliqua* is to
transform it into something rich and strange but something without its original first-person force:

> Although we have in this type of utterance a "that"-clause following a
> verb, for example "promise," or "find," or "pronounce" (or perhaps such
> verbs as "estimate"), we must not allude to this as "indirect speech."
> "That"-clauses in indirect speech or *oratio obliqua* are of course cases
> where I report what someone else or myself elsewhen or elsewhere did

say: for example, typically, "he said that... ," but also possibly "he promised that... " (or is this a double use of "that"?), or "on page 456 I declared that... " If this is a clear notion [A footnote here says, "My explanation is very obscure, like those of all grammar books on 'that' clauses: compare their even worse explanation of 'what' clauses." Actually Austin's explanation is extremely clear, elegant, and correct.—JHM] we see that the "that" of *oratio obliqua* is not in all ways similar to the "that" in our explicit performative formulas [He means formulas like "I declare that this conference has begun."—JHM]: here I am not reporting my own speech in the first person present indicative active. [This *is* a little obscure. Does he mean by "here" in *oratio obliqua* or in felicitous performatives? He must mean here in an explicit performative, since reporting even my own speech is not the same as actually uttering that speech in a living situation even though I use a "that"-clause in both cases. In any case the distinction between "I say that I promise to do so and so" (a real performative) and "I said that I promised to do so and so" (a report, *oratio obliqua*) is perfectly clear, though the second locution could be said in such a way that it repeats or intensifies the promise: "I *said* that I promised... " "He said that he promised... " is true indirect discourse and not open to that ambiguity.—JHM] (*HT*, 70–71)

Turning the living performative utterance into an example, as Austin does throughout, is like reporting it in indirect speech, as though it were being narrated in a novel. Indirect discourse is a primary narrative convention in the novel as a genre, for example in the novels of Anthony Trollope or Henry James. Thoughts or assertions, including performative utterances, reported in *oratio obliqua* in a novel are doubly etiolated. They are imaginary in the first place. They are then further deprived of force by being reported by the narrator, who denatures them by transforming what was originally (imagined to be) said in the first-person present tense into third-person past tense. "I promise that... " becomes "He said that he promised that... "

A reader of my remarks might at this point object that of course Austin's examples are in that sense "mention," not use, but that in another sense they are seriously used as examples to make clear Austin's argument and to help it proceed further. That is just my point. The "literary" in the sense of etiolated utterances, utterances that are used not seriously to carry out the performative intention they express but merely to illustrate, are absolutely necessary to Austin's argument. His own discourse is, necessarily and not contingently, infected with the literary. In some cases it even becomes wildly and exuberantly literary, as when Austin says:

> Similarly
> In buzzing I was thinking that butterflies buzzed
> accounts for my buzzing. (*HT*, 127)

This is followed on the next page by more buzzing alliteration: "In buzzing, I was pretending to be a bee," and "In buzzing I was behaving like a buffoon" (*HT*, 128). These lines are not just about poetry. They are (rudimentary) poetry.

I have adduced the fragmentary fictional dialogues as a third category of the literary that haunts *How to Do Things with Words*. Often, but not always, these are an aspect of the examples, as when Austin imagines accusing a woman of adultery by asking whether it was her handkerchief that was found in X's room (the allusion to *Othello* mentioned earlier), or when he exemplifies the way a gesture may work as a wordless performative by saying, "I may persuade some one [*sic*] by gently swinging a big stick or gently mentioning that his aged parents are still in the Third Reich" (*HT*, 119), or when he exemplifies the use of "tempt" by imagining someone saying, "Do have another whack of ice cream," and being answered, "Are you tempting me?" (*HT*, 125). Some of Austin's imaginary dialogues, however, are not examples but part of his own rhetoric of persuasion, as when he makes up an interchange with a listener or reader:

> You will say "Why not cut the cackle? Why go on about lists available in ordinary talk of names for things we do that have relations to saying, and about formulas like the 'in' and 'by' formulas? Why not get down to discussing the thing bang off in terms of linguistics and psychology in a straightforward fashion? Why be so devious?" Well, of course, I agree that this will have to be done—only I say *after*, not before, seeing what we can screw out of ordinary language even if in

what comes out there is a strong element of the undeniable. Otherwise we shall overlook things and go too fast. (*HT*, 123)

Bogging down, it might be said, can be defined as going so slowly as not to go anywhere at all. One of the ways Austin goes slowly is in such fictional dialogues. They count as another intrusive apparition of the etiolated, of literature. Such dialogues belong in a novel and would be at home there, at home in the domain of unreal specters. Such spooks may nevertheless haunt us, as we are haunted by characters in novels we have read or by our memories of Austin's admirable examples, like the one about the patient in the insane asylum accidentally scalded to death by the keeper.

Lurid Tales: The Ideology of Austin's Examples

Austin's examples tell a surreptitious story. This story goes counter to, or at any rate is not told explicitly by, the overt argument of his book. What is that story? What does it performatively, if covertly, accomplish? I call the story an ideology because it seems not to be self-conscious or deliberate but to be tacitly taken for granted. That an ideology is unconscious, that it goes without saying, is what gives it such power to determine belief and behavior.

Most but by no means all of Austin's most memorable examples are of "misfires." They are performatives that are for one reason or another infelicitous. The series of examples drawn from game rules and game playing, for example, tends to be drawn from cases in which the rules are infringed or in which there is a controversy arising from what someone, the umpire most often, said performatively, such as "Over!" or "Out!" Even the examples of felicitous performatives, however, contribute to what may be called a lurid undertext of violence and catastrophe. This undertext presents, in counterpoint to the serious argument, a continuous story of seriocomic disaster. Austin's sensibility and culture is that of an extraordinarily gifted, irreverent, sexist, nationalist, cricket-playing, English-public-school- and Oxbridge-trained male intellectual of his time, the time of the vogue of the English metaphysical poets and of T. S. Eliot, the time of the Third Reich and of British hostility to Stalinism. Austin has

the sensibility, say, of the creators of the comic songs and skits in
"Beyond the Fringe." Such a person knows Greek, Shakespeare,
Donne, and the Bible, as well as the slang of the day (e.g., "cock a
snook," *HT*, 119) and the clichés of philosophical argumentation
(e.g., "The cat is on the mat," *HT*, 146). Such a person also takes
pleasure in violence, in sexual misconduct, particularly by women,
and in situations in which things go wrong in spectacularly
grotesque and comic ways.

In Austin's examples Murphy's law is abundantly obeyed. What
can go wrong does go wrong. People marry monkeys. Horses are
appointed consul. British warships are christened the *Generalissimo Stalin* by some "low type" who happens to come by. Someone
is tempted not to eat an apple, as Adam was tempted by Eve to
do, but to have another whack of ice cream, perhaps even more
unhealthy than the Edenic apple. Patients in lunatic asylums are
boiled alive. The purser rather than the captain tries to marry people on shipboard. Someone in a football game breaks the rules by
picking up the ball and running with it, thereby inventing rugby.
Monkeys utter the command "Go!" Donkeys are shot. Cats are
drowned in butter. Dogs or penguins are baptized. The command
is given, "Shoot her!" A ferocious bull paws the field, ready to
charge, or a thunderstorm threatens, and all you can do is shout
"Bull!" or "Thunder!" People bequeath objects they do not own.
Other people "cock a snook" (which means making a particular
defiant gesture), or throw a tomato at a political rally, or say "Get
out." Cats are let out on the table. People, probably Jewish, are
threatened by being reminded that their aged parents are still in
the Third Reich.[21]

Women come out especially badly in Austin's examples. A vein
of misogyny runs all through *How to Do Things with Words*. It is
the misogyny characteristic of Austin's gender, class, and national
culture. Marriage, in the first mention of it, is said to be something
in which you "indulge." It is the woman, not the man, who throws
a monkey wrench into the marriage ceremony by saying "I will
not." Women are also unable to keep the marriage bond, as in the
example of the woman accused of adultery. If worst comes to worst

you can try saying "Shoot her!" or "I promise to send you to a nunnery," or "I wish you at the bottom of the sea," or "I divorce you," though the last unfortunately (Austin almost seems to think) will not work in a Christian country, only in a Muhammadan one. The reference to Euripides' *Hippolytus*, discussed above, is another sexist and misogynist reference, since Hippolytus came to a bad end because he had the misfortune to have his stepmother fall in love with him. This was a revenge instigated by Aphrodite, who resented Hippolytus's chaste fidelity to Artemis. In another example Austin imagines someone denigrating a woman by saying a sentence in a certain way: "One can mimic not merely the statement in quotation marks 'She has lovely hair,' but also the more complex fact that he said it like this: 'She has lovely *hair*' (shrugs)."[22]

The last citation, by the way, is one place where Austin recognizes that iterability is an essential feature of any utterance: "The phatic act, however, like the phonetic, is essentially mimicable, reproducible (including intonation, winks, gestures, &c.)" (*HT*, 96). I shall show later how Derrida makes iterability the lever with which he overturns the apparent certainties of speech-act theory, including the distinction between felicitous and "literary" ones, the cornerstone of Austin's doctrine.

Austin's running series of examples of women who betray or perform infelicitously the oaths they should keep suggests that only men can be certainly counted on to utter felicitous performatives and be true to the obligations they have sworn to fulfill. A hierarchy as old as Plato is strongly enforced by Austin's examples, with men on top. The hierarchy shades down through women to various animals—monkeys, horses, donkeys, cats—with each lower stage increasingly unable to utter happy performatives.

This static hierarchy is also a temporal one. Another entirely traditional part of Austin's implicit ideology is a belief that both language and the concomitant levels of civilization, as measured by the ability or inability to make discriminations and to utter effective speech acts, suitably nuanced, have gradually developed over the centuries. They have evolved from primitive simplicity to present-day sophistication and subtlety, the sophistication and subtlety of an Oxford ordinary-language philosopher. This is expressed in a symptomatic passage, an important accidental letting of Austin's cats (now in the sense of ideological prejudices) on the table. Primitive language was vague and imprecise, says Austin, with different uses all conflated or smorged up together, as Walt Kelly's Pogo would say. We philosophers, with all our respect for ordinary language, are participating in making discriminations, making language clearer and less ambiguous. We do this by creating distinctions that are performative fiats, not discoveries of what is already there. I once more interrupt my citation with dialogical interpolations as commentary:

JLA: The plausible view (I do not know exactly how it would be established) would be that in primitive languages it would not yet be clear, it would not yet be possible to distinguish, which of various things that (using later distinctions) we might be doing or were in fact doing.

[JHM: You do not know because it is not open to science or to certain knowing. It is not open to verifiable knowledge because it is a myth, a "view" that seems irresistibly "plausible," an ideological fiction required by positings Austin now wants to make. Austin echoes here Rousseau's myth of primitive man before the social contract.]

JLA: For example "Bull" or "Thunder" in a primitive language of one-word utterances

[JHM: Here a footnote is given: "As in fact primitive languages probably were, cf. Jespersen." Do linguists still believe that today? I do not know. Probably not.]

JLA: could be a warning, information, a prediction, &c.

[JHM: But Austin shows that even the most sophisticated and grammatically refined sentences remain fundamentally ambiguous in just this way. Even a sentence using the most complex syntax is still open to being viewed as either constative or performative. It depends on circumstances and on how you take it, as well as on the particular verb and syntax used. This is another fundamental contradiction in Austin's thought. He needs to believe in primitive ambiguity in order to have confidence that he is making progress. His actual experience, however, is of bogging down. He finds that his distinctions do not hold, are inapplicable abstractions. Sophisticated language is just as vague or equivocal or ambiguous as was the hypothetical primitive language that no one speaks or can ever be shown to have spoken.]

JLA: It is also a plausible view

[JHM: I don't necessarily hold it, he implies, but someone might. This is like "If anyone wishes to call it the greatest and most salutary {revolution} in its history," etc., in the opening paragraphs.]

JLA: that explicitly distinguishing the different *forces* that this utterance might have is a later achievement of language, and a considerable one; primitive or primary forms of utterance

[JHM: So to women and animals like horses and monkeys can be added, in Austin's hierarchy of those excluded from uttering felicitous performatives, primitive man speaking in one-word sentences: "Bull!" or "Thunder!"—"hopelessly ambiguous," as Austin says (*HT*, 100).]

JLA: will preserve the "ambiguity" or "equivocation" or "vagueness" of primitive language in this respect;

[JHM: But has Austin not been showing throughout the lectures that sophisticated language is sophisticated precisely in the sense of being adulterated, equivocal, even vague?]

JLA: they will not make explicit the precise force of the utterance.

[JHM: But, as Austin shows, it is impossible to do that. It is always possible, for example, that I am being insincere.]

JLA: This may have its uses: but sophistication and development of social forms and procedures

[JHM: such as the need to put people in jail and keep them there with a clear conscience]

JLA: will necessitate clarification. But note that this clarification is as much a creative act

[JHM: i.e., a performative fiat, like his dubbings, callings, and christenings]

JLA: as a discovery or description! It is as much a matter of making clear distinctions as of making already existent distinctions clear.

[JHM: This was cited earlier. I am now giving the clarifying context.]

JLA: . . . It seems much more likely that the "pure" statement is a goal, an ideal, towards which the gradual development of science

[JHM: A touching confidence in science! Here is another ideological presupposition: that science is making things better and better because clearer and clearer.]

JLA: has given the impetus, as it has likewise also toward the goal of precision. Language as such and in its primitive stages is not precise,

[JHM: You can see here how "ordinary-language philosophers," whatever they say, are not content to leave language as they find it, but want to purify it, to make it more precise, more scientific. Austin exemplifies the comedy of the precise, scientific, logical mind dealing with the messy, a messy he is smart enough to see is irredeemably messy.]

JLA: and it is also not, in our sense

[JHM: *Our* sense?]

JLA: explicit: precision in language makes it clearer what is being said—its *meaning*: explicitness, in our sense, makes clearer the *force* of the utterances, or "how" (in one sense; see below) it is to be taken. (*HT*, 71–73)

[JHM: But, as Austin abundantly shows, you can never wholly control "how" a given utterance is going to be taken, by different people for different uses in different circumstances, or just what its force will be. "Force" is an important word here, as elsewhere in Austin. It indicates his sense that words really can "do things."]

The paradox here is easy to see. On the one hand, Austin wants to remain dependent on ordinary language and not go one inch beyond what everyday people say in everyday circumstances. Ordinary-language usage is the ground, measure, and guarantee of everything he says. On the other hand, a covert but unmistakable disdain for common language pervades his discourse. Ordinary language is untidy, full of irrational complexities, such as the fact that "we do not have 'I tempt you,'" while it is acceptable to say "Let me tempt you to have another whack of ice cream." The philosopher, Austin himself, to be specific, is needed to come along and tidy up the untidy, to create distinctions where none existed before by a series of creative, performative speech acts, and generally to help the evolution of language along toward a higher level of sophistication. Ordinary people speaking ordinary language do not speak of "performatives" as against "constatives," or of "perlocutionary utterances," or, "save the mark!" (*HT*, 62), of "behabitives," "expositives," and "exercitives." Austin himself in "A Plea for Excuses" expresses elegantly this double attitude toward ordinary language: "And it must be added too, that superstition and error and fantasy of all kinds do become incorporated in ordinary language and even sometimes stand up to the survival test (only, when they do, why should we not detect it?). Certainly, then, ordinary language is *not* the last word: in principle it can everywhere be supplemented and improved upon and superseded. Only remember, it *is* the *first* word" (*PP*, 185).

Keeping Law and Order

What is the effect or covert purpose of this massively reinforced ideology, the ideology present in what I have called the "undertext" of the examples Austin happens to choose to make his distinctions clear? One effect I have already named. The examples demonstrate that it is impossible, either when talking about performative language or when using it, to keep poetry out, even though poetry seems fatally to etiolate any attempt to do things with words or to tell someone how to do things with words.

Another effect is more a covert intent. The lurid violence in Austin's examples suggests that social equilibrium is precarious. The examples indicate that the maintaining of law and order is extremely difficult. Pure felicitous performatives are rare and hard to come by, even harder to ascertain that you actually have in hand. The whole of *How to Do Things with Words* can be seen as an argument for rigorous concentration of power and rigor in using it. The lectures tacitly justify bringing in the police. Austin's stories are therefore not just casual examples that are voided by being literary, or by being citations, or by being indirect discourse. They also have a powerful performative force of their own, one of which Austin seems unaware, though one can never be sure of that with someone as smart as Austin was.

The examples reinforce a picture of personal and social life as violent and dangerous. The extreme difficulty of getting a pure explicit performative to work and to do what we want it to do; plus the demonstrations that so many ways exist to "misfire," as a gun fails to go off or is "a flash in the pan"; plus the general way *How to Do Things with Words* is the chronicle of bogging down, not a clear narrative account of how to do things with words, leads to a sense that social law and order are extremely fragile. This works, not surprisingly, as a strong argument for the use of force (whether by language or by other means) for repression, for example the firm control of poetry, women, playacting, soliloquies, animals, "primitive men" who speak archaic languages, and so on. The examples also indirectly insinuate, reinforce, or impose a complex hierarchical ideology whose outlines emerge from the stories when you abstract them from their contexts, as I have done. This ideology contradicts the open, democratic, tentative, reasonable, mild, self-mocking tone, the tone of the man who is completely secure in his institutional placement and authorized by it to be playful and speculative. The examples keep telling the reader that though things may seem to be going along smoothly as we marry, make bets, utter excuses or warnings, sign wills, undertake contractual obligations, christen warships, play games, take care of people in insane asylums, and so on, we are always skating on thin ice, on the verge of catastrophe. A huge bull in the field is always about to charge, and my warning ("Bull!") may always come too late or be misunderstood as a constative description of a "Landscape with Bull." There are so many ways for things to go wrong that it is a miracle that things ever go right, that felicitous performatives get uttered, that we can ever do with words just that thing we intend that they should do.

The effect of all this unhappy violence is to make a strong case for an authoritarian, patriarchal imposition of law and order. If women, for example, say the wrong thing and cannot keep their marriage pledges, then they must be kept forcibly in a subordinate position. You "indulge" in marriage by saying "I do," and in no time at all your wife betrays you. She must be carefully watched.

A rhythmic counterpoint of multitudinous references to law, lawyers, judges, and courtroom scenes punctuates *How to Do Things with Words.*[23] These serve as an explicit reminder of what is at stake in making performatives work. "A Plea for Excuses" uses a legal term in its title ("plea") and gives a detailed account of an actual criminal case from the nineteenth century. Austin's attitude toward law and lawyers is slightly ambiguous. On the one hand, he more than once blames lawyers for their timidity in being unwilling to recognize explicitly the performative dimension of their language:

"Of all people, jurists should be best aware of the true state of affairs. Perhaps some now are. Yet they will succumb to their own timorous fiction, that a statement of 'the law' is a statement of fact" (*HT*, 4). Lawyers want "to apply rather than to make law" (*HT*, 32). Lawyers are timorous because they are, understandably, unwilling to acknowledge what Austin sees clearly about judges and juries if not about lawyers, the somewhat terrifying fact that "As official acts, a judge's ruling makes law; a jury's finding makes a convicted felon" (*HT*, 154). On the other hand, Austin admires the realm of law because it has clear conventions, rules, and protocols to make sure that performative utterances work: "The whole point of having such a procedure [a preordained, ritualized assembly of performative words and rules along with infallible ways to identify who is authorized to use them] is precisely to make certain subsequent conduct in order and other conduct out of order: and of course for many purposes, with, for example, legal formulas, this goal is more and more nearly approached" (*HT*, 44). Austin's entire theory presupposes that for a performative to work, as I have already cited Austin as saying and now need to remind the reader of again, "there must exist an accepted conventional procedure having a certain conventional effect, that procedure to include the uttering of certain words by certain persons in certain circumstances" (*HT*, 14).

It can be argued, without much exaggeration, that the underlying purpose and *raison d'être* of *How to Do Things with Words* is to make it possible for a judge speaking in the proper circumstances to say, "I find you guilty" (*HT*, 58), and have it work to get the miscreant punished. As Austin recognizes, the circumstances are crucial: "The performative nature of the utterance still depends partly on the context of the utterance, such as the judge being a judge and in robes on a bench, &c." (*HT*, 89).

The ultimate goal of Austin's work is to secure the conditions whereby law and order may be kept. This explains the urgency and determination with which Austin seeks to establish a sound doctrine of performative utterances. The stability of civil society and the security of the nation depends on it. We must have some justified way to hold people to their promises, to put people in jail for perjury, for breach of promise, or for bigamy, or for welshing on a bet, and so on. We need ways to be sure that the rules of the game are obeyed, that ships get christened correctly, and that people do not marry monkeys. "But of course lawyers," says Austin in "Performative Utterances," "who have to deal very much with this kind of thing, have invented all kinds of technical terms and have made numerous rules about different kinds of cases, which enable them to classify fairly rapidly what in particular is wrong in any given case" (*PP*, 240).

Though Austin may not at first seem to be much concerned with morality, he is in the end entirely faithful to the implicit charge of the post he held as the White's Professor of Moral Philosophy in Oxford. His examples indirectly assert and reinforce a powerful set of presumptions: the ideal of the male at the top in full possession of his "I," speaking from a position of authority in the right circumstances, with the conventions and the law all already firmly in place, and then women, animals, poets, "low types," actors and actresses, soliloquizers who mutter *sotto voce*, and so on, beneath the men of authority, firmly kept in place.

How to Do Things with Words also reinforces a certain vision of history, as well as of class and (implicitly in what he says about "primitive man") of race. This vision of history has the white male English philosopher, not surprisingly, as its evolutionary goal. This superior man is ceaselessly at work purifying the dialect of the tribe, making distinctions, therefore making law and its enforcement possible, as was not the case for our primitive ancestors who spoke in one-word sentences that were vague and ambiguous. For all his homage to ordinary language, Austin wants to make it better. He believes the philosopher (that is, Austin himself, in spite of his demurrer about not wanting to write a manifesto) is the man to do it. *How to Do Things with Words* is the manifesto (another explicit performative) that establishes that right. Moreover, though Austin asserts that his work is constative, not performative, he explicitly recognizes that the distinctions he is (we are) making (he claims it is collective) are not discovered but invented, created. And he claims the distinctions are a big advance.

That *How to Do Things with Words* is the record of a failure to achieve its goal, securing law and order, that it is the record rather of a bogging, by logical stages, down, is the underlying "serious" drama of the lectures. That so much is at stake in this failure, the reader may surmise, explains Austin's determination at the end, Socrates-like, to keep trying, to go back to even more foundational principles, to keep working at his doctrine until he gets it to work. This may also explain why he was unwilling to publish the lectures as a finished book, or at any rate never got around to doing that before his death. In spite of Austin's efforts, *How to Do Things with Words* is more subversive of law and order than supportive of them.

Two Technological Regimes in Collision

Derrida recognized clearly the way Austin's writing is an attempt to secure law and order. I shall cite what he says as a transition to my discussion in the next chapter of Derrida's theory (and practice) of speech acts. Derrida sees that Austin's entire effort is oriented toward making politics, law, and ethics work, as is appropriate for a professor of moral philosophy:

> I will simply add that it is not necessary to point to a flesh-and-blood example, or to write moralizing pamphlets demanding the exclusion of wicked parasites (those of language or of the *polis*, the effects of the unconscious, the *pharmakoi*, people on welfare, nonconformists or spies) in order to speak an ethical-political language or—in the case of Austin at least, this is all that I wished to indicate—to reproduce in a discourse said to be theoretical the founding categories of all ethical-political statements. I am convinced that speech act theory is fundamentally and in its most fecund, most rigorous, and most interesting aspects (need I recall that it interests me considerably?) a theory of right or law, of convention, of political ethics or of politics as ethics. It describes (in the best Kantian tradition, as Austin acknowledges at one point) the pure conditions of an ethical-political discourse insofar as this discourse involves the relation of intentionality to conventionality or to rules. What I wanted to emphasize above, however, in this regard was simply the following: this "theory" is compelled to reproduce, to reduplicate in itself the law of its object or its object as law; it must

submit to the norm it purports to analyze. Hence, both its fundamental, intrinsic moralism and its irreducible empiricism. And Hegel
knew how to demonstrate how compatible both are with a certain
kind of formalism.[24]

Derrida expresses succinctly here the point I have been demonstrating: that Austin's discourse exemplifies the theory he is expounding, and its "law," even the disturbing law that says the
judge makes the law. The concept of the perdurable, unitary, freely
willing ego, essential to speech-act theory, is, I add in conclusion
to this section, a concomitant of the age of the printed book. It is
no accident that Descartes appeared at the time the hegemony of
the printed book was being firmly established. Along with the separate self-conscious ego ("Cogito, ergo sum") goes the separation of
each ego from all the others, the opacity of the other person's ego,
along with various other inside/outside splits (subject/object; inside the house / outside the house; inside the national borders / beyond them; inside a certain language / outside it; inside a certain
gender, race, or class / other to it; and so on). The subject/object
opposition generates the system of representation that reaches its
apex with realism in the novel. The world is out there. The responsibility of art is to represent it accurately by way of language
or some other medium. Our familiar systems of ethics, law, and society are another concomitant of this system: judicial assigning of
responsibility; laws of contract and copyright; the concept of the
democratic nation-state with its free, responsible citizens; literature
in the modern sense with its (hypothetical) right to say or write
everything as a salient feature of modern democracies; the notion
that fictions ("literature," "poetry") are "etiolated," parasitic on rep-
resentational, verifiable truth-telling; the subordination of women
and animals.

Austin presupposes and reinforces all this complex system of
presumptions. Nevertheless, since the upshot of *How to Do Things
with Words* is not to protect these values and the social order they
sustain but to endanger them, Austin marks the moment of the
breakdown of all these assumptions and of the complex paradigm
they constitute, rather than its secure foundation in the light of

new knowledge about the way language works. The apparently small discovery (or invention) of the performative utterance and the unsuccessful attempt to secure its felicitous working endangers the whole shebang it was meant to shore up.

Derrida, on the other hand, already belongs to the age of cyberspace. For him, as I shall show, the self is multitudinous and variable, permeable, remade from moment to moment by speech acts. Felicitous speech acts are parasitic on infelicitous ones, on literature in fact, rather than the other way around. All those presuppositions of the print age about the self, about social institutions, about the hierarchy of creatures, about gender, class, race, and about literature on which Austin's thinking depends are put in question by Derrida, including even the exclusion of animals from the realm of beings able to execute happy performatives. Derrida's entire effort as a political and ethical thinker has been to invent or discover new ways of thinking that will work toward what he calls "the democracy to come." His recent work challenges the concept of the citizen located in one topographically delimited *polis*. This concept was sustained by print media, with their fact/fiction, real/imaginary, inside/outside, private/public dichotomies. The Cartesian self of the age of the book is now being replaced by the televisionary or cinematic or Internet "self" who dwells within a new transnational regime of telecommunications. That regime is a place of spectral, fleeting, impermanent selves created and decreated by media. In those media the distinction between fact and fiction, real and imaginary, no longer firmly holds or no longer holds in the same way as it did in the era of the printed book.

By a strange and quite extraordinary coincidence, both Derrida and de Man were present at Harvard at about the same time Austin was giving his lectures there (1955), though neither attended them. De Man was a junior fellow at Harvard in 1955, and Derrida was at Harvard as an exchange student from the École Normale Supérieure in Paris in 1956–57. As de Man once told me, the word around Harvard was that a somewhat odd and quirky Oxford don was giving a series of rather dull and fairly inscrutable lectures. That, however, may have been just de Man's view of it at the time.

I gather, on the contrary, that for one distinguished auditor, Stanley Cavell, hearing Austin's lectures was a decisive turning point in his thinking. Austin, Derrida, and de Man, fortuitously assembled at more or less the same time in the same university, brought together in one place and time the old at the moment of its dissolution and the new in its dawning. The age of print and the first glimmers of the age of the World Wide Web, cyberspace, and hypertext (the latter strikingly anticipated in Derrida's *Glas*) came together and overlapped. As I shall show in my discussions of Derrida and de Man, the difference between these two thinkers is that while the latter was the most astute critic of the assumptions of the print age, the former has done more to indicate what new ethics, what new forms of responsibility, community, and democracy, might replace the old. Both have also indicated the place literature should have in this new realm, in the possible/impossible democracy to come. In both cases the appropriation and transformation of Austin's speech-act theory is essential to the work they do.

§ 2 Jacques Derrida

Jacques Derrida does not just take up the question of speech acts at a certain moment in the trajectory of his work, the moment of "Signature Event Context" and "Limited Inc a b c... ," but instead includes a new concept and practice of performative utterances as a fundamental part of all his work, especially his later writing and teaching. The new concept and new practice are associated with new notions of ethical and political decision, action, and responsibility. Derrida's recent seminars and books have almost all centered on particular examples of performative utterances and gestures: the gift, the secret, testimony, hospitality, responsibility, pardon and perjury (*pardon* and *parjure* in French, words whose prefixes echo one another), the distinction between law and right, ethical decision, political declaration, capital punishment, and so on. This prolonged meditation about speech acts has been closely intertwined, as I shall show, with a continued interrogation of the relation of speech acts to literature and with an interrogation of literature itself. As Derrida asserts in the "Afterword" to *Limited Inc*:

> The rules, and even the statements of the rules governing the relations of "nonfiction standard discourse" and its fictional "parasites," are not things found in nature, but laws, symbolic inventions, or conventions, institutions that, in their very normality as well as in their normativity, entail something of the fictional. Not that I assimilate the different regimes of fiction, not that I consider laws, constitutions, the declara-

tion of the rights of man, grammar, or the penal code the same as novels. I only want to recall that they are not "natural realities" and that they depend upon the same structural power that allows novelesque fictions or mendacious inventions and the like to take place. This is one of the reasons why literature and the study of literature have much to teach us about right and law.[1]

This role of literary study in the investigation of ethical and political commitment, the role of "speech acts in literature," is my focus in this book. This dimension of Derrida's work might be defined as an attempt to understand, to make clear, and to secure the possibility of a new kind of performative. A recent example is the remarkable meditation on the promise in "Avances," Derrida's preface to Serge Margel's *Le tombeau du dieu artisan* (The tomb of the artisan god).[2] This new kind of performative is different from the "standard," "serious," "nonetiolated" Austinian one. It is foreshadowed nevertheless by Austin's work, for example when Austin says, "The judge makes the law."

Derrida's *Specters of Marx*, to cite one case of recent concern with speech acts, is among many other things a book attempting to identify and validate this new kind of performative. Derrida makes this explicit in one passage near the beginning. There he speaks of "the originary performativity that does not conform [*qui ne se plie pas*] to preexisting conventions, unlike all the performatives analyzed by the theoreticians of speech acts, but whose force of *rupture* produces the institution or the constitution, the law itself, which is to say also the meaning [*le sens*] that appears to, that ought to, or that appears to have [*qui paraît, qui devrait, qui paraît devoir*] to guarantee it in return. *Violence* of the law before the law and before meaning, violence that interrupts time, disarticulates it, dislodges it [*le démet*], displaces it out of its natural lodging: 'out of joint.'"[3] Somewhat later in *Specters of Marx*, Derrida speaks of "this dimension of performative interpretation, that is, of an interpretation that transforms the very thing it interprets [*qui transforme cela même qu'elle interprète*]."[4]

Though many such formulations punctuate Derrida's more recent work (and I shall analyze some of them), nevertheless full understanding of Derrida's theory and practice of performatives depends on a direct confrontation with *Limited Inc*. I shall concentrate, at least at first, primarily on that.

"These Things Are Difficult": Not Being Able to Mean What You Say

What Derrida says about speech acts is not easy to get straight, as he himself acknowledges. In the "Afterword: Toward an Ethic of Discussion," he says of the first two essays in *Limited Inc*: "I consider them very difficult, overdetermined, and extremely intricate," and he exhorts us "to *reread* attentively" (*LI*, 114). Elsewhere in the "Afterword" Derrida comments, "These things are difficult, I admit; their formulation can be disconcerting" (*LI*, 119). What Derrida writes is, by his own admission, intrinsically hard to understand. Why? Partly because it goes against "our" most habitual and ingrained ways of thinking, but also because those ideological mystifications about Derrida's work and about so-called "deconstruction" with which "we" have been bewitched possess great power.

An incredible example of this is a statement on the back cover of the paperback *Limited Inc*. This amazing text asserts again a mistaken presumption about what Derrida says, a presumption that Derrida patiently denounces in *Limited Inc* itself, as well as in many other places. So forceful is this presumption that it is imperturbably reaffirmed even on the cover of a book by Derrida himself, in a statement written no doubt with the best will in the world, and perhaps even approved by Gerald Graff, the editor of the volume. Referring to the three essays gathered in *Limited Inc*, the statement observes: "They are perhaps the clearest exposition to be found of Derrida's most controversial idea, that linguistic meaning is fundamentally indeterminate because the contexts which fix meaning are never stable." Derrida states, within the very book so labeled: "I do not believe I have ever spoken of 'indeterminacy,' whether in regard to 'meaning' or anything else. Undecidability is something else again. . . . Undecidability is always a *determinate* [*déterminée*] oscillation between possibilities (for example, of meaning, but also of

acts). These possibilities are themselves highly *determined* in strictly
defined situations (for example, discursive—syntactical or rhetorical—but also political, ethical, etc.). They are *pragmatically* determined" (*LI*, 148; *LI/F*, 274). If the book gets advertised under a false
slogan that Derrida has earnestly and repeatedly denounced, wary
readers will not take it for granted that they can read this text without distorting it through the lens of their presumption to know
what Derrida is going to say, *must* be going to say.

What a change in tone and atmosphere we encounter in the
shift from *How to Do Things with Words* to *Limited Inc*! In the former we found the coolly ironic, self-assured yet self-deprecating
tone of the Oxford don. Austin speaks from a powerful tradition of
apparently casual but actually severely rule-bound "analytical"
philosophical discourse, a tradition he reveres and cultivates even
as he labors for his "revolution." When we open *Limited Inc*, however, we find the parodic and aggressive tone of the polemicist
(though Derrida denies that this work is polemical). Derrida, unlike Austin with his politely generalized foils, ridicules a real figure,
John Searle, who had attacked Derrida's first essay on speech-act
theory, "Signature Event Context" (reprinted in *Limited Inc*). Derrida draws his terminology from the realm of phenomenological or
"continental" discourse, a realm no less rule-bound than Austin's
tradition, but one whose rules Derrida breaks. Throughout *Limited Inc*, words like "absolutely," "radical," "transcendentality," "destruction," and "rupture" abound, and the reader is plunged into a
terminology of death and absence, the terminology of French ex-
istentialism, of Nietzsche, Husserl, and Heidegger—but turned to
new uses by Derrida. The terminology, the tone, the whole ambiance, would probably have driven Austin up the wall and certainly did drive Searle up the wall. Here is an example from early
in "Signature Event Context":

> To be what it is, all writing must, therefore, be capable of functioning
> in the radical absence of every empirically determined receiver in gen-
> eral. And this absence is not a continuous modification of presence
> [as, Derrida observes, Condillac would have it—JHM], it is a rupture
> in presence, the "death" or the possibility of the "death" of the receiver

inscribed in the structure of the mark (I note in passing that this is the point where the value or the "effect" of transcendentality is linked necessarily to the possibility of writing and of "death" as analyzed). The perhaps paradoxical consequence of my here having recourse to iteration and to code: the disruption, in the last analysis, of the authority of the code as a finite system of rules; at the same time, the radical destruction of any context as the protocol of code. (*LI*, 8)

One way to define the difference between Austin and Derrida is to say that Austin claims to be making a revolution within philosophy, whereas Derrida is making a revolution beyond philosophy. Derrida defines Plato's condemnation of writing, in the *Phaedrus*, for being iterable and for being cut off from the speaking "I," as "the philosophical movement par excellence" (*LI*, 8). Derrida wants to reverse that 2,500-year-old movement, whereas Austin claims to be continuing a movement already begun within philosophy and therefore to be continuous with it, even if the discovery (or invention) of speech acts is a revolution within philosophy, the "greatest and most salutary in its history."[5] Yet another preliminary way to define the difference is to say that Austin was a polysemist. He was admirably sensitive to the different grammatical and logical ways a given word can be used in different contexts. Derrida, however, is a disseminationist or a dehiscentist, to coin two words. He distinguishes dissemination sharply from polysemy. Words, for Derrida, scatter like seed or break open, like a dehiscent seedpod, and in doing so are inaugurally productive. They are always already broken open, divided within themselves.

Yet another salient way to define the difference or even abyss that separates Derrida from Austin is to note what Austin says at the beginning of his BBC talk, "Performative Utterances." "I remember," says Austin, "once when I had been talking on this subject that somebody afterwards said: 'You know, I haven't the least idea what he means, unless it could be that he simply means what he says.' Well, that is what I should like to mean."[6] As I have shown in the previous chapter, Austin often loses control of what he is saying and inadvertently (at least it seems inadvertent) says quite other things. He does not (apparently) mean what he says. For

Derrida, however, this is a regular feature of any discourse. "Iterability" (about which more later) means that you can never be sure that you mean what you intend to mean or mean to say: "Iterability alters, contaminating parasitically what it identifies and enables to repeat 'itself'; it leaves us no choice but to mean (to say) something that is (already, always, also) other than what we mean (to say), to say something other than what we say *and* would have wanted to say, to understand something other than... etc." (*LI*, 62; the "etc." is Derrida's).

A final preliminary point of comparison is that both *Limited Inc* and *How to Do Things with Words* are politically exigent and committed, as no careful reader can doubt. Derrida's political commitments in his speech-act theory and in his theory of literature as it is related to that are, however, radically different from Austin's.

Derrida's Dual Writing

Perhaps the best place to begin to account for *Limited Inc* is to note that it is inhabited by two quite different kinds of language, like an ellipse that is controlled by two centers. One is a patient and logical language of philosophical argumentation. "Signature Event Context" is written primarily in this style, so that Derrida can refer to it near its conclusion as "this very *dry* discussion [*ce propos très* sec]" (*LI*, 20; *LI*/F, 49). The other style is a violent language of comic parody or ridicule. In the main essay of *Limited Inc*, "Limited Inc a b c... ," Derrida makes scornful fun of John Searle, as part of his response to Searle's attack on his "Signature Event Context." Irony is mixed with austere and difficult philosophical argument. The latter involves careful citation of and commentary on practically all of Searle's essay, "Reiterating the Differences: A Reply to Derrida."[7] The reader experiences a kind of overkill in Derrida's use of both styles. Moreover, the styles shade into one another, without an identifiable frontier between them.

Limited Inc is one of Derrida's most joyous and exuberant works. It is evidence of amazing intellectual energy and inventiveness, prime testimony to the inimitable eloquence in many different stylistic modes that is characteristic of his work. It also makes one hope not ever to be the target of such an essay. Derrida more or less mops the floor, as one says, with Searle, though it is doubtful if it changed Searle's mind, as Derrida in one place testifies. "I perceive even today," he says in the "Afterword,"

> in this violence of mine [He means in "Limited Inc a b c... "—JHM] the very clear—and I hope distinctly formulated—concern to distinguish and submit to analysis the brutality with which, beneath an often quite manifest exterior, Searle had read me, or rather avoided reading me and trying to understand. And why, perhaps, he was not *able* to read me, why this inability was exemplary and symptomatic. And for him lasting, doubtless irreversible, as I have since learned through the press. [He probably means Searle's attack on him in *The New York Review of Books*.—JHM].[8] (*LI*, 113)

Searle will most likely go to his grave convinced that Derrida has misunderstood speech-act theory.

Examples of Derrida's ironic violence come in the opening pages of *Limited Inc*. "Signature Event Context" begins by picking up and making problematic the word "communication" in the invitation proffered him to present just that, a "communication," before a conference entitled "Communication" held by the Congrès international des Sociétés de philosophie de language française at Montreal in August 1971. Similarly, "Limited Inc a b c... " (that is the full title of the long second essay in *Limited Inc*) begins by noting that the manuscript of Searle's "Reply," sent as an advance copy to Derrida with an invitation to reply in turn, has on the top, at the left, above the title, as something the reader encounters even before the title, so that it is even more on the margin of the work, outside and inside at once, than the title, the following: "Copyright © 1977 by John R. Searle." The date, 1977, Derrida tells the reader, was handwritten above the copyright symbol. With this little bit of professorial solemnity and expression of anxiety (as if Searle fears that if he does not establish copyright right away someone, Derrida perhaps, will steal his essay and publish it under his own name), Searle inadvertently hands himself over to the man his attack has made into his antagonist. As Derrida observes, it is Searle's strategy, in assaulting "Signature Event Context" for being full of mistakes and misunderstandings, to claim, as Derrida quotes Searle as writing, to "concentrate on those [points] that seem to me to [be] the most important and especially on those where I disagree with his conclusion." Derrida, on the other hand, explicitly focuses on the apparently peripheral, marginal, unimportant: "I do not 'concentrate,' in my reading (for instance, of the *Reply*), either exclusively or primarily on those points that appear to be the most 'important,' 'central,' 'crucial.' Rather, I deconcentrate [*déconcentre*], and it is the secondary, eccentric, lateral, marginal, parasitic, borderline cases which are 'important' to me and are a source of many things, such as pleasure, but also insight into the general functioning of a textual system" (*LI*, 44; *LI*/F, 90).

The same thing might be said, I note in passing, of my focus in the previous chapter on the subtext, the more or less hidden story, that Austin's examples inadvertently tell. They tell how the power of Murphy's law, which says that what can go wrong will go wrong, applies to performative utterances as to other human endeavors. They also tell the story of a woman's inability to give her word and keep it. In a somewhat similar way, in the opening or "false beginning," as he calls it, of "Limited Inc a b c... " Derrida shows how Searle's ridiculous anxiety to copyright his essay before it has even been published gives him away. It reveals not only his vanity and his naiveté, but also his inability to comprehend how speech-acts work. As Derrida points out, if Searle's article speaks the truth, then that truth is universal. It belongs to everyone, and it is absurd or even improper to try to copyright it. Searle should be glad if someone steals it, since that would confirm the truth of what he has said. It would be appropriate to copyright it only if it is fictional, something that Searle, or whoever has copyrighted the essay in his name, has made up and therefore can legitimately try to protect as his own fabrication. You do not copyright the multiplication table. (I note that changes in copyright law and copyright convention now mean, as I understand it, that it is not necessary to make an explicit copyright statement in order to copyright what one writes. These words

I am writing now are automatically copyrighted as soon as they appear on my computer screen. That is, I guess, reassuring or at least ought to reassure someone who is anxious, like Searle, to preserve his original inventions. As for me, I would of course be glad to have what I write stolen because I believe it is true.)

In order to analyze and ridicule Searle's copyright notice, Derrida cites it verbatim, as I have cited Derrida's citation, though I have omitted to cite the quotation marks that Derrida, conventionally enough, puts around the citation. Derrida calls attention to his conventional practice by citing his citation and then citing it yet again, ending with three sets of quotation marks nested one within the next. I add a fourth to show that I am citing Derrida's citation of a citation of a citation: " " " "Copyright © 1977 John R. Searle." " " "

This multiplication of the clothespins of citation works in three different ways at once:

1. To demonstrate that any sign or set of signs can be cited, put within quotation marks, and that you can even cite a citation, ad infinitum.
2. To demonstrate that any sign or set of signs can be repeated, iterated, which is not quite the same thing as citing it, since the iteration may not be a citation but a new act of copyrighting, for example copyrighting with the same words a different essay that Searle might have written in 1977. Derrida says this explicitly later on: "Iteration . . . was never confused with citation. . . . Iteration alters, something new takes place [*L'itération altère, quelque chose de nouveau a lieu*]" (*LI*, 40; *LI*/F, 82). One might respond to this that something new takes place in citation as well. Derrida says as much in the detailed discussion of the two. Nevertheless the difference between citation and iteration is clear enough. Citation is supposed to drag its original context implicitly along with it, while iteration may use the same words in a radically new context.
3. To raise questions about the efficacy of the speech act that writing "Copyright © 1977 by John R. Searle" apparently is, though it would, as Derrida says, be imprudent and hasty to presume that we know it "is" a performative (*LI*, 31). If a performative utterance or writing can be repeated and cited in this way, how can one be sure of the efficacy or "felicity" of any one of the elements in this series, even the apparently "first" one? Is only the first one "use," all the others "mention"? It would

seem so, and yet it is also obvious, when you come to think of it, that a citation can, in the proper circumstances, itself be an inaugural speech act, for example when I indict someone by citing exactly what he or she said, as Derrida does with his abundant citations of Searle. (He says, correctly, that he cites nearly all of Searle's "Reply," many parts more than once, as in the case of the "marginal" copyright notice.) And, to iterate a point made in the previous chapter, who would disqualify a marriage ceremony because what the participants say is citation, which parts of it must be if it is to be performatively efficacious?

Derrida then goes on to raise questions about the unity and power to utter felicitous performative speech acts, for example the act of copyrighting performed by "John R. Searle," whoever he is or purports to be. The standard theory of performative utterances depends, as I have shown in my discussion of Austin, on the unitary "I" or ego in full possession of its senses and intentions. Is it, however, demonstrably certain that whoever or whatever inscribed "Copyright © 1977 by John R. Searle" at the top left-hand corner of the manuscript sent to Derrida for his possible response is such an ego or responsible subject? Derrida does not think so. He dismantles with gay exuberance the presumed unity of "John R. Searle." This act of dismantling is a splendid example of this penchant of Derrida's style in "Limited Inc a b c... ":

> And, of course, how can I be absolutely sure that John R. Searle himself (who is it? [*qui est-ce?*]) is in fact the author? Perhaps it is a member of his family, his secretary, his lawyer, his financial advisor, the "managing editor" of the journal, a joker [*un farceur*] or a namesake [*un homonyme*]?
>
> Or even D. Searle (who is it?), to whom John R. Searle acknowledges his indebtedness: "I am indebted to H. Dreyfus and D. Searle for discussion of these matters." This is the first note of the Reply. Its acknowledgment of indebtedness does not simply fit into the series of four footnotes since its appeal is located not in the text but in the title, on the boundary, and is directed, curiously enough, at my name— "*Reply to Derrida*[1]"—
>
> If John R. Searle owes a debt to D. Searle concerning this discussion, then the "true" copyright ought to belong (as is indeed suggested along the frame of this *tableau vivant*) to a Searle who is di-

vided, multiplied, conjugated, shared. What a complicated signature! And one that becomes even more complex when the debt includes my old friend, H. Dreyfus, with whom I myself have worked, discussed, exchanged ideas, so that if it is indeed through him that the Searles have "read" me, "understood" me, and "replied" to me, then I, too, can claim a stake in the "action" or "obligation," the stocks and bonds, of this holding company, the Copyright Trust [*je peux préten-dre aussi à quelque "action" ou "obligation," sinon à quelque "holding" dans la société de ce "copyright"*]. And it is true that I have occasionally had the feeling—to which I shall return—of having almost "*dictated*" this reply. "I" therefore feel obliged to claim my share of the copyright of the *Reply*.

But who, me? [*Mais qui, moi?*] (*LI*, 31; *LI*/F, 66, 68)

As Derrida demonstrates later on in the essay, he feels that he has, almost, dictated Searle's "Reply" because one of the most ludicrous, but also most sinister, aspects of the "Reply" is that it uses arguments and takes positions against *Sec* (Derrida's abbreviation for "Signature Event Context") that are drawn from *Sec* itself and clearly stated there. Derrida's hyperbolic and joyful disintegration of "John R. Searle" leads a few pages later to a stroke of invective genius: calling Searle "Sarl." If the entity that signs the copyright statement is an indeterminate number ($3 + n$) of people, including even Derrida himself, joined together in a "Copyright Trust," then it would be proper to give that entity the official legal name of such an entity. In the United States that name is "Incorporated," abbreviated as "Inc." In Great Britain it is "Limited," or "Ltd." In France it is "Sarl," short for "Société à responsabilité limitée." Derrida drops two "e's" from Searle's name, and for the remainder of the essay refers to the author of the "Reply" as Sarl. (The translation, incorrectly I think, says he has also dropped an "r," unless Searle's middle initial is meant, but "John" also is dropped [*LI*, 36]). This transformation, as Derrida says, has the advantage of avoiding what might be offensive in criticizing John R. Searle, the presumed individual person:

I hope that the bearers of proper names will not be wounded by this technical or scientific device. For it will have the supplementary advantage of enabling me to avoid offending individuals or proper names in the course of an argument that they might now and then consider, wrongly, to be polemical. And should they, perchance [*d'aventure*], see this transformation as an injurious or ironic alteration, they can at least join me in acknowledging the importance of the desires and fantasms [*des enjeux, désirs, phantasmes*] that are at stake in a proper name, a copyright, or a signature. And, after all, isn't this the very question which, posed by *Signature Event Context*, will have involved us in this improbable confrontation? It is as a reminder of this, and not to draw the body of his name into my language by subtracting one *r* and two *e*'s [The French just says "*avec deux e en moins.*"—JHM], that I thus break [*sauter*] Searle's seal (itself already fragmented or divided). (*LI*, 36; *LI*/F, 76)

I shall return to the question of what Derrida means by saying that Searle's seal (*sceau* in French, usually referring to a stamp used as a signature) is already fragmented and divided.

This passage is admirably ironic polemic, whatever Derrida says about not being polemical, and however often he repeats a (performative) exhortation to himself: "Let's be serious [*Soyons sérieux*]" (*LI*, 34 twice, 39, etc.; *LI*/F, 73, 80). At the same time, the canny reader of "Limited Inc a b c... " will note, at least in retrospect, that all the chief serious issues are raised in this passage: division of the signature; iterability; citationality (if there is such a word); the impossibility of identifying the origin of an utterance with a single "I"; the question of what constitutes an event, a "taking place," in the present; the questioning of the Austinian distinction between serious and nonserious or parasitic; and so on. In order to be faithful to Derrida's argument I shall occasionally follow him and use "Sarl" rather than "Searle." Like Derrida, I shall use "Searle" for the person, "Sarl" for the textual persona, though this distinction is difficult to maintain. That difficulty is one of Derrida's main points in *Limited Inc.*

In addition to openly ironic passages, *Limited Inc* contains many passages written in a different style, the style of clear, cogent, rigorous, unironic, "serious" logical argument. The terminology is of logical implication, of the distinction, for example, between necessity and possibility, and so on. This is the style of professional philosophical argumentation. It shows Derrida's mastery of that. Nevertheless, an unmistakable ingredient of ironic excess, as though he were speaking to a slightly dense student and had to go slowly and repeat himself, makes these passages readable as parody of the philosophical style of which they nevertheless demonstrate mastery. That is one meaning of the "a b c... " in the title. Derrida is producing a little elementary primer or "a b c" of speech-act theory that he hopes is at a level Searle may be able to understand, dense though he is, and in spite of the fact that he has demonstrably not read or understood even the most obvious things about "Signature Event Context," for example the central importance of what Derrida says about signatures in the last section of that essay. As Derrida himself observes, another meaning of the "a b c," and of the labeling of the essay's sections by the rest of the letters in alphabetical order from d to z, is that these devices call attention to the fact that the interchange or "debate" (it is not either a dialogue or a confrontation) between Derrida and Searle takes place in particular written languages (Searle's American and Derrida's French): "One of the conventions of this debate (and, says *Sec*, not the least determining, in the final analysis) is that it should take place, if it takes place [*qu'il a lieu, s'il a lieu*], in a graphic element of a type that is phonetic, and more precisely, alphabetical" (*LI*, 45; *LI*/F, 90).

An example of the logical, pedagogical style in "Limited Inc a b c... " is the following crucial passage about iterability:

> I repeat, therefore, since it can never be repeated too often [A joke there, since he is talking about repeatability.—JHM]: if one admits that writing (and the mark [*la marque*] in general) *must be able* to function in the absence of the sender, the receiver, the context of production, etc., that implies that this power, this *being able*, this *possibility* is *always* inscribed, hence *necessarily* inscribed *as possibility* in the functioning or the functional structure of the mark. (*LI*, 48; *LI*/F, 96)

Why does Derrida deploy these two styles (and every mixture in between)? One answer is that he does it for the fun of it. As he more than once remarks, he takes great pleasure in what he is doing (e.g.,

LI, 35). This is evident in the joyful exuberance of passages I have cited. But there are two other good reasons. The ironic ridiculing of Searle allows Derrida to exemplify rather than simply to describe the issues that are at stake in the confrontation. This means that "Limited Inc a b c... " is deliberately and self-consciously a tissue of (written) performative utterances. The performative aspect of *Limited Inc* is not more or less covert, as is the case with Austin's *How to Do Things with Words*, but up front, in your face, underlined, salient. Derrida wants *Limited Inc* to do something with words, for example, to disqualify what Sarl says, and he wants the reader to notice that this is happening.

These speech acts are gestures of displacement and inauguration. They "deconstruct" Sarl's assumptions and at the same time generate a new theory and practice of speech acts. This double doing defines, for Derrida, the work of so-called deconstruction: "What is called [*Ce qu'on appelle*] deconstruction endeavors to analyze and if possible to transform this situation" (*LI*, 138; *LI*/F, 255). He means the political and institutional situation, with its "enormous networks of presuppositions" (ibid.), within which Austin and Searle, and also Derrida himself and I, here, wrote or write. Derrida's double performative gestures thereby make way for a new politics and a new ethics based on this new form of speech acts. This is stated explicitly both at the end of "Signature Event Context" and in a passage in the "Afterword." In the former, Derrida asserts, "Deconstruction cannot be restricted or immediately pass to a neutralization: it must, through a double gesture, a double science, a double writing [*par un double geste, une double science, une double écriture*]—put into practice a reversal of the classical opposition *and* a general *displacement* of the system" (*LI*, 21; *LI*/F, 50). In the "Afterword" the strategy of "Limited Inc a b c... " is made explicit:

> On the one hand, I try to submit myself to the most demanding norms of classical philosophical discussion. I try in fact to respond point by point, in the most honest and rational way possible, to Searle's arguments, the text of which is cited almost in its entirety. On the other hand, in so doing I multiply statements, discursive gestures, forms of writing, the structure of which reinforces my demonstration

in something like a practical manner; that is, by providing instances of "speech acts" which by themselves render impracticable and theoretically insufficient the conceptual oppositions upon which speech act theory in general, and Searle's version of it in particular relies [*se fie*] (serious/nonserious; literal / metaphoric or ironic; normal forms / parasitical forms; use/mention; intentional/nonintentional; etc.). This *dual writing* [*double écriture*] seemed to me to be consistent with the propositions I wanted simultaneously to demonstrate on the theoretical level and to exemplify in the *practice* of speech *acts*. Of speech acts concerning which I did not want it forgotten that they are *written*, and that this opens up possibilities and problems which are not negligible. (*LI*, 114; *LI*/F, 206)

Deconstructive analysis, productive displacement—these are the two moves accomplished simultaneously by Derrida's dual writing.

What Is Iterability?

The lever or fulcrum for this double operation is iterability. The three essays in *Limited Inc* taken together make up an extended treatise on iterability and its implications. As Derrida indicates more than once, iterability, which is neither a concept nor not a concept, is a new name for what is given many different names in the course of Derrida's work: *différance*, hymen, *supplément, pharmakon*, dissemination, writing, margin, parergon, the gift, the secret, and so on. Each name works differently. Each is part of a different semantic or tropological system. Derrida says just this in a footnote to the "Afterword." The footnote also indicates what is peculiar about the word "iterability" within this series. It is both a member of the series and at the same time also a feature of each member of the series. They all are marked by iterability or all are iterable or all name a form of iterability:

The list of these words is not closed, by definition, and it is far from limiting itself (currently) to those that I cite here or see often cited (*pharmakon, supplement, hymen, parergon*). . . . If the list remains indeed open, there are already many others at work [*au travail*]. They share a certain functional analogy but remain singular and irreducible

to one another, as are the textual chains from which they are inseparable. They are all marked by iterability, which however seems to belong
to their series. (*LI*, 155; *LI*/F, 211–12)

That there are so many of these words, potentially a limitless
number, indicates that no one of them is proper. What these words
name has no proper name, only deferred, displaced, figurative, or
improper names, that is, catachrestic labels.

What Derrida means by iterability seems straightforward enough
and easy enough to understand. The reader, nevertheless, should be
wary, since it turns out to be "difficult," almost unfathomably so,
to understand iterability. Iterability is nothing more, as a passage already cited indicates, than the possibility for every mark to be repeated and still to function as a meaningful mark in new contexts
that are cut off entirely from the original context, the "intention to
communicate" of the original maker of the mark. That originator
may be absent or dead, but the mark still functions, just as it goes
on functioning after the death of its intended recipient. Dickens's
novels were intended primarily for English and American readers
who bought them when they were first published in volume form,
or even read them, before that, in monthly or weekly "parts." That
does not keep them from being readable today. I must repeat again
here the passage already cited, so the reader can be sure that Derrida says what I say he says. The passage can never be repeated too
often. My repetition is an example of iterability: the first time, I
made the citation to exemplify Derrida's "logical" style; and this
time, I make it to highlight the way the passage defines "iterability." The same words in a new context are altered, which, as I shall
show, is one of Derrida's chief points about iterability. Here is the
passage again:

> I repeat, therefore, since it can never be repeated too often: if one ad-
> mits that writing (and the mark in general) *must be able* to function in
> the absence of the sender, the receiver, the context of production, etc.,
> that implies that this power, this *being able*, this *possibility* is *always* in-
> scribed, hence *necessarily* inscribed *as possibility* in the functioning or
> the functional structure of the mark. (*LI*, 48)

"Mark" is Derrida's general name for any sign or trace, including a word, but it also includes, for example, a deictic gesture, a gesture that has meaning and is therefore more than itself. Similarly, the red paint on the sign Tess of the d'Urbervilles reads in Hardy's novel ("THOU, SHALT, NOT, COMMIT—") is more than just red paint. Even the color red becomes significant, a "mark," when the terrified Tess fills in the missing last word: "adultery."[9]

To say "mark" rather than "word" or even "sign" has important implications, as Derrida indicates. It allows him, for example, to challenge the age-old notion, going back to Aristotle, that man is the only animal with language and therefore radically distinct from the other animals. Cats, for example, make and use marks of many sorts. They must therefore, it might appear, be included in the human family; or rather, the border between human and animal in this case breaks down. Nevertheless, what Derrida means by iterability seems simple and clear enough: A mark can be iterated. Who could dispute it? And, as Derrida notes, neither Austin nor Searle does dispute it. What they would dispute is the consequences Derrida draws from this simple fact about "marks." The consequences are far-reaching.

The first consequence is radically to disqualify the basic strategy of Austin's and Sarl's theory of speech acts, that is, the exclusion from analysis and definition of the marginal, the etiolated, the non-standard, the nonserious, the fictional, the parasitic, the impure. These are "further matters which we are not trenching upon," comments Austin (*HT*, 122). "I must not," the reader will remember him saying, "be joking, for example, nor writing a poem" (*HT*, 9), nor acting on the stage, nor speaking in soliloquy, not, that is, if I want my performative utterance to be felicitous. Austin's and Searle's doctrines of speech acts, in somewhat different ways, both depend on an assumed subordination of the nonserious to the serious, the impure to the pure. First, for example, comes the standard promise made by an "I," ego, or subject, a person, ideally male, in full possession of his senses, speaking in the present with deliberate intention, and uttering "I promise so and so." Then come all the impure promises as deviations from that, for example promises imitated in a novel, or acted on the stage, or said with intent not to keep them, or under coercion, or by someone who is insane or drugged, or by someone from a culture that does not share our assumptions about promises. Since all these are secondary, impure, etiolated, fictive deformations of real promises they can be safely set aside so the standard, serious promise can be analyzed. This sounds reasonable enough. Such subordination of the fictive to the real is reason itself, from Plato and Aristotle on.

Derrida, in a characteristic gesture, reverses this hierarchy. For him, the pure promise is a "fictional" phantasm derived from the impure one. Why is that? Because what exists "originally" are speech acts marked, from the beginning or even before the beginning, by iterability, that is, by impurity. The impure is the original. The pure, normal, standard speech act, if there were such a thing, would be derived from that. Derrida's reproach to Austin and Searle is that they do not recognize that since impurity is always possible, that possibility cannot be set aside. It must always be considered in the analysis of any speech act or other utterance, even the apparently most verifiable constative ones.

Derrida has much fun with the example Sarl cites, from a "dead author," of an apparently straightforward and unequivocal sentence. The sentence is perfectly understandable and functional even though its author is dead: "On the twentieth of September 1793 I set out on a journey from London to Oxford" (quoted in *LI*, 60). Derrida undoes this apparent simplicity by suggesting the many different ways Sarl's sentence might be used. Just as I am using citations from Austin and Derrida for the purposes of my own argument, wresting them from their contexts in the writings of each, so Derrida suggests that Sarl's sentence might function in many different contexts, potentially an infinite number. He compares Sarl's sentence with the enigmatic but suggestive "I forgot my umbrella," "abandoned like an island among the unpublished writings of Nietzsche" (*LI*, 63):

> A thousand possibilities will always remain open, even if one understands something in this phrase [the one cited by Sarl about setting

out for Oxford] that makes sense [*fait sense*] (as a citation? the beginning of a novel? a proverb? someone else's secretarial archives? an exercise in learning language? the narration of a dream? an alibi? a cryptic code—conscious or not? the example of a linguist or of a speech act theoretician letting his imagination wander for short distances, etc.) (*LI*, 63; *LI*/F, 122)

Sarl's sentence may indeed not be entirely fortuitous, not be just one randomly chosen example of a presumably transparent sentence. It may indeed be a cryptic code, since John R. Searle did set out for Oxford, though rather later than September 20, 1793. Searle received at Oxford the training that made him an ordinary-language philosopher, a disciple and defender (as he thought) of Austin. He was called to the vocation of finishing the work that Austin, alas, did not live to complete. We all, the sentence may be read as implying, ought to set out for Oxford, leaving not only London but, especially, Paris far behind. We all ought to become ordinary-language philosophers like Searle, or Sarl. The sentence appears purely constative but contains a cryptic performative exhortation when it is transferred to the use Sarl makes of it.

To imagine using Sarl's cited sentence in all the wildly divergent ways Derrida proposes exemplifies another all-important feature of iterability. When a sentence or other mark is reused in a different context, it does not remain the same. It is altered. Derrida recalls that the Latin root *iter* in "iterability" probably comes from a Sanskrit word meaning "other." Derrida here quotes in a new context in "Limited Inc a b c..." a passage from "Signature Event Context":

> Limiting the very thing it authorizes, transgressing the code or the law it constitutes, the graphics of iterability inscribes alteration irreducibly in repetition (or in identification): a priori, always and already, without delay, *at once* [*toujours déjà, sans attendre, aussi sec*]: "Such iterability—(*iter*, again, probably comes from *itara*, *other* in Sanskrit, and everything that follows can be read as the working out of the logic that ties repetition to alterity) structures the mark of writing itself, no matter what particular type of writing is involved" (*Sec* [as reprinted in *LI*], 7). (*LI*, 62; *LI*/F, 120)

These sentences already involve a further feature of iterability, the most counterintuitive, enigmatic, and difficult to grasp of all the aspects of Derrida's concept/nonconcept of iterability. It is easy enough to accept the fact that a given sentence can function differently in many different contexts, though perhaps not so easy to accept the fact that this means the impure is the original, the putative pure is the derived and secondary. Even more difficult to understand and accept (perhaps it is the un-understandable and unacceptable as such) is Derrida's assertion that even a sentence or other collection of marks that appears only once never to appear or be used again, never to be iterated or altered by being inserted in a new context, is already, from the beginning, divided within itself. There is no such thing as a pure, standard, nonfictive, self-identical utterance. Such marks are divided within "a priori, always and already, without delay, *at once, aussi sec.*" (The play here is between the French idiom *aussi sec,* meaning at once, and the acronym *Sec,* meaning "dry," that Derrida has chosen for "Signature Event Context." The same play governs Derrida's admission at the end of *Sec* that it has been a "very *dry* discussion [*propos très* sec].") Here is Derrida's way of saying this:

> But let's go a bit further. Does this kind of *fact* [a pure utterance that exists only once and is tied to a single sender and a single receiver] really exist? Where can we find it? How can we recognize it? Here we reach another type of analysis and of necessity. Isn't the (apparent) *fact* of the sender's or receiver's presence complicated, divided, contaminated, parasited by the *possibility of an absence* inasmuch as this possibility is necessarily inscribed in the functioning of the mark? This is the "logic," or, rather, the "graphics" to which *Sec* seeks to do justice: As soon as [*aussi sec*] a possibility is essential and necessary, *qua possibility* (and even if it is the possibility of what is named, *negatively,* absence, "infelicity," parasitism, the non-serious, non-"standard," fictional, citational, ironical, etc.), it can no longer, either de facto or de jure, be bracketed, excluded, shunted aside [*laisser de côté*], even temporarily, on allegedly methodological grounds. [This is what Austin does when he says he won't trench on the nonserious.—JHM] Inasmuch as it is essential and structural, this possibility is always at

work [*cette possibilité travaille*] marking *all the facts*, all the events, even those which appear to disguise it. Just as itera*bility*, which is not iteration, can be recognized even in a mark which *in fact* seems to have occurred only once. I say *seems*, because this one time is in itself divided or multiplied in advance by its structure of repeatability. This obtains *in fact*, at once [*aussi sec*], from its inception on [*dans l'unique fois*: this means rather "in the singular occurrence"]; and it is here that the graphics of iterability undercuts [*brouille*] the classical opposition of fact and principle [*le droit*], the factual and the possible (or the virtual), necessity and possibility. In undercutting these classical oppositions, however, it introduces [*contraint à*] a more powerful "logic." (*LI*, 48; *LI/F*, 97)

The hardest part of iterability to understand is the way it "broaches and breeches" (Samuel Weber's translation of the difficult French word *entame*) the utterance even the first and perhaps only time it is spoken. Iterability is *différance*, that is, an opening within the utterance itself that makes it differ from itself, within itself. Iterability opens a gap within the utterance, but also makes it defer itself, opening up abysses of temporality before and after, in a kind of future anterior. This temporality makes the present never present because it always reaches toward a past that was never present and a future that will never be reached as present, as in what Derrida says about the way the democracy to come [*à venir*] is always future. Iterability, because of its gapping or gaping, is dehiscent, disseminative.

The word "dehiscent" is a botanical word meaning "opening at pores or by splitting to release seeds within a fruit or pollen from an anther." "Indehiscent" means not splitting open at maturity. "Dehisce" means to burst or split open along a line or slit, as do the ripe capsules or pods of some plants. These words come from Latin *dehiscere*: *de*, off + *hiscere*, to open, split, inceptive of *hiare*, to be open, to gape, from *ghei* to yawn, gape, suffixed variant form of Greek *khasma*, yawning gulf, related to modern English "chasm," "gap," "gape," "gasp." Related English words are "gill," meaning ravine, chasm; "gyrfalcon," meaning voracious or yawning bird. The connection to "chasm" is provocative. It stresses the yawning gap from which the seeds are cast forth, as from a mysterious, in a certain sense empty, and in any case not wholly intelligible or masterable, source. Iterability comes from the *iter*, the *alter*, what Derrida has more recently called *le tout autre*, the wholly other.

One can see the connection, nevertheless, of dehiscence and dissemination. It is because both the coded message of the speech act and the intention of the one who speaks or writes it is dehiscent, breached, divided, with a yawning gap, that it is not so much polysemic (Derrida firmly dismisses that) as disseminated, like seed broadcast by a bursting seed pod. As a result, consciousness, intentionality, meaning, and intention unequivocally identifiable by the hearers, or promisees, are effects of iterability, rather than the other way around. As Austin well recognized, and as Derrida also knows, the whole traditional juridico-political system depends on believing the opposite, on having the opposite fully institutionalized and operative. Otherwise, how could you hold someone responsible for a promise or for a signature to a contract and then put them in jail if he or she failed to live up to the commitment?

An example of dehiscence might be my own discourse here. It is a feature of iterability that I am able to cite Derrida's words, repeat them exactly. That citation would seem to deprive Derrida's words of force. If, for example, I quote him as saying, "Through these difficulties, another language and other thoughts seek to make their way. This language and these thoughts, which are also new responsibilities, arouse in me a respect which, whatever the cost, I neither can nor will compromise [*transiger*]" (*LI*, 153; *LI*/F, 282), no one is likely to think that I am myself affirming that something arouses in me a respect that I neither can nor will compromise. Nevertheless, the demand on me to "teach Derrida," or write about his work, whatever exactly that means, comes not from my institution but from the texts of Derrida's work and to some degree against the institution, since there are some features of the institution that would *not* want Derrida to be repeated in the classroom or written about. This demand on me to teach Derrida and to write about him, imposed on me by the texts he has written, means that when I do so my own words have or may have an independent performative force, even when I am citing and commenting on what Derrida wrote.

Derrida, in his recent seminars on witnessing, has repeatedly cited Celan's striking phrase, "Nobody bears witness for the witness":

> Niemand
> zeugt für den
> Zeugen.[10]

One sees the force of what this means. The witness I bear, the testimony I give, can be given only by me alone. I alone can bear witness for what I witnessed. Witnessing is absolutely individual, sui generis, unique, private, singular. Derrida draws an extreme conclusion from this, namely that no act of testimony can be verified. It is Derrida alone who knows what demand is being made on him by that other law, the demand that arouses his respect and that he cannot and will not compromise. Nevertheless, as Derrida also reminds us, the word "testimony" comes from *testis*, from *terstis*, meaning the third. The witness testifies as a third to some transaction between at least two others. In this case I bear witness to the transaction between Derrida and that other law that arouses in him an infinitely exigent respect. As a witness or third to Derrida's witnessing, I come to testify to my respect for what Derrida has said. This respect leads me to wish to bear witness in my turn in an act of teaching or writing that wants to be as faithful as possible to just what Derrida said. I want to pass it along to my own auditors or readers in a repetition with difference, a dissemination, a dehiscence that will have incalculable effects, or perhaps no effects. Who can know beforehand? How would you confirm even afterwards the effect of teaching or writing? Another way to put this is to say that even the most exact repetition of Derrida's words on my part does not exonerate me from responsibility. Far from it. That act of repetition or manifestation of iterability is a speech act that puts a heavy burden, debt, responsibility, or obligation on my shoulders. I am responsible for what I say even if what I say stems from an attempt to say again as exactly as I can just what Derrida says, with abundant citation to prove he said just that.

The Domino Effect

Let me look now a little more closely at how each of the features necessary to Austin's or Sarl's normal, serious, felicitous, standard speech act is undone by iterability. This happens in a domino effect—each element knocking down the next in a cascade—though this figure is itself disqualified in a way I shall specify. The existence of each of these features, the reader must remember, is not denied. What is denied is the possibility of their pure unadulterated existence, as well as their status as original and originating stabilities of which their nonserious or infelicitous counterparts are parasitic derivations that can be safely set aside. Derrida's fundamental gesture here is a reversal: what Austin and Searle see as secondary and derived, Derrida sees as the original matrix, and what Austin and Searle see as original and originating, Derrida sees as no more than fragile and always contaminated effects. "By no means," says Derrida in "Signature Event Context,"

> do I draw the conclusion that there is no relative specificity of effects of consciousness, or of effects of speech (as opposed to writing in the traditional sense), that there is no performative effect, no effect of ordinary language, no effect of presence or of discursive event (speech act). It is simply that those effects do not exclude what is generally opposed to them, term by term; on the contrary, they presuppose it, in an asymmetrical way [*de façon dissymétrique*], as the general space of their possibility. (*LI*, 19; *LI*/F, 47)

The key words here are "effect" and "asymmetrical." Consciousness, intention, being the right person in the right place at the right time speaking certain words conventionally taken to produce certain effects—christening a ship or marrying a couple, for example—are not original and originating sources from which certain results felicitously flow and of which the infelicitous nonserious nonstandard are secondary and parasitic versions. They are secondary to a general matrix that makes them possible and impossible at once. In a gesture that is Nietzschean through and through, Derrida reverses the assumed cause and effect and makes the presumed cause (the self-presence of consciousness to itself, for example) the fragile and impure effect of a more general "graphematics." The latter simultaneously makes such effects possible and makes it impossible for them ever to be pure. This is that "asymmetry" of which Derrida speaks. What Austin and Searle presume to be original is only one effect among many other possible ones within a general space of potentiality with which they are not commensurate and which they do not exhaust. Other effects are the parasitic ones, such as irony, jokes, and literature, which Searle and Austin condemn as "etiolated."

Elsewhere in "Signature Event Context," Derrida speaks of "the increasingly powerful historical expansion of a general writing [*une écriture générale*], of which the system of speech, consciousness, meaning, presence, truth, etc., would be only an effect, and should be analyzed as such" (*LI*, 20; *LI*/F, 49). Derrida's more recent work on the new media, what he calls "the new regime of telecommunications," develops what he meant in 1971 by "the increasingly powerful historical expansion of a general writing." As Derrida demonstrates, and as I have also asserted at the end of Chapter 1 of this book, Austin's speech-act theory and its reductive codification by Searle belong to the age of print. Austin and Searle imperturbably repeat, apparently without being aware that they do so, assumptions that belong not only to the general tradition of Western philosophy but more specifically to continental philosophy from Descartes to Husserl. Austin and Searle are not "ordinary-language philosophers" if we mean by that something novel and revolutionary, broken off from the tradition. "Ordinary-language philosophy" is a version of that tradition. Derrida, on the contrary, belongs to the age of the new communications technologies that are bringing the age of traditional print media to an end.

Farewell to the Ego

The first requisite undone by iterability is the self-presence of the ego, the "I" that says "I promise." For an Austinian performative to work, the ego must be self-identical and self-present, fully conscious of itself and of its intentions, its *vouloir-dire* or will to say, to mean, and to mean what it says. The ego must be self-identical and self-present not only in the moment it utters a speech act but also continuously through time, so that I can be held tomorrow to promises I made yesterday. The link to Cartesian and post-Cartesian assumptions is evident, as is the (unconscious or inadvertent) link to Husserl—inadvertent since perhaps neither Austin nor Searle has read Husserl. Austin, however, makes explicit his indebtedness to Kant as predecessor (*HT*, 2, 3).

The possibility of holding someone to his or her promise would, it seems evident, depend on the self-presence of the ego. In place of that, Derrida, as the exuberant passage about Searle as copyright holder exemplifies, proposes that the utterer of a performative is an anonymous horde, Sarl for Searle. How can we be sure that John R. Searle wrote those words, "Copyright © 1977 by John R. Searle"? It may have been his financial advisor or an impostor. Derrida makes this point forcefully in a parenthesis in "Limited Inc a b c... ":

> (Perhaps it should be said in passing that the *différance*, as we have just seen, removes from itself what "seems to have been written *in its* name." Namely, the proper name, which suddenly finds itself removed. It can thus transform itself, at once [*aussi sec*], and change itself into a more or less anonymous multiplicity. This is what happens to the "subject" in the scene of writing. That Searle's seal should become at once and without waiting for me, Sarl's seal, is therefore anything but accidental. It is a little like the multitude of stockholders and managers [*la multiplicité des actionnaires et des gestionnaires*] in a company or corporation with limited liability [*une société à responsabilité limitée*], or in a limited, incorporated system; or, like that limit which is supposed to distinguish stockholders from managers. Even here, the signatory is no exception.) (*LI*, 57; *LI*/F, 112)

This passage explains the title, "Limited Inc" and explains also the ironic hijinks in the opening pages of "Limited Inc a b c... " As is characteristic of Derrida, those pages are the enactment, one might say the performative act of putting in place, of what is then later more objectively or conceptually expressed. This act of displacement/replacement always involves wordplay, doing something with or to words, as in what is done with the word "communication" at the beginning of "Signature Event Context," in a passage to which I have already referred. This overture is an example of displacing and thereby positing something new that Derrida sees as essential to deconstruction. It is deconstruction at work, as working, or, as Austin would put it, as having illocutionary or perlocutionary *force*. In the opening paragraphs of "Signature Event Context," Derrida turns the word "communication" against its expected use in a conference on linguistic communication by recalling that the word can also mean the transmission of force or energy; he does so again later on in his "communication" by noting that Austin correctly sees performative utterances not as communicating information but as having force (*LI*, 1–3, 13).

"Communicating, in the case of the performative," says Derrida, paraphrasing Austin, "if such a thing, in all rigor and in all purity, should exist (for the moment I am working within that hypothesis and at that stage of the analysis [Later of course Derrida will find numerous reasons why that rigor and purity are impossible.—jhm]), would be tantamount to [*ce serait*] communicating a force through the impetus [*impulsion*] of a mark" (*LI*, 13; *LI/F*, 37). Exemplifying this, the opening pages of "Limited Inc a b c... " enact, bring about through the force of language, the doubling and redoubling of the ego, multiplying to infinity, $x + n$, the named subject who is the apparent emitter of a performative (or constative, for that matter) statement. Derrida, here as elsewhere, wants to do what he talks about. He wants to communicate an impetus through the force of the marks he inscribes on paper or emits as modulated currents of air when he speaks what he has written, for example when he presented the English version of "Limited Inc a b c... " as a lecture at Yale in 1977, his first presentation in English at that university.

Just how, I ask, do marks turn into forces? Derrida is certainly right to say that "force" is a key word in Austin's discourse about speech acts. The notion of force is also buried in the prefix "per" in Austin's term "perlocutionary." And Derrida is right, of course, to say that Austin's notion that words have force has a Nietzschean ring to it. But just how does that force "communicate" itself? This process seems to me extremely mysterious and problematic. A children's chant in the United States, said in taunting reply when someone has called you a bad name, goes like this: "Sticks and stones may break my bones, but names can never hurt me." I call it a chant because it is a magical, apotropaic incantation. It is not just a constative statement of fact but a performative speech act intended to ward off the effect of the name-calling. As a constative statement, the chant is false, however effective it may be as a performative. Names *can* hurt you. But just how does that happen? How do little marks on paper or trivial modulations of air, ripples that would not even cause a leaf to tremble, come to have earthshaking physical effects, as when the right person in the right circumstances says, "I declare war," or when I say "I love you" and am believed?

Certainly force *is* communicated by the impetus of marks to which meaning is ascribed or posited. Who could doubt it? It happens all the time. But just how and why it happens is the whole mystery of performative language. This mystery is the secret transference from meaningful marks to physical force that makes it possible to do things with words. Is this transference after all no more than a metaphor, the figural displacement involved in the sleight of hand when one moves from "communication" in the sense of conveying an intended meaning (as when we speak today of new communications technologies or as when Derrida speaks of "telecommunication") to "communication" in the sense of transferring a force or energy (as when one billiard ball smacks against another)? Which of these two senses of the word "communication" is the literal, which the figurative? Or are two incompatible and heterogeneous literal senses enclosed in the same word?

What I have called a sleight of hand is visible in Derrida's sentence in the little phrase "would be tantamount to" (*ce serait* in the French original of *Sec*, more literally "that would be" [*LI*/F, 37]) and in the tautology that is not a tautology in the iteration of "communicating," first in one sense and then in the other: "Communicating, in the case of the performative, . . . would be tantamount to communicating a force through the impetus of a mark."

"Tantamount to"? "Impetus" (French: *impulsion*)? In just what senses? As literal equivalence or as figurative displacement or stand-in? Where is the impetus? That the translator, Samuel Weber, found it necessary to translate the more straightforward "ce serait" in "Communiquer, dans le cas du performatif, . . . ce serait communiquer une force par l'impulsion d'une marque" as "would be tantamount to" indicates Weber's sense that something slightly more than tautological equivalence is present in the stuttering iteration joined by that "would be": "To communicate . . . would be to communicate." That is what Derrida says; in French: "communiquer . . . ce serait communiquer." Just how does one "communication" turn into the other? That is the question, perhaps an unanswerable one, though no one can doubt that this communication between two senses of "communication" happens.

Farewell to the Receiver

Along with the suspension of the ego as the single so-called "emitter" of the speech act goes also the suspension of the single so-called "receiver" as destination of the message. If iterability and "graphematics," as the general matrix of all forms of language and other codes or systems of marks, oral and written, phonetic and hieroglyphic, mean that any utterance or writing can function in the radical absence of the sender, they also mean that any utterance or writing must be able to function in the radical absence of any particular receiver. On the one hand, "for a writing to be a writing [One must remember how Derrida has extended the term 'writing' to include readable 'marks' in general, including oral ones, pictures, gestures, etc.—JHM] it must continue to 'act' [*'agir'*] and to be readable even when what is called the author of the writing no longer answers for what he has written, for what he seems to have signed, be it because of a temporary absence, because he is dead or, more generally, because he has not employed his absolutely actual and present intention or attention, the plenitude of his desire to say what he means [*son vouloir-dire*], in order to sustain what seems to be written 'in his name'" (*LI*, 8; *LI*/F, 28–29). On the other hand, "in order for my 'written communication' to retain its function as writing, i.e., its readability, it must remain readable despite the absolute disappearance of any receiver, determined in general. My communication must be repeatable—iterable—in the absolute absence of the receiver [*destinataire*] or of any empirically determinable collectivity of receivers" (*LI*, 7; *LI*/F, 27). Since a determined collectivity of receivers is an essential component of the context Austin presupposes as essential to the working of a felicitous performative, Derrida's claim that a mark can function in the absence of its destined receivers deconstructs yet another of Austin's essential presuppositions. In a somewhat later work, *The Post Card* (*La carte postale*, 1980), this takes the form of claiming that a post card in its openness determines as its receiver whoever happens to read it.

Intention Disabled

The next domino to fall is "intention." I mean intention not only in the sense of a desire to achieve a certain end through a performative utterance—for example to marry the couple, if you are the right person in the right circumstances, by saying, "I pronounce you husband and wife"—but also in the sense of the intention to say what you mean to say, to control the meaning of what you say. It is easy to see what iterability does to intention in both these senses. If the sign is already divided within itself by iterability, and if it can act and be readable both in the absence of its "origin" in an emitting consciousness and in the absence of any determinable or "intended" receiver, then my intention to say something, my *vouloir-dire*, which in French means "meaning" but literally says "wish to say or mean," has, distressingly, no power to control the meaning of what I say.

At one moment in his "Afterword" Derrida scornfully dismisses Searle's book on intention[11] for the way it makes a boastful virtue out of being ignorant of continental work on intention, most obviously that of Husserl (*LI*, 130). In Husserl's work, as most people know, the concept of intention is crucial. Derrida asserts that the problem of intention has become increasingly puzzling to him, a deep question, not an answer: "What does 'intention' properly mean as the *particular* or *original* work [*mise en oeuvre*] of iterability? I admit that this enigma grows increasingly obscure for me" (*LI*, 130; *LI*/F, 236). Working within the Husserlian tradition but radically displacing it, Derrida affirms, in a passage I have already cited, that we can never mean what we say or say what we mean. Whatever we say or write is broadcast or disseminated by the fundamental dehiscence of all marks. Whatever marks I make are cut off from my intention and left free to have meanings and ever new meanings in all the potentially different contexts in which they may be read. These meanings can never be controlled or seen beforehand, even though they are not limitless and are controlled or limited by the specificity of the marks in question, for example that they are in one language rather than another. This means not that intention does not exist or have effects, as Sarl mistakenly understands Derrida to be saying, but that it never straightforwardly and in all rigor and purity achieves what it intends. In a typology of different forms of iteration,

> the category of intention will not disappear; it will have its place, but from that place it will no longer be able to govern the entire scene and system of utterance [*l'énonciation*]. . . . Given that structure of iteration, the intention animating the utterance will never be through and through present to itself and to its content. The iteration structuring it a priori introduces into it a dehiscence and a cleft [*brisure*] which are essential. (*LI*, 18; *LI*/F, 45–46)

The result of this division within intention is that the goal or telos of a serious, standard, felicitous speech act can never be certainly attained. If unitary origin vanishes or becomes a phantasmal "effect," end suffers a similar fate. Basic to a normal performative utterance is the assumption that it will bring about what it aims to bring about. If intention, however, does not control or limit the iterable grapheme, then one can never be sure that it will bring about what it intends:

> Intention or attention, directed toward something iterable which in turn determines it as being iterable, will strive or tend in vain to actu-

alize or fulfill itself, for it cannot, by virtue of its very structure, ever achieve this goal. In no case will it be fulfilled, actualized, totally present to its object and to itself. It is divided and deported [*déportée*] in advance, by its iterability, towards others [*l'autre*], removed [*écartée*] in advance from itself. This re-move makes its movement possible [*Cet écart est sa possibilité même*]. Which is another way of saying that if this remove is its condition of possibility, it is not an eventuality, something that befalls it here and there, by accident. Intention is a priori (at once [*aussi sec*]) *différante*: differing and deferring, in its inception. (*LI*, 56; *LI*/F, 111)

The Unconscious as Matrix

In the rich and overdetermined sequence of essays that makes up *Limited Inc*, Derrida shifts at certain important moments to the way speech-act theory must repress the unconscious. In texts written before and after "Limited Inc a b c... ," Derrida has commented brilliantly on Freud and on psychoanalysis generally, for example in "Freud and the Scene of Writing" and in many other essays.[12] The psychoanalytic vector is an essential dimension of Derrida's work. In "Limited Inc a b c... ," the invocation of the Freudian unconscious functions as yet another way to put in question the notion of the self-conscious ego present to itself and to its intentions. What Derrida says also works to assimilate the Freudian unconscious, or at least Derrida's reading of that, to the general space of graphematics that is the matrix both of "felicitous" and of "parasitic" speech acts. He calls the graphematic unconscious "a type of 'structural unconscious' [*inconscience structurelle*]." This existence of this hidden space is betrayed in the way "*no* intention can *ever* be fully [*de part en part*] conscious, or actually present to itself" (*LI*, 73; *LI*/F, 139).

In order to get on with its business, standard speech-act theory has to lock up the unconscious and pretend there is no such thing. Derrida's wants to use language performatively to break that lock. Only this will make way for a new kind of ethics and politics that will be compatible with iterability and its consequences. This is said in so many words in an important passage in "Limited Inc a b c... " (about that new ethics and politics I shall say more later):

Each time that the question of the "ethical and teleological discourse of consciousness" [cited from *LI*, 18, that is, from *Sec*] arises, it is in an effort to uncover and to break the security-lock [*le verrou de sécurité*] which, from *within the system*—inside of the prevailing model of speech acts that govern the current theory in its most coherent and even most productive operation [*dans son agencement philosophique*]—condemns the unconscious as one bars access to a forbidden place. By placing under lock and key, by sealing off; here, by prohibiting that the Unconscious—what may still be called the Unconscious—*be taken seriously*, be taken seriously, that is, *in (as) a manner of speaking*, up to and including its capacity for making jokes [*son pouvoir de Witz*].[13] The Unconscious not only as the great Parasite of every ideal model of a speech act (simple, serious, literal, strict, etc.), but the Unconscious as that parasite which subverts and dis-plays [*déjoue*], parasitically [*en le parasitant*], even the concept of parasite itself as it is used in the theoretical strategy envisaged by Austin or by Searle. (*LI*, 73–74; *LI*/F, 139–40)

A characteristic reversal or invaginating inversion, turning the outside in, is present in the citation just made. Not only does the parasite contaminate the purity of the normal, but the concept of parasite itself is thereby shown to be an invalid concept derived from the mistaken assumption of the priority of the normal. The overall goal of both "Signature Event Context" and "Limited Inc a b c… " is to show, patiently or not so patiently, that there is no such thing as a pure, normal speech act, even though there are "effects" that make such a thing appear to be. The effects are derived from a matrix that also generates the contaminated, impure, parasitic speech act. The impure, etiolated, hollow, void, fictional performative is not parasitic on the normal ones. It is the other way around, or rather, both are effects of the same matrix. "Signature Event Context" and "Limited Inc a b c… " attempt to bring this reversal into the open, to make it happen where it can be seen. They do this by a complex, prolonged speech act.

The astute reader will perhaps at this point wonder whether what Derrida says about performative speech acts in general—that their intention can never be accomplished—would apply also to the explicit performative dimension of his own discourse. Can Derrida mean what he says and do with words what he means to do? On the one hand the answer must be that he cannot. What is sauce for the goose must be sauce for the gander. On the other hand, Derrida has in various ways allowed for this. For one, he has accepted and embraced the aleatory and unpredictable aspects of his own performative utterances. They are dehiscent and disseminative. There is no way to be sure that they will do exactly what he intends. Their effects will be multiple and contradictory, though this does not mean that they will not be controlled as an oscillation within the bounds of a determinable undecidability. Nor is this any reason not to act decisively with words. Nor is it a reason not to take responsibility for their effects. One must say, "I said or wrote that, and I take responsibility for what those words have brought about."

Derrida's concept of the radically inaugural quality of performatives, discussed in detail below, means that for him each performative utterance to some degree creates its own new conditions and laws. It transforms the context into which it enters. Derrida's performative utterances, moreover, are not just autonomously and freely made. They are made, as I shall show, in response to an exigent call or demand from what Derrida in more recent writings calls "le tout autre," the wholly other. That wholly other authorizes and endorses the performatives Derrida utters. What emerges from Derrida's analysis and enactments is, in short, a new concept of performatives and their efficacy, not just a disqualification of the Austinian normal serious literal one.

That disqualification or displacement depends at crucial moments on the invocation of the unconscious as a name for that "wholly other." The unconscious as wholly other is not just an accidental and temporary permutation of consciousness. It is the forever unreachable matrix from which consciousness has arisen. The effect of unlocking the unconscious from its crypt, the result of taking it seriously, is devastating for the project of Austin and Sarl:

> It is sufficient merely to introduce, into the manger [*dans la bergerie*] of speech acts, a few wolves of the type "undecidability" (of the *pharmakon*, of the *Gift* [meaning in German "poison," but with a play on English "gift"—JHM], of the supplement, of the hymen) or of the type

"unconscious" (an unconscious pleasure may be experienced as pain, according to *Beyond the Pleasure Principle*), of the type "primary masochism," etc., for the shepherd to lose track of this flock [*pour que le pasteur ne puisse plus compter ses moutons*]: one is no longer certain where to find the identity of the "speaker" or the "hearer" (visibly identified with the conscious ego), where to find the identity of an intention (desire or non-desire, love or hate, pleasure or suffering), or of an effect (pleasure or non-pleasure, advantage or disadvantage, etc.). This is only another reason why, at the "origin" of every speech act, there can only be Societies which are (more or less) anonymous, with limited responsibility or liability—Sarl—a multitude of instances, if not of "subjects," of meanings highly vulnerable to parasitism—all phenomena that the "conscious ego" of the speaker and the hearer (the ultimate instances of speech act theory) is incapable of incorporating as such and which, to tell the truth, it does everything to exclude. (*LI*, 75; *LI*/F, 143)

If the "I" cannot know what its intentions are, whether it is serious or nonserious, someone hearing the utterance is even less able to tell what the intention may be. The apparent speech act may be a citation, perhaps a parodic or ironic one, like Derrida's allusion to Descartes, or a distorted citation of him, that Searle misses. He misses it because of course he knows little about the history of Western philosophy, on principle, since he assumes it was mostly nonsense. After the revolution effected by ordinary-language philosophy, it is not necessary to know anything about it. As Derrida argues in his discussion of his cryptic allusion to Descartes (*LI*, 82–85), to turn Descartes's title (for the fifth of his *Meditations*) from "On the Essence of Material Things; And Likewise [*iterum* in the original Latin] of God, That He Exists" into "Parasites; Iter, of Writing: That It Perhaps Does Not Exist" is not just a trivial philosophical "in joke." It is a way of indicating the extreme consequences of the possibility of "graphematics" for ontology and for the whole system of Western philosophical assumptions. These assumptions both Austin and Searle, to a considerable degree unwittingly, though in quite different ways, take for granted as unquestionable:

In leaving the existence of writing undecidable, the "perhaps" marks the fact that the "possibility" of graphematics places writing (and the rest) outside the authority of ontological discourse, outside the alternative of existence and non-existence, which in turn always supposes a simple discourse capable of deciding between presence and/or absence. The rest of the trace, its remains [*le restance de la trace*], are neither present nor absent [*ni une présence ni une absence*]. They escape the jurisdiction [*la prise*] of all ontotheological discourse even if they render the latter at times possible. (*LI*, 83; *LI*/F, 156–57)

To understand these implications of Derrida's Cartesian title, however, it would be necessary to recognize the allusion, that is, to understand that the title manifests a certain form of iterability in action, not just in theory. Searle's ignorance, and probably the ignorance of a good many of his readers, prevents that. Unless you see that it is an iteration, you cannot fully feel its force, though it may seem like an unconscious echo of something.

Unsaturable Context

The next domino to fall is the assumption of determinable or saturable context. My image of dominos, however, is, as the reader will have seen, inadequate or imperfect. In this case the dominos all fall at once. They are organized in a row only for the commodity or exigency of my presentation, not because they are logically or causally connected in a fragile chain in just this order, like a row of dominos set on end. The factors assumed to make a serious, felicitous speech act possible are not in a sequence. They are simultaneous, intertwined elements. When one falls, they all fall. Understanding that catastrophic falling, however, requires a separate exposition for each element in order.

What does Derrida mean by "context"? The word is one of the three highlighted in Derrida's title for the essay that caused John Searle such pain and raised his incautious ire: "Signature Event *Context*" (my italics). The words Austin most often uses are "circumstances" and "situation" rather than "context." For Austin it is "the total speech-act in the total speech-situation" that must be considered in evaluating the felicity or infelicity of a given performative (*HT*, 148). Derrida's word "context" names more or less all that Austin means by "circumstances," though perhaps not quite exactly the same field is covered, as I shall show.

Derrida's goal is to show how iterability means that the "context" can never be fully determined or "saturated." If this is the case, then Austin's (and Searle's) conditions for a demonstrably felicitous performative can never be met. Derrida also wants to show that the same words can function well enough in radically different contexts. This means a given mark or set of marks can never be wholly delimited by any context within which it is inserted.

"Context" is an important word these days. In cultural studies it is often used to name all determining historical and social circumstances within which a given human artifact, for example a given literary work, is embedded. These circumstances are called by the general name "culture." "Traditional" or "formal" critics are reproached for not taking sufficient account of historical "context." This distinction depends on a fairly firm inside/outside dichotomy. The sense Derrida gives to the word "context" to some degree blurs that boundary between inside and outside. We often think of the context as everything surrounding the text, everything that goes along with (the root meaning of "con-" here) the text.

The word "context," however, is double or duplicitous. The two basic meanings given by the *American Heritage Dictionary* are "1. The part of a written or spoken statement in which the word or passage at issue occurs; that which leads up to and follows and often specifies the meaning of a particular expression. 2. The circumstances in which a particular event occurs; a situation."[14] The reader will see the equivocation. On the one hand, the first definition implicitly recognizes that no word or phrase has definite, determinable, or delimited meaning in itself. It has meaning only in the context of surrounding words. These allow one to choose among different possibilities in reading a given use of the word, for example to choose between the two meanings of "context" as defined in the dictionary. On the other hand, the second definition implies that meaning is determined and delimited not so much by other surrounding words as by the nonverbal "circumstances" or "situation." The same words spoken in different circumstances can have radically different meanings and effects, that is, both different constative and different performative efficacies. I shall return to this somewhat disquieting fact. It is a fact of which Austin was by no means unaware, though Searle needs to minimize it.

By "context" Derrida appears to mean everything else but the actual words or, in his lingo, "marks." Included in that "everything surrounding the text" are the consciousness and unconscious of the speaker or writer, her body, the interpersonal and social circumstances, the historical situation, and so on, that is, the whole environment of the marks as made. Though Derrida does not make much of the difficulties of defining a context a priori, before a speech act intervenes in it, a context in the sense of total circumstances is always overdetermined, always heterogeneous. It is uncontrollably diverse in itself. It stretches out to vaguer and more distant fringes that are neither quite part of the context nor able to be put firmly beyond its borders as something we need not "trench upon," to borrow Austin's somewhat peculiar topographical figure. For a performative to be felicitous, its context would need to be exhaustively determinable, with no ambiguities or loose threads, no heterogeneity, no problems about its frontiers or edges. To use Derrida's distinctly odd term, the context would need to be not only determinable but *saturé*, "saturated."

What does *saturé* mean in this context? It is an odd word, not a common one, to my knowledge, in theoretical or philosophical writings. My *Petit Robert* gives a series of meanings for *saturé*: an initial scientific sense to describe, for example, a liquid that has dissolved all of a given substance that it can hold at that temperature and pressure, and then a series of derived senses, for example as when we say a sponge is saturated with water, or when we say a market is saturated with a given product, or when we say the public is saturated with detective novels. A curious but provocative mathematical meaning asserts that *saturé* "is said of a set [*ensemble*] possessing a given property when that property does not apply to any set including the first."[15] A set has the property when taken by itself, but when it is included in a larger set the property no longer applies. That is very strange, when you think of it, as is the use of

the word *saturé* to name it. I say this meaning is provocative because Derrida invokes set theory in his argument against Searle in
"Limited Inc a b c… " In one place he says that the "set of texts" in
his debate with Searle will not

> have been discourses dominating the *ensemble* of this field [the "set" of
> speech acts, of performatives, of illocutionary and perlocutionary
> phrases, etc.] and stating the truth about it. Rather, they will have con-
> stituted elements of that *ensemble*, parts of an open corpus, *examples* of
> events, to which all the questions and categories accredited by the the-
> ory of speech acts will still be applicable and reapplicable [*repliant* {fold-
> ing back} *ou réappliquant*]: whether or not they are performatives, in
> what measure and aspect they depend upon the per- or illocutionary,
> whether they are serious or not, normal or not, void or not, parasitic or
> not, fictional or not, citational or not, literary, philosophical, theatrical,
> oratorical, prophetical or not, etc. (*LI*, 39; *LI*/F, 80–81)

Speech-act theory cannot dominate the field of speech acts because
it is itself made up of utterances that may themselves be speech
acts, indeed certainly *are* speech acts. They are inside, not outside,
the ensemble. They are parts of the set, not its sovereign master
dominating it from without. This set, however, has the peculiarity,
to return to the mathematical meaning of the French word *saturé*,
of not being saturated or saturable. As a consequence of the graphematics of iterability, each member of this set contains properties
that are not applicable to other parts, and each member is nonsat-
urated and nonsaturable within itself. The whole ensemble is heterogeneous, porous, bubbly, full of gaps or at least of substances
that would always be able to take on more soluble material.

Derrida draws amusing consequences from this inclusion of
speech-act theory in the set it purports to dominate when he demonstrates that Sarl is not serious. Sarl's claim to model what he is
doing-by-saying on scientific methodology, Derrida comments, is
a figure of speech and therefore excluded by Sarl's theory itself;
moreover, it is a false analogy at that, since science deals with objects of study that are other than itself, whereas speech-act theory
is itself made of examples of what it purports to "theorize." Having
made these points, Derrida observes:

This fundamental theoretical preamble [*protocole*] . . . already involves a lax [*lâche*] (or non-strict, if you prefer) recourse to a resemblance, indeed to a non-literal figure. . . . By contrast with *all* the other sciences, the theory of speech acts has as its object . . . speech acts said to be ordinary in languages said to be natural. This fact, far from facilitating the process of abstraction and of idealization, which in turn is always a process of objectification, on the contrary limits it. The language of theory always leaves a residue that is neither formalizable nor idealizable in terms of that theory of language. Theoretical utterances are always speech acts. (*LI*, 69; *LI*/F, 133)

Derrida draws from this distressing example of the impossibility of lifting yourself by your own bootstraps the conclusion that Searle and other speech-act theorists cannot be serious, however hard they try to be so. I have identified in my discussion of *How to Do Things with Words* the strand of jokes and irony in Austin's discourse and its consequences. In Austin these are self-conscious and deliberate, but Searle tries to be serious and nothing but serious. Here is what Derrida says about Searle and all that ilk:

We must add this: the necessity, assumed by classical theory, of submitting itself to the very normativity and hierarchy that it purports to analyze, deprives such theory of precisely what it claims for itself: seriousness, scientificity, truth, philosophical value, etc. Because the model speech act of current speech act theory claims to be serious, it is normed by a part of its object and is therefore not impartial [*neutre*]. It is not scientific and cannot be taken seriously [*pris au sérieux*]. (*LI*, 72; *LI*/F, 136–37)

Not only can it not be taken seriously, it is not serious. In spite of all its attempts to remain solemn (mimed in Derrida's repeated "Let's be serious"), speech-act theory is full of jokes, irony, literature, parasites of all those kinds explicitly expelled by a many-times-repeated attempt to exorcise the ghost of poetry. This nonserious strain is the source of great power, a performative power, if speech-acts theorists only knew it and had the courage to take advantage of it:

Which is what constitutes the drama of this family of theoreticians: the more they seek to produce serious utterances, the less they can be taken seriously. It is up to them whether they will take advantage of this opportunity to transform infelicity into delight [*jouissance*]. For example, by proclaiming [Such a proclamation would be a performative speech act, a happy or felicitous one.—JHM]: everything that we have said-written-done up to now wasn't really serious or strict; it was all a joke: sarcastic, even a bit ironic, parasitical, metaphorical, citational, cryptic, fictional, literary, insincere [*mensonger*: lying], etc. (*LI,* 72; *LI/F,* 137)

Though Searle can hardly be said to have an instinct for the power that lies in irony and literature, Austin, as I have shown, certainly does. It spite of his attempts to expel irony, literature, jokes, he uses them all the time as powerful self-subverting tools of argumentation, without overtly recognizing that he is doing so or that this force is the underlying reason why he "bogs down." Derrida, however, both uses, in positive and productive ways, and says that he uses, these forces of the nonserious, while showing why it is impossible to be serious, thereby turning this loss into a gain. Thinking of what it might mean to embrace the fatal necessity of being nonserious and to make something positive of it, to take advantage of the immense accretion of force, the immense *jouissance,* that would result and to use it as the basis of a productive ethico-political decision and intervention, Derrida exclaims: "What force they would gain by doing this!! But will they take the risk? Will we have to take it for them? Why not?" (*LI,* 72; *LI/F,* 137). *They* will not, at least not in so many words, but he will. That taking of the risk is the basis of the new ethics Derrida proposes and performatively affirms, as I shall show later.

The word *saturé* can mean in French simply, *dégoûté, fatigué,* as when I might say, "I'm sick to death of that, saturated," as the reader may already be of all this talk about a single word, *saturé.* Our slang version would be, "I've had it up to here," accompanied by a hand gesture. We are not, however, through with *saturé* yet. The English word "saturated" and the French word *saturé* mean "stuffed, filled to capacity or satisfied even beyond satiety." Both have the same root as "satire": all three words come from Latin *saturare,* "to fill, satiate," from *satur,* "full of food, sated." By saying the context cannot be saturated, Derrida seems to mean that the emitted words, whether written or spoken, always fail to fill the "context" completely. The context always remains porous, unsaturated, able still to take on more from a different source. But who or what, in Derrida's figure, fails to do the saturating? Is it the uttered words, failing to perform felicitously? Or the conscious intention with which the words are uttered, failing to command its context and make sure that what it intends actually happens? Or a witness to the utterance, a speech-act theorist for example, or a policeman or a judge, failing to ascertain that the circumstances are all in order for an indubitably felicitous speech act, an utterance that succeeds in doing things (and the things it intends) with words?

In all these cases the image would be in one way or another that of an emitting source, a radiating center of energy that organizes and transforms what is around it, just as the jar in Wallace Stevens's "Anecdote of the Jar," made by human agency and placed in Tennessee by the "I" of the poem, "took dominion everywhere." Stevens's poem might be taken as an allegory of a happy speech act, perhaps that of the poem itself as it organizes the superabundant richness of language and gives it limits along with a sharp rhetorical and rhythmic shape. The poem describes its own performative activity.[16]

Derrida seeks to persuade the reader that this happy assertion of dominion can never take place. "Is there a rigorous and scientific concept of *context*?" Derrida asks in *Sec*. "Or does the notion of context not conceal, behind a certain confusion, philosophical presuppositions of a very determinate nature? Stating it in the most summary manner possible, I shall try to demonstrate why a context is never absolutely determinable, or rather, why its determination can never be entirely certain or saturated [*assurée ou saturée*]" (*LI*, 3; *LI/F*, 19–20). "Saturated"? Just what does Derrida mean by that? It still seems an odd word, even when we have looked it up in a deskful of dictionaries. Derrida's notion seems to be that there is no context without text, defining the text here as a mark or set of marks that is a center having a radiating power, like Stevens's jar, to expand outward to dominate an environment. Since any mark or set of marks is always already riven with iterability, it is incapable of dominating in the sovereign way Stevens's poem dramatizes. The context is never saturated by the mark's force. Parts of the context are only partially transformed. In one place in *Sec* Derrida defines this weakness in terms of the deconstruction (if I dare use that word) of intention and the introduction of that "structural unconscious" I have already discussed:

> This essential absence of intending the actuality of utterance [*de l'intention à l'actualité de l'énoncé*], this structural unconsciousness, if you like, prohibits any saturation of the context. In order for a context to be exhaustively determinable, in the sense required by Austin, conscious intention would at the very least have to be totally present and immediately transparent to itself and to others, since it is a determining center [*foyer*] of context. (*LI*, 18; *LI/F*, 46)

This can never be. The marks that make up a speech act seem to have an unfortunate propensity to forget the intention that initially inhabited them and gave them force. This propensity is a counterforce within the speech act that makes it, to use Derrida's term, "break" with its context and function in any number of other contexts. The speech act is already divided within itself and so cannot remain a single central force organizing a single context. This is both a strength and a weakness: a weakness in that the speech act cannot saturate any given context; a strength in that it can function in innumerable other contexts.

Derrida's eloquent expression of this in *Sec* shows that he did not need to have read W. K. Wimsatt, Jr., and Monroe C. Beardsley's "The Intentional Fallacy" to know that neither authorial intention nor surrounding verbal context can control the meaning of a set of words.[17] Derrida begins by describing the qualities of the presumedly "saturated" context that is ruptured by iterability. This ideal saturating power would be constituted by presence in the present, the presence to himself or herself of the writer as an emitting source that would soak through and through not only the "inscription" but also the context within which the inscription is written and in which it actively intervenes as an invitation to be read, understood, and acted upon according to the intentions of the writer: "This allegedly real context includes a certain 'present' of the inscription, the presence of the writer to what he has written, the entire environment and the horizon of his experience, and above all the intention, the wanting-to-say-what-he-means [*le vouloir-dire*], which animates his inscription at a given moment" (*LI*, 9; *LI*/F, 30).

This smooth working of the inscription animated by intention seems invulnerable to rupture, but, Derrida avers, the inscription itself contains within itself a "force of rupture." What is this force? It is the power the inscription has, once it is inscribed, to continue working in the complete absence of the intentional structure that originally inhabited it. Recognition of this truth underlies Wimsatt and Beardsley's "The Intentional Fallacy"; but while the separation of an "inscription," for example a lyric poem, from the author's intentions or affects is a basic presupposition of the New Criticism, Wimsatt and Beardsley hardly conclude that an inscription has, so to speak, a life of its own, an ability to take on different meanings in different contexts. These are the radical ethical and political conclusions, however, not to speak of interpretative ones, that Derrida draws. Far from separating poetry from history, politics, and social life, as the New Criticism is said to do, Derrida, as I shall show, sees in the force iterability has to enter history the chance for a new ethics and a new politics, the politics of what he calls "the democracy to come."

"At the same time," says Derrida, "a written sign carries with it a force that breaks with its context, that is, with the collectivity of presences organizing the moment of its inscription. This breaking force [*force de rupture*] is not an accidental predicate but the very structure of the written text [*l'écrit*]. In the case of the so-called 'real' context, what I have just asserted is all too evident" (*LI*, 9; *LI*/F, 30). Derrida's definition of this "force" does not differ greatly from what Plato says in the *Phaedrus* about the inferiority of writing to speaking. A piece of writing, Plato (or rather Socrates) says, wanders or drifts about the world like an orphan cut off from its paternal authorizing force, able to do no more than repeat itself interminably, like a robot. Writing is a "drifter," a homeless vagrant. The difference, and it is a big difference, is that what Plato sees as a danger and an enfeebling, Derrida sees as a new force and as a chance, a piece of good luck, the chance or opportunity he imbues with a political and ethical inflection later on in "Limited Inc a b c... " and in many other more recent works. Derrida's expression of this distinguishes two forms of rupture, drift, or breaking out of the original context, one external, the other internal. In the external form, an inscription goes on functioning in new nonverbal contexts. In the internal form, an inscription goes on functioning in new verbal contexts. This might be called the Wellerism effect, after the jokes Sam Weller tells in Dickens's *Pickwick Papers*. A Wellerism plays on a phrase's ability to have different meanings in different contexts.[18] The two forms of rupture are not unrelated, however, nor absolutely detachable from each other, since a new verbal context for a "syntagma" implies a new external context too:

> But the sign possesses the characteristic of being readable even if the moment of its production is irrevocably lost and even if I do not know what its alleged author-scriptor consciously intended to say at the moment he wrote it, i.e. abandoned it to its essential drift [*sa dérive essentielle*]. As far as the internal semiotic context is concerned, the force of the rupture is no less important: by virtue of its essential iterability, a written syntagma can always be detached from the chain in which it is inserted or given without causing it to lose all possibility of functioning, if not all possibility of "communicating," precisely. One can perhaps come to recognize other possibilities in it by inscribing it or *grafting* [*greffant*] it onto other chains. No context can entirely enclose it. Nor any code, the code here being both the possibility and impossibility of writing, of its essential iterability (repetition/alterity). (*LI*, 9; *LI*/F, 30–31)

Some pages later in *Sec*, Derrida expands this analysis to include all spoken and written signs, as well as all linguistic and nonlinguistic signs (such as gestures or facial expressions). This expansion is of signal importance. It must be noted carefully, since it gives the lie to the common assumption, present for example in Sarl, that Derrida leaves the speech/writing distinction untouched and wants to privilege writing over speech. For him, rather, speech and writing are just different forms of signs, both equally subject to the consequences of iterability:

> Every sign, linguistic or nonlinguistic, spoken or written (in the current sense of this opposition), in a small or large unit, can be *cited*, put between quotation marks; in so doing it can break with every given context, engendering [*engendrer*] an infinity of new contexts in a manner which is absolutely illimitable (non saturable). This does not imply that a mark is valid outside of a context, but on the contrary that there are only contexts without any center or absolute anchorage [*ancrage absolu*]. This citationality, this duplication or duplicity, this iterability of the mark is neither an accident nor an anomaly, it is that (normal/abnormal) without which a mark could not even have a function called "normal." What would a mark be that could not be cited? Or one whose origins would not get lost along the way? (*LI*, 12; *LI*/F, 36)

I shall indicate below how Derrida's commentary on this passage in "Limited Inc a b c... " modifies it in one crucial feature. "Limited Inc a b c... " also gives an example of what Derrida means when he claims that any set of signs can break with any context and function in innumerable new contexts. Derrida, as I have shown, ridicules Sarl's example of that supposedly unequivocal or univocal sentence about setting out from London for Oxford, a sentence that is, according to Sarl, entirely controlled by a determinable and saturable context. On the contrary, Derrida argues, the sentence could function in innumerable quite diverse contexts. Derrida describes this possibility as a general and inevitable fate befalling all signs or marks. He begins with a characteristic *concesso non dato* by saying, in effect, that he takes for granted yet by no means concedes that the present can be fully present: ". . . at the very moment (assuming that this moment itself might be full and self-identical, identifiable—for the problem of idealization and iterability is already posed here, in the structure of temporalization)" (*LI*, 61). Derrida frequently, as here, makes the gesture of halting in the middle of a formulation and stepping back once more to put the terms he is using in question. He does the same thing with the word "concept" when he speaks of the "concept" of iterability; it is not, he pauses to say, really a concept. Here he stops to relate iterability to the structure of temporality, a structure that for Derrida—as for Heidegger, in a different but related way—is always before and after itself, never fully present to itself. Temporality is made up of differential relations in which the present moment is hollowed out by reaching back to a past that was never present and forward toward a future anterior that is always about to be, like the democracy that is always "to come" (*à venir*; the future, in French, is *l'avenir*).

Derrida, notoriously, calls this structure *la différance*, so he is reminding the reader in this parenthesis that iterability is a feature of *différance*, that it is *différantial*. This must be held in the mind when Derrida picks up his argument after the parenthesis:

> at the very moment when someone would like to say or to write, "On the twentieth... etc.," the very factor that will permit the mark (be it psychic, oral, graphic) to function beyond this moment—namely the possibility of its being repeated *another* time—breaches, divides, expropriates [*entame, divise, exproprie*] the "ideal" plenitude or self-presence of intention, of meaning (to say) [*vouloir-dire*] and, a fortiori, of all adequation between meaning and saying. (*LI*, 61–62; *LI*/F, 120)

"Psychic" in Derrida's formulation here is important. Iterability breaches and divides even the mute marks made by thought within the psyche as much as it does oral and graphic marks. Psychic marks, the sign and generator of consciousness, are just one more kind of mark, subject to the same iterability and dehiscence as writing and speaking. This fact supports the rejection of the self-present ego uttering with full intention sentences in the first-person present indicative. That perpetual nonpresence of the self to itself is what, in another of Searle's examples that Derrida ridicules, makes it possible for Searle to write grocery lists to himself, or makes it possible for Proust's protagonist in *À la recherche du temps perdu* to carry on a silent conversation with himself in Mme de Villeparisis's drawing room, even though one of those inner voices says something that Marcel does not believe:

> "What a goose! [*Quelle buse!*]" I thought to myself, irritated by her icy greeting. I found a sort of bitter satisfaction in this proof of her [refer-

ring to the Duchess of Guermantes, whom he loves] total incomprehension of Maeterlinck. "To think that's the woman I walk miles
every morning to see. Really, I'm too kind. Well, it's my turn now to
ignore her." Those were the words I said to myself, but they were the
opposite of what I thought; they were purely conversational words
such as we say to ourselves at those moments when, too excited to remain quietly alone with ourselves, we feel the need, for want of another listener, to talk to ourselves, without meaning what we say, as we
talk to a stranger [*c'étaient de purs mots de conversation, comme nous
nous en disons dans ces moments où trop agités pour rester seuls avec nous-
mêmes nous éprouvons le besoin, à défaut d'autre interlocuteur, de causer
avec nous, sans sincérité, comme avec un étranger*].[19]

This possibility of interior dialogue may be what motivated
John Searle to write grocery lists to himself. Even the secret regions
of the silent self are divided by the iterability of the mark. "Iterability," I iterate, "alters, contaminating parasitically what it identifies and enables to repeat 'itself': it leaves us no choice but to
mean (to say) something that is (already, always, also [*déjà, toujours, aussi*]) other than what we mean (to say), to say something
other than what we say *and* would have wanted to say, to understand something other than... etc. In classical terms, the accident is
never an accident" (*LI*, 62; *LI*/F, 120). This is another example of
the reversal we saw in Derrida's assessment of Austin in *Sec*. Austin
wants to make misfires, infelicities, and etiolations accidental,
make them something that might have been otherwise and that is
parasitic on the normal, proper, ordinary use of the performative in
the right context or circumstances. The accidental is a kind of footnote to the normal (though Austin spends an inordinate amount of
time on these footnotes; he is obsessed by them). Derrida, on the
contrary, sees Austin's "normal" as a special (illusory) case or "effect" within the truly normal situation of iterability. This is a re-
versing displacement. It presupposes that consciousness, intention,
and so on exist all right but are effects, not originating causes.

In "Limited Inc a b c... " Derrida returns to what he had said
about context in "Signature Event Context" and reproaches Searle
for taking the question of context so lightly: "How can a theoreti-

cian of speech acts treat a contextual criterion as though it were of secondary importance [*un critère secondaire*] . . . ?" (*LI*, 78; *LI*/F, 148). Either a contextual difference changes everything, says Derrida, in which case it is of crucial importance, or, as *Sec* holds, it leaves certain aspects of the speech act intact, in which case Searle's hypothesis of a determinable context does not hold and his theory breaks down. This either/or, asserts Derrida, leads to the elaboration of a new notion of context based on "a new logic, . . . a graphematics of iterability [*une graphématique de l'intérabilité*]" (*LI*, 78; *LI*/F, 148). To move forward with that, Derrida returns to his view in *Sec* that "every sign . . . can . . . break with every given context, engendering an infinity of new contexts in a manner which is absolutely illimitable." He now modifies that as follows: "It would have been better and more precise to have said 'engendering *and* inscribing itself,' or being inscribed *in*, new contexts. For a context never creates itself *ex nihilo*; no mark can create or engender a context on its own, much less dominate it [*encore moins dominer absolument son contexte*]. This limit, this finitude is the condition under which contextual transformation remains an always open possibility" (*LI*, 79; *LI*/F, 149). This is an important revision. It also shows how difficult it is to do without latent personifications or prosopopoeias, however astute you are about the mystifying power of apparently casual or effaced tropes, as when Derrida, in the passage in *Sec* now being modified, grants to speech acts a power of "engendering."

The revisionary passage also shows that Derrida wants to have it both ways. The context is there already, but it becomes a context only when the speech act intervenes within it, however weakly and without power to saturate it. The speech act nevertheless transforms the context it enters, even though in retrospect that context seems to have been there already as the ground of the speech act's efficacy. This power to intervene in the context, even if not to dominate it, is the emancipatory chance opened by a speech-act theory based on iterability. This radical transformation of traditional speech-act theory is basic to Derrida's new notions of politics and ethics, to which I now turn.

Declarations of Independence

Derrida's new conceptions of politics and ethics depend on a reversal of speech-act theory whereby the performative utterance creates the conventions it needs in order to be efficacious, rather than depending on their prior existence for its felicity. It thereby transforms the context it enters rather than presupposing it and being based on it. Such a speech act is a historical event in the sense that it deflects, in however small a degree, the course of history. Only a performative theory of the historical event can account for historical change. Only such an understanding of speech acts will go beyond the sterile opposition between, on the one hand, a static structural concept of history that sees a given historical "episteme" or discursive regime replaced suddenly and inexplicably by another one and, on the other hand, some oversimple idea of material determinism.

The notion of a performative that creates its own grounds appears in many places in Derrida's work of the last 25 years. One eloquent and succinct formulation appears in "Declarations of Independence," the preamble to a seminar on Nietzsche given at the University of Virginia in 1976 to help celebrate the 200th anniversary of the United States Declaration of Independence, and then published as part of a book entitled *Otobiographies: L'enseignement de Nietzsche et la politique du nom propre* (Otobiographies: The teaching of Nietzsche and the politics of the proper name).[20]

The relation between ethical and political performatives in Derrida's thought is indicated in the characteristically indirect or unostentatious way the opening sentences of this seminar enact the thing the lecture is about. These opening sentences are predominantly performative rather than constative, though, as Austin knew and as Derrida argues in this little essay, all performatives are also a little or a large bit constative and vice versa. The distinction is undecidable, and that apparent disaster gives us our opportunity. In this case Derrida's opening sentences do what they say by giving an ethical example rather than a political one, even though the main topic is political. This implies the homology between the two regimes of human life, the political and the ethical, that it is one purpose of the essay to declare.

Derrida had been invited by Roger Shattuck to give a lecture comparing the United States Declaration of Independence with the French Declaration of the Rights of Man. He had promised to do so. He had, as he puts it, "engaged" himself to do so. He had even, we can imagine, signed a contractual commitment to do so, probably by giving his agreement in a letter, although in order to be paid he probably also had to sign official university documents giving his social security number and other information. His lecture was given in the material, institutionally defined, and highly overdetermined situation of facing an audience at the University of Virginia, founded by Thomas Jefferson. Thomas Jefferson, as everyone knows, was the "redactor" of the Declaration of Independence, the author of the first draft. This document was then greatly shortened and altered, to Jefferson's distress, by the time it was signed by our courageous forefathers.

The opening paragraph of the second section of the seminar, given both in Virginia and in Montreal, entitled "Logique de la vivante" (Logic of the living feminine), shifts from the Declaration of Independence to Nietzsche. It calls attention explicitly to Derrida's pedagogical situation. In order to avoid boring his audience, he says, he is not going to fulfill the regular requirements of a seminar. These are the obligations to proceed by a chain of arguments, to make one's methodological presuppositions explicit, to refer to previous authorities, and so on. These are, as Derrida says, "but some of the imperatives of classical pedagogy with which, to be sure, one can never break once and for all [*sans appel*]. Yet, if you were to submit to them rigorously, they would very soon reduce you to silence, tautology, and tiresome repetition [*ressassement*]" (*O/F*, 37; *O/E*, 4). While he promises that "the place I am now occupying will not be left out of the exhibit or withdrawn from the scene" (*O/F*, 37, 38; *O/E*, 4), to avoid the tedium of pedagogy he will also take advantage of the leeway allowed him by "academic freedom."

The latter phrase is a problematic formula and a concept in which every syllable counts. Derrida writes it thus: "la li-ber-té a-ca-dé-

mi-que" (*O*/F, 37; O/E, 4). He will speak aphoristically, discontin-
uously, omitting liaisons as well as full developments, documenta-
tions, and demonstrations of his ideas. His performance, in short,
declares its independence from the normal protocols of a seminar.
It does something unauthorized and radically inaugural. As Derrida somewhat defiantly puts it: "I do not teach truth as such; I do
not transform myself into a diaphanous mouthpiece of eternal pedagogy [*en porte-parole diaphane de la pédagogie éternelle*]" (*O*/F, 38;
O/E, 4). The pedagogical situation, as you can see, duplicates in
another register the political one. If the colonists had gone on accepting and repeating the systems of law and authority they had
brought from England, if they had not, in the words of the Declaration itself, had the courage "to dissolve the political bands which
[had] connected them with another," we should still be a British
colony. To do something new, the colonists needed to make a radical and unauthorized break with tradition, however much that
break's lack of grounds needed to be obscured by the rhetoric of the
"Declaration." In an analogous way (the analogy is Derrida's point
in the citation above), if a teacher rigorously obeys the obligations
of a seminar he will speak tautologies and become a transparent
mouthpiece for what is already known: He or she breaks with that
obligation, however, only at his or her peril. Someone can always
come along with the charge: "What you are teaching has no authority, no validity. You are not speaking the truth."

The opening of the second section, as I have just shown, describes, constatively, the situation Derrida is in and the way he proposes to deal with it. What is described there, however, had already
been done in the opening of the first section, "Declarations of Independence." In the latter opening Derrida performs, in rapid sequence, a promise, a confession, an apology, a request for pardon,
and an excuse, all explicit forms of speech act. The lecture opens, or
is marked on its liminal border, with a promise, the promise made
by the title of his seminar's first section: "Declarations of Independence." That title was perhaps openly advertised in posters and an-
nouncements around the university. The reader of the book version
certainly encounters it on page 11. Derrida's audience has come ex-

pecting his lecture to live up to the promise of its title and to what Derrida had contractually promised or engaged himself to Roger Shattuck to do. This probably happened, as I have suggested, in a letter, or perhaps in a telephone call in which Derrida said, in effect, "Yes, I'll do what you ask. I promise to do so."

The seminar proper then begins with a confession: "It is better that you know right away: I am not going to keep my promise.[21] [*Il vaut mieux que vous le sachiez toute de suite, je ne tiendrai pas ma promesse* {O/F, 13}]." Derrida is in a shrewd ethical situation if there ever was one. In order to deal openly with the way he knows he is going to fail to fulfill his promise, he decides it is better to confess right off that he is not going to keep it, so members of the audience can leave now if they want. This is said explicitly in the opening of the second section: "In any case, let us agree to hear and understand one another on this point: whoever no longer wishes to follow may do so [*quiconque ne veut plus suivre peut le faire*]" (O/F, 38; O/E, 4). I was not there and do not know in what tone Derrida delivered that first sentence of the first section, in which he says he is not going to keep his promise, or how he uttered the invitation to leave I have just quoted. There is, however, surely something cheeky or even a little insolent in beginning a lecture by telling your audience that it is better (better than what?) to begin by confessing that he is not going to fulfill the contract that has brought them all there, with the addendum that if they do not like that they can leave now. This opening sentence brings out the way the situation of an academic lecture involves several different performative layers. These layers are surrounded by a whole set of unspoken protocols: the assumptions that a speaker will give a lecture about the topic on which he or she was invited to speak, that the announced title of the lecture accurately describes its subject matter, that the speaker guarantees he is qualified to speak on the topic announced, that the audience will listen respectfully and ask pertinent questions afterwards, and so on.

The first sentence of Derrida's "Declarations of Independence" is a declaration of independence from all that. It implicitly defines the lecture the audience is about to hear as radically initiatory, lawless, infelicitous (in Austin's sense), revolutionary, not able to be validated by anything that has come before or that is already in place in the academic situation within which it intervenes. In this Derrida's lecture is like Austin's own *How to Do Things with Words* as Austin himself defines it, that is, as a revolution in the history of philosophy. The first sentence of "Declarations of Independence" does what the lecture is about. It declares independence.

The initial confession is followed by a plea for pardon. I would like to be able to do what I promised, says Derrida, but that is impossible: "I beg your pardon, but it will be impossible for me to speak to you this afternoon, even in an indirect style, about what I was engaged to deal with [*engagé à traiter*]" (DI/E, 7; O/F, 13). Asking for pardon is a speech act in a specific sense. It does not name or describe anything. It puts the recipient of the "demand" in the position of having either to grant the plea or to deny it. In that sense it is a way of doing things with words. It is a speech act that pleads for a speech act in return, an act of forgiveness or pardon.

Whether or not Derrida's auditors, or Roger Shattuck, forgave him for not talking about what he had engaged himself to talk about I do not know, but the plea for pardon that must be answered in one way or another by another speech act (either "Yes, I forgive you," or "What you are doing is unforgivable") calls attention to the tendency of speech acts to be reciprocal. One speech act invites, demands, or requires another. Speech acts often generate an interpersonal situation in which the necessary response to one speech act is another speech act, even if the latter act is silence or a mute gesture, as when a street beggar asks for alms and I pass by without giving anything or lift my hand and shake my head in a gesture of refusal. The border between speech acts proper and gestures that function as implicit speech acts is blurred. The distinction between gestural and verbal speech acts is impossible to draw, as both Austin and Derrida knew. It might be better to speak of "sign acts," a more inclusive term.

If Derrida demands pardon, you must do something. Doing nothing magically becomes doing something, that is, failing to forgive. In the exemplary case that opens Derrida's "Declarations of

Independence," Derrida has been put in the situation he is in by Roger Shattuck's initial speech act in the form of an invitation to compare the United States Declaration of Independence with the French Declaration of the Rights of Man. Derrida had to say yes or no. He apparently said yes, then had to admit publicly that he was unable to carry through. He was unable to keep his promise, and therefore had to ask pardon, then had to offer an excuse, yet another specific form of speech act.[22] "But as I'd rather not simply remain silent [*faire le silence*] about what I should have spoken about to you," continues Derrida, "I will say a word about it in the form of an excuse. I will speak to you, then, a little, about what I won't speak about, and about what I would have wanted—because I ought—to have spoken about" (DI/E, 7; O/F, 13). These sentences are really weird, if you think about them: I ought to have spoken about it, but I'm not going to do that, yet I don't want just to "remain silent [*faire le silence*, literally 'make silence']" (an odd phrase that, in spite of being idiomatic French; one would think silence would make itself without any help from us), so I'll say a word in the form of an excuse about what I'm not going to talk about, though I would have liked to talk about it, since I ought to do so, have an obligation to do so." How can you talk about something without talking about it, or not talk about something by talking about it? How could doing that, if you could do it, be a felicitous excuse? Does Derrida's admirable following discussion of the Declaration of Independence function as a felicitous excuse? Only his auditors and readers can decide whether to excuse him. I for one am happy to do so and grateful to accept what he does say as an adequate substitute and as a happy performative, a felicitous excuse, though I have some small lingering anxiety about the irony that runs all through these opening sentences.

The irony lies in the way Derrida has, the canny reader can see in retrospect, so cleverly set up these opening sentences to give living examples, embedded in a particular situation, of the particular problematic of speech acts he is going to discuss through readings of the Declaration of Independence and then, at greater length, in readings of *Ecce Homo* and other works by Nietzsche. These opening sentences work, the reader can see, on two registers at once, each undercutting, ironically, the "sincerity" of the other. How can someone who is speaking ironically be uttering a felicitous performative, particularly one so evidently needing sincerity, as a confession, a "demand" for pardon, or an excuse? What happens to our faith in his sincerity or to our willingness to pardon or excuse Derrida if we come to believe he is speaking ironically when he says, "Very sincerely, I would have liked to be able to do it [*Très sincèrement, j'aurais aimé pouvoir le faire*]" (DI/E, 7; O/F, 13).

I shall return to the question of how an ironic discourse can be performatively efficacious in my discussion of Paul de Man in Chapter 3 of this book. De Man, surprisingly—surprisingly to me at least—comments, "Irony consoles and it promises and it excuses."[23] What de Man says must of course be true (that's an irony, dear reader!), though it will take some doing to figure out how that can be so in the case of this sentence. However we may deal with Derrida's irony here, he concludes the preamble to his preamble to his seminar on Nietzsche by saying in so many words that just the speech acts he has exemplified will be the subjects of his seminar: "Still, it remains that I fully intend to discuss with you—at least you will be able to confirm this [*le vérifier*]—the promise, the contract, engagement, the signature, and even what always presupposes them, in a strange way: the presentation of excuses" (DI/E, 7; O/F, 13–14). This sentence is yet another speech act, a species of promise. I intend to talk about promises, contracts, and so on. You can check it out and will find it to be the case that I do what I intend. I guarantee it.

Derrida's preamble not only exemplifies a series of classic performatives—confession, contract, promise, prayer for forgiveness, excuse—but also shows how problematic these become as soon as you move from their ideal concepts to actual examples. In this case the examples also show how tangled in difficulties the ethical situation between teacher and auditors in a seminar room can become if the teacher wants to do something at all original. This is so however much the situation, context, or "circumstances" may seem to be stabilized by institutional presuppositions and requirements that should be easy enough to fulfill, particularly for a distinguished thinker like Derrida.

The discussion of the Declaration of Independence that follows shows how the same thing turns out to be the case with a political speech act as soon as you begin to look at it closely. No one doubts that the Declaration of Independence was a felicitous speech act. We have the United States as evidence, the "only remaining superpower," the model Western-style democracy, the world's largest economy, the greatest global force politically, militarily, economically, and so on. The Declaration inaugurated all that. How did it do so?

Derrida's "prudent" and "minute" study of the Declaration of Independence focuses on a few sentences and on just one question, the question of signature. *"Who signs,"* asks Derrida, *"and with what so-called proper name* [nom soi-disant propre], *the declarative act which founds an institution?"* (DI/E, 8; O/F, 16, Derrida's italics). A signature is clearly a speech act, as opposed to the constative answer to the question: "What's your name?" A legal document such as a mortgage, a contract, or a marriage certificate is valid only when it is signed with a proper name, in the presence of witnesses. A check is an efficacious transfer of money only when it is signed by the right person. Part of what makes people so uneasy about the shift nowadays to electronic transfers of money is that they no longer depend on actual signatures. The Declaration of Independence became a potentially felicitous speech act only when it was signed: "The declaration which founds an institution, a constitution or a State requires that a signer engage himself or herself [*il est requis qu'un signataire s'y soit engagé*]" (DI/E, 8; O/F, 16).

The answer to the question of who signed and thereby validated the Declaration of Independence seems only too easy to give. It is all those courageous men who risked their necks (literally) and signed their names at the bottom of the original document. If the revolution had failed, these men would most likely have been hanged, as is the usual fate of failed revolutionaries. Those signers included, by the way, an ancestor of mine, Samuel Hopkins, of Rhode Island, whose somewhat shaky signature is in the lower right-hand corner. As Derrida observes (DI/E, 11; *O*/F, 24), if Samuel Hopkins and his colleagues had not signed the Declaration, I would not today be able to sign my name to a check in United States dollars, carry a passport, marry, or sign a mortgage guaranteed by United States law, and so on.

Things, nevertheless, are not so simple here, as is pretty certain always to be the case with Derrida's analyses. ("Things aren't so simple," he observes [DI/E, 12; *O*/F, 29].) I shall identify four salient features of this complexity. All four are simultaneously present mutual presuppositions, but they can be distinguished and discussed separately as an aid to understanding Derrida's text.

The first major feature of Derrida's elegant and succinct analysis of the Declaration of Independence is his demonstration that, in this case at least, signatures are implicitly countersigned, or, to put it another way, one signs as the representative of others who appear to have the real authority, in a perpetual round of deferral. The actual signers of the Declaration define themselves as "the representatives of the United States of America in General Congress assembled." They signed, as the Declaration says, "in the name and by authority of the good people of these Colonies," colonies that are defined as "free and independent States."

Other scholars have noted what is equivocal about the word "good" here. The phrase "good people" implies that there may also be some "bad people," people not qualified to sign: women, loyalists, slaves. "All men are created equal," but that does not include slaves or women, for example Jefferson's black mistress. It includes only the "good people." Or, to put this more precisely, white women may be included among the "good people," but only as a kind of good people who cannot be directly represented by delegates of their own gender, who do not vote, cannot serve in Congress, and so on. In addition, the contradiction between "United States of America" and "free and independent States," like remnants of the fine grain of the "big bang" that determine the present large-scale structure of the universe, remains today a crucial problem of political authority in the United States. This problem has the name "states' rights."

Derrida does not call attention to these problems. His concern is with the structure of delegated representation. Behind the "good people," whom the actual signers represent, is God, in whose supremely proper name all the others sign. God is the author and guarantor of the "laws of Nature," to which the Declaration appeals as the source of their claim "that all men are created equal; that they are endowed by their creator with certain inalienable rights." They appeal also "to the Supreme Judge of the world for the rectitude of [their] intentions." The buck has to stop somewhere, and in this case, as in many others, it stops with the positing of God. A solid foundation somewhere must be presupposed in order to hide the baseless autonomy of the act of revolution. It is really God, the Declaration claims, who signs the Declaration of Independence, as "a last instance." "There must be a last instance [*une dernière instance*]," says Derrida. "God is the name, the best one, for this last instance and this ultimate signature" (DI/E, 12; O/F, 27). The word "instance" (French *instance*) is important here, for it carries within it a crucial equivoque. On the one hand, an instance is an example, one item selected from among many without displacing the many, as when, in English, we say, "for instance." God is named, constatively, as one example among many signers, albeit the last example, the end of the line of deferred delegation. On the other hand, an instance is a stand-in, a replacement for the many, for the "sta" in "instance" also carries the notion of a standing, a position, the result of a positing. God is posited, performatively, as the last "in-stance," or stand-in: "God—who had nothing to do with any of this [*Dieu, qui n'y fut pour rien*] and, having represented god knows whom or what in the interest of all those nice people [*toutes ces bonnes gens*], doubtless doesn't give a damn [*s'en moque*]—alone will have signed. His own declaration of independence. In order, neither more nor less, to make a state-ment of it [*en faire état*]" (DI/E, 13; O/F, 31).

The sequence of delegated representation is not yet complete, however. Derrida will show it to be a circle, starting from and returning to Thomas Jefferson. At the start, for Derrida, are Jefferson's embarrassments and anxieties, as he watched his draft being cut and altered, "mutilated." The latter is Franklin's word, used when he tried to console Jefferson for what had happened to his text. As Derrida says, Jefferson would not have been so anxious and unhappy if he had really thought of himself as no more than the representative or amanuensis of those who physically signed the Declaration. It is as though Jefferson secretly and perhaps even unconsciously desired to be the real and sole signatory of the Declaration, the single founder of the new state, a kind of god in himself. As Derrida puts this, it is "as if he had secretly dreamed of signing all alone" (DI/E, 9; *O/F*, 19).

After moving from Jefferson to the other signers to the good people to God, Derrida returns again to Jefferson through the anecdote about Franklin. Attempting to reassure Jefferson, Franklin told him about the hatter whose friends gradually cut away his proposed text for the sign outside his shop, reducing it from "John Thompson, hatter, makes and sells hats for ready money" down to a picture of a hat and the name "John Thompson." Though Derrida does not explicitly call attention to this, the anecdote exemplifies a feature of speech acts that Austin notes, though with some ironic dismay. It is by no means necessary or good always to employ the classic form of performative—composed of a first-person pronoun and a present indicative active verb (e.g., "I promise")—to produce a felicitous performative. You don't bother to say, "I respectfully warn you that there is in that field a ferocious bull about to charge." You just say "Bull!" Similarly elided, the Declaration of Independence might just have said "Thomas Jefferson," under a map of the United States. What is gained in succinct economy, however, is lost in the increasing ambiguity of meaning. "John Thompson" might be the signature of the man who painted the sign or the name of the brand of hats sold there or any number of other things. From Franklin's anecdote, Derrida draws the ironic conclusion that Jefferson might have seen in the story of the hatter the true fulfillment of his secret desire, the desire to replace God and be the sole founder of the new nation: "Taken as a whole [*À tout prendre*], a complete and total effacement of his text would have been better, leaving in place, under a map of the United

States, only the nudity of his proper name: instituting text, founding act and signing energy" (DI/E, 13; O/F, 31).

A second crucial element in Derrida's analysis is his demonstration, via the problematic of the signature, that this round of delegated representation—moving by stages up to God and back again to the first drafter of the Declaration, Thomas Jefferson—exemplifies the structure of temporalization that Derrida calls *la différance*, meaning both differentiation and deferral. Derrida works this structure out as essential to the functioning of all signs, or what he calls "traces." In the case of the Declaration, whatever signer one chooses is only the deferred and differentiated representative of some other signers before or after. The word "represent" contains this notion of displacement or deferral. Though it is essential to the felicity of those speech acts that are ratified by signatures (mortgages, marriage certificates, and the like, as well as declarations of independence) that their signatures be dated precisely, as a way of indicting that they took place in a particular present moment, this is only a "false appearance of the present [*une apparence fausse de présent*]," to borrow Mallarmé's phrase in "Mimique," analyzed by Derrida in *Dissemination*.[24] The false present looks before and after in a constant to and fro of perpetual delegation and deferral. In order for the Declaration to work, to be efficacious, however, this must be forgotten, ignored, or covered over. "But this future perfect [*ce futur antérieur*]," says Derrida, "the proper tense for this coup of right (as one would say coup of force), should not be declared, mentioned, taken into account. It's as though it didn't exist. . . . By this fabulous event, by this fable which implies the structure of the trace and is only in truth possible thanks to [*par*] the inadequation to itself of a present, a signature gives itself a name" (DI/E, 10; O/F, 22–23).

The word "fable" here is a reference to Francis Ponge's "Fable," cited on the previous page and analyzed by Derrida in detail several years later in "Psyche: The Invention of the Other."[25] Ponge's "Fable" begins: "Par le mot *par* commence donc ce texte / Dont le première ligne dit la vérité" ("By the word *by* begins therefore this text / Of which the first line says the truth"). The turning back on itself and curious act of self-foundation in these lines will allow a turn to the third essential feature of Derrida's analysis.

The most important example of the to and fro, future-anterior temporalization I have named as the second essential feature of Derrida's analysis is the way the Declaration of Independence depends on the thing it creates. It lifts itself by its own bootstraps, itself makes the foundation on which it builds the new state. Prior to the Declaration the "good people" did not exist as citizens of the United States able to delegate their authority to their representatives or to be authorized by "the laws of nature and Nature's God." This motley crew became the good people of the United States only through the presumed success of the Declaration of Independence as a speech act, though the felicity of this speech act depends on presuming the priority of that which it posits or creates. The Declaration creates that in the name of which it speaks. "But this people does not exist," says Derrida. "They do *not* exist as an entity, it does *not* exist, *before* this declaration, not *as such*. If it gives birth to itself, as free and independent subject, as possible signer, this can hold only in the act of the signature. The signature invents the signer [*La signature invente le signataire*]" (DI/E, 10; *O*/F, 22). This happens, as Derrida says, "in a sort of fabulous retroactivity [*dans une sorte de rétroactivité fabuleuse*]" (ibid.). It is fabulous both in the sense that it is fictive or invented and in the sense that it is like those fables of origin that often are projected back to some mythical preoriginary time, the story of Romulus, Remus, and the mothering wolf for Rome, for example, or the story of George Washington and the cherry tree for the United States ("I cannot tell a lie. I did it with my little hatchet."). Such fables are invented as necessary fictions in order to account for the founding moment of a new nation. Derrida generalizes this act of self-founding as true for all acts of signature. In all cases, the power to sign is given by the signer to himself or herself in the act of signing: "I will have given myself a name and an 'ability' or 'power' [*pouvoir*], understood in the sense of power- or ability-to-sign by delegation of signature" (DI/E, 10; *O*/F, 22).

Even the self of the signer is created in this self-referential or auto-affective foundationless act of establishing a foundation:

By this fabulous event . . . a signature gives itself a name. It opens *for it-self* a line of credit, *its* own credit, for itself *to* itself. The *self* [*Le soi*] surges up here in all cases (nominative, dative, accusative) as soon as a signature gives or extends credit to itself, in a single coup of force, which is also a coup of writing, as the right to writing. The coup of force makes right, founds right or the law, gives right, *brings the law to the light of day, gives birth and day to the law* [*donne le jour à la loi*]. Brings the law to the light of day, gives both birth and day to the law: read "The Madness of the Day," by Maurice Blanchot. (DI/E, 10; O/F, 23)

The reference to Blanchot's *récit*, and implicitly to Derrida's analysis of it in *Parages*,[26] is important, but must await my discussion elsewhere of Derrida's literary theory and criticism. Here already, however, we must ask, "Brings to light from where?" From where does the light come? The answer is "from the realm of the wholly other, *le tout autre*," but just what *that* means must also await later discussion.

The final entity magically brought into existence by the force of this autonomous self-generating act is the law or right itself that has nevertheless to be presupposed as something to be obeyed in order to make the declaration of independence lawful and rightful. The United States Declaration of Independence cuts itself off from British law, "dissolves the political bands" that joined it to England. It creates a new law, the law of the newborn nation, even though it needed that new law as something already there to justify what it was doing.

The reader will see how the Declaration of Independence as read by Derrida, if it is taken as exemplary of speech acts in general, even including ethical ones, as the opening paragraphs about promise, confession, and excuse invite the reader to do, demonstrates that paradigmatic performatives disobey all the requisites for a felicitous speech act as laid down by Austin, at least in his initial analyses early in *How to Do Things with Words*. The Declaration of Independence creates the law by which it acts rather than depending on preexisting rules. It breaks the preexisting law rather than sustaining it. It generates the ego that utters it rather than depending on that ego's preexistence for its felicity. Rather than leaving the surrounding circumstances, rules, conventions, and protocols as they were before the speech act was uttered, the Declaration of Independence is radically inaugural. It intervenes decisively to deflect the course of history, leaving it thereafter never the same. From Austin's perspective the Declaration of Independence is hideously infelicitous, like naming a great new British warship the Joseph Stalin. It ought not to have worked, but it did. If, as there is every reason to believe, the United States Declaration of Independence can, for Derrida, also be taken as the model for local, interpersonal speech acts—declarations of love, promises, lies, and the like—then, if we believe Derrida, a quite different way of reading literature from the one that would appear to be derived from Austin would be opened up.

The fourth and final essential feature of Derrida's analysis of the sort of speech act the Declaration of Independence exemplifies also disobeys a fundamental Austinian assumption laid down in the initial pages of *How to Do Things with Words*. This is the presupposition that it ought to be possible to distinguish clearly between performative and constative utterances and to know for sure in a given case which kind of utterance you have in hand. As I have shown, the distinction breaks down for Austin, too, but he does not draw from that the radical consequences Derrida draws. For Austin this breakdown means that a given utterance is constative or performative depending on how you take it and use it. Once you have done that it is easy enough to decide which you have or what mixture of the two you have. For Derrida it is impossible to decide in a given case whether the locution is constative or performative. That undecidability is absolutely necessary to whatever efficacy or felicity a given utterance has. In the case of the Declaration of Independence it is impossible to decide whether the text does no more than describe an act that has already occurred or whether the text itself as duly signed brings about the independence from England it names.

> One cannot decide—and that's the interesting thing, the force and the coup of force of such a declarative act—whether independence is stated [*constatée*] or produced by this utterance. . . . Is it that the good

people have already freed themselves in fact and are only stating the fact of this emancipation in [*par*] the Declaration? Or is it rather that they free themselves at the instant of and by [*par*] the signature of this Declaration? (DI/E, 9; O/F, 20)

Derrida then asserts that this undecidability is not a contingent accident in this particular case, or something that could be cleared up by a little more analysis, or something that results from an unfortunate ambiguity in Jefferson's phrasing. It is necessary and intrinsic to performative utterances in general and to this one in particular. Moreover, far from being a catastrophe that renders them all infelicitous, this undecidability is a piece of good luck that is altogether necessary to making them work. Undecidability is required for their felicity as ways to do things with words. "This obscurity," says Derrida, "this undecidability between, let's say, a performative structure and a constative structure, is *required* in order to produce the sought-after effect. It is essential to the very positing or position of a right as such, whether one is speaking here of hypocrisy, of equivocation, of undecidability, or of fiction" (DI/E, 9–10; O/F, 21).

Why is this? It is necessary because for an ungrounded or self-grounding performative to work, it must convey the illusion, fable, or fiction of having a solid, preexisting ground or law to erect itself on, while claiming for itself autonomous performative force. The document itself is open to both interpretations. Textual support for either way of reading can be cited, though the two readings are incompatible. This is quite different from the relativism of Austin's "It depends on how you take it." In Derrida's understanding, both ways of reading are commanded by the text, though it is impossible, logically, to have both at once. Nevertheless, the text needs both possibilities in order to bring about what it names. The example Derrida gives is the declaration in the Declaration that "these united Colonies are and of right ought to be *free and independent states.*" This at once states a fact and enunciates a prescription. "'Are and ought to be,'" says Derrida; "the 'and' articulates and conjoins here the two discursive modalities, the to be and the ought to be [*l'être et le devoir-être*], the constation and the prescription, the fact and the right" (DI/E, 11; O/F, 27). According to

Derrida's reading it must be a case of both are and ought, constative and performative joined by an "and" that disguises their incompatibility, if the Declaration is going to work, just as the Declaration must both appeal to a God of Nature who is presupposed
as already existing and at the same time posit the existence of that
God through its own language. "One can understand this Declaration as a vibrant act of faith, as a hypocrisy indispensable to a
political-military-economic, etc. coup of force, or, more simply,
more economically, as the analytic and consequential deployment
of a tautology" (DI/E, 12; *O*/F, 27).

As David Arndt has observed in a brilliant dissertation chapter
on the Declaration of Independence,[27] a perhaps even better example, not specified by Derrida, of this undecidability is the phrase
"We hold these truths to be self-evident." The self-evidence of the
truths "that all men are created equal" and "that they are endowed
by their creator with certain inalienable Rights" is both affirmed,
constatively, as a preexisting, self-evident truth, and at the same
time posited, performatively, in a more or less covert, groundless,
and self-grounding speech act: "*We hold* these truths to be self-
evident," an assertion in which the performative "holding" is the
only security for the self-evidence of these truths.

These four elements, then—the endless round of deferral of signatures and countersignatures, the specific temporal structure of
the *différantial* trace, the generation by the Declaration of Independence of the grounds it presupposes, and the impossibility of
deciding whether the Declaration is constative or performative—
characterize paradigmatic speech acts in Derrida's reformulation of
Austin. This reformulation gives rise to a new vision of political
and ethical action as radically inaugural—a vision already anticipated in *Limited Inc*, as I shall now show.

An Ethics and Politics of Iterability

Limited Inc is, among other things, a particular kind of performative utterance. It is a declaration of vocation. Derrida's vocation
is to displace the phallogocentric system of law, based on a certain

hierarchical evaluation, which the Austinian and Searlean notion of serious performatives supports. The performative aspect of Derrida's writings responds to a call to work toward that other language, those other thoughts, those other responsibilities that, Derrida says in the "Afterword," "arouse in me a respect which, whatever the cost [*quoi qu'il en coûte*], I neither can nor will compromise [*transiger*]" (*LI*, 153; *LI*/F, 282). Derrida comes to this defiant formulation by way of a discussion of the "unconditionality" (the Kantian echo is made explicit) of the demand that he resist apartheid in South Africa. "I have," says Derrida, "on several occasions spoken of 'unconditional' affirmation or of 'unconditional' 'appeal' [*appel*]. This has also happened to me in other 'contexts' and each time that I speak of the link between deconstruction and the 'yes' [*le 'oui'*]" (*LI*, 152; *LI*/F, 282).

Just what does "unconditional" mean in this context? The answer is a little surprising. It means, says Derrida, a demand, call, or injunction that comes from an opening in any given context. It arises from the way no context can be "saturated," as I have already shown Derrida to be asserting and as I have tried to explain. The unconditional demand on Derrida arises from the fact that no context can be closed off or completed. The wholly other enters through these gaps into any given context and makes an unconditional demand on the one who dwells within the context to intervene in a certain way within it. Derrida expresses this in the following passage. It is one of those places (there are many among his interviews) where Derrida, in response to a question that betrays a certain incomprehension, in this case one from Gerald Graff in the "Afterword," patiently and courteously tries to explain once more what he means now and has meant in earlier writings:

> Now, the very least that can be said of unconditionality (a word that I use not by accident to recall the character of the categorical imperative in its Kantian form) is that it is independent of every determinate context, even of the determination of a context in general. It announces itself as such only in the *opening* [*ouverture*] of context. Not that it is simply present (existent) elsewhere, outside of all context; rather, it intervenes in the determination of a context from its very in-

ception [*depuis son ouverture*], and from an injunction, a law, a responsibility that transcends this or that determination of a given context. Following this, what remains is to articulate this unconditionality with the determinate (Kant would say, hypothetical) conditions of
this or that context; and this is the moment of strategies, of rhetorics,
or ethics, and of politics. The structure thus described supposes both
that there are only contexts, that nothing *exists* [*existe*] outside context, as I have often said, but also that the limit of the frame or border of the context always entails a clause of nonclosure [*une clause de
non-fermeture*]. The outside penetrates and thus determines the inside. This is what I have analyzed so often, and for so long, under the
words "supplement," "parergon," and each time that I have said of the
trait of writing or of inscription (for instance, that which marks the
limit of a corpus or of a context) that it was divisible and that it erased
itself in the very process of marking [*dans son marquage même*]. (*LI*,
152–53; *LI*/F, 281–82)

This passage says a mouthful. It is by no means easy to grasp
apart from its context in all that other work by Derrida to which he
here refers. This is true because the expression of Derrida's thought
here is paradoxical. The unconditional demand, for example the injunction to resist apartheid, comes, it seems, from outside the context. It "transcends" any given context. That might mean, for example, that the resistance to apartheid cannot be justified by South
African law or even by "Western" law, by the Bill of Rights or by
the Rights of Man. The injunction is more universal and unconditional than that. At the same time the injunction does not "exist"
outside the context. We cannot hear it speaking at a distance, calling us from somewhere else. Nothing "exists" outside one context
or another. The word "exist," italicized by Derrida, is not innocent.
It has a Heideggerian context, the reader may guess. It is used in
the Heideggerian sense of "stand out," as Heidegger speaks of human existence or of objects as "existants," that is, as things or persons that stand out against a local background, though they also in-
corporate it, in fundamentally different ways in each case. Neither
human beings nor objects can exist without a context, nor, Derrida
is saying, can an unconditional ethical or political demand exist
without a context. Nevertheless, such a demand arises from what

might be called the outside of the inside. It depends on the fact that no context is closed or bounded but has at its limit or boundary what Derrida, in a wonderful oxymoron, calls "a clause of nonclosure [*une clause de non-fermeture*]." "Clause" etymologically means "enclosed," as a grammatical clause entails a closure of meaning. "A clause of nonclosure" is a closure of nonclosure. That nonclosure offers the chance for an ethical or political intervention that is justified by an unconditional injunction.

Nevertheless, that intervention must employ particular local strategies or ruses to be effective. There is no use just saying, "I am responding to an unconditional demand." You have to figure out how to intervene effectively, "and this is the moment of strategies, of rhetorics, of ethics, of politics." Rhetorics, ethics, and politics are pragmatic forms of conduct that take into account in the most urgent way the circumstances, the situation in which that conduct is performed, though they are justified by an unconditional injunction. One form this conduct takes is what Derrida here calls "deconstructing": "This unconditionality also defines the injunction that prescribes deconstructing [*Cette inconditionnalité définit aussi l'injonction qui prescrit de déconstruire*]" (*LI*, 153; *LI*/F, 283).

An example of the unconditional prescription to deconstruct would be the responsibility to show how the trait of writing or inscription that marks the limit of a corpus or of a context is divisible and how it erases itself in the very process of marking. One case of that is the reading of Austin or Searle in *Limited Inc*. This reading depends, as I have shown, on iterability. Iterability is one example of that divisibility that erases itself in the very process of marking. Derrida's "deconstruction" of Austin and Searle was enjoined by that unconditional demand of which he here speaks and by the attempt to develop "another language and other thoughts." These "seek to make their way [*cherchent à travers*]" through the complexities of Derrida's deconstruction of Austin and Searle or "Sarl" to emerge as ethico-political injunctions (*LI*, 153; *LI*/F, 282).

What is this other language, these other thoughts, these other responsibilities that arouse in him a respect and that Derrida neither can nor will compromise? "Compromise [*transiger*]" is used here in the strong sense of the failure to keep a promise, just as "perjury" is a failure to remain true to an oath, the prefixes in each case serving as quasi-negatives: positive acts that have a negative valence. Where does the call or injunction that Derrida will not compromise come from? The word "respect" here is Kantian. It translates the word *Achtung* in Kant's ethical works. An earlier passage in the "Afterword" contrasting two types of ethics gives an answer and shows how Derrida's other language and other thoughts are derived from the "law of iterability."

"It is clear," says Derrida, "that seriousness and literalness are exemplary qualities for the phrases Searle wishes to study and which form the point of departure for what he calls the 'idealization of the analyzed concept.' Such phrases are defined precisely in terms of the 'realization' of intentions in expression. This prescriptive normativeness is not overtly moralistic [*moralisante*]" (*LI*, 122; *LI*/F, 221). Austin's examples, it may be said, are more explicitly "moralistic." He was, after all, as I have said, a professor of moral philosophy and had a professional obligation to raise moral issues. Austin wants among other things, as I have shown, to guarantee that bigamists, welshers, and other such "low types" can be both morally deplored (it was an infernal shame that someone without authority christened that English ship *The Generalissimo Stalin*) and legally, juridically, punished. Hence the frequent references to the law, to lawyers, judges, and legal theorists, as in "A Plea for Excuses." On the other hand, Austin's pervasive ironies, as well as his constant use of "perhaps" and "maybe," undercut at every turn the seriousness of what he says. Derrida, however, wants to bend over backward to give speech-act theorists the benefit of the doubt and not to claim that they are always ponderously "moralistic." "Moralistic" is a dyslogistic word. Almost anyone would want to be "ethical," but hardly anyone would want to be "moralistic." "I have already said," Derrida continues, "that I never suspected speech act theoreticians of purely and simply giving us moral lessons and telling us to be serious, to avoid metaphors and ellipses [*soyez sérieux, évitez les métaphores et les ellipses*]. But often while analyzing a certain ethicity inscribed in language—and this ethicity is a metaphysics (there is nothing pejorative in defining it as such)—they reproduce, under the guise of describing it in its ideal purity, the given ethical conditions of a *given* ethics [une éthique *donnée*]" (*LI*, 122; *LI*/F, 221). I have attempted to identify just what that given ethics is in Austin's case, have given it the name "Austin's ideology," and have claimed that it is revealed in the examples he adduces. What Derrida wants to stress is how speech-act theorists tend to leave out or marginalize crucial features of the ethics they espouse. For example, they tend to obscure or take for granted the way their ethics justifies bringing in the police: "There is always a police and a tribunal ready to intervene each time that a rule (constitutive or regulative, vertical or not) is invoked in a case involving signatures, events, or contexts. . . . The police [are] always waiting in the wings [*La police est toujours dans les coulisses*]" (*LI*, 105; *LI*/F, 195). Speech-act theorists in Austin's wake also, not surprisingly, fail to acknowledge the possibility of that other ethics toward which Derrida wants to gesture:

> They exclude, ignore, relegate to the margins [*laissent dans leurs marges*] other conditions no less essential [*irréductibles*] to ethics in general, whether of *this given* ethics or of *another*, or of a law that would not answer to Western concepts of ethics, right, or politics. Such conditions, which may be anethical with respect to any given ethics, are not therefore anti-ethical in general. They can even open or recall the opening of another ethics, another right, another "declaration of rights," transformation of constitutions, etc." (*LI*, 122; *LI*/F, 221)

Austin, it might be argued, performs such a different ethical and political act in declaring a revolution in philosophy on the basis of ungrounded or unauthorized performatives, though he does not overtly admit this. It is the case, however, whatever Austin says about merely continuing a general direction that philosophy, meaning Oxford ordinary-language philosophy, is already going. He invents new terminologies by performative fiat, and thereby founds a whole new discipline. Nevertheless, as I have shown, and as Derrida is here also saying, Austin, like Sarl, remains caught in the metaphysics he claims to be revolutionizing, including the ethical assumptions associated with that metaphysics. "It is such conditions," Derrida continues,

> that is, conditions of ethical thought and action not noted by speech act theoreticians, that interest me when I write of iterability and of all that is tied to this quasi concept in a discourse and in other texts that I cannot reproduce here [and in many others written since then, I would add, or in recent seminars, for example those on the secret, on witnessing, on responsibility, on pardon and perjury, on capital punishment—JHM]. The ethical-legal-political implications [the French says: *Les consequences ou les implications éthico-juridico-politiques*] of all these gestures would be easy enough to show. (*LI*, 122; *LI*/F, 122)

I do not think such implications would be easy to show, or that they follow as transparent consequences, without saying. A start toward making those implications explicit has already been attempted in my section above in this chapter entitled "Declarations of Independence." I turn now, however, as a conclusion to this chapter, to an example of the relation of Derrida's unorthodox "quasi concept" of speech acts to a specific ethical situation, the situation in which I say "I love you" to another person. My hope and belief is that this will clarify what Derrida means by that new language and new thoughts, "which are also new responsibilities" that he neither can nor will compromise.

"Je t'aime"

Derrida explores the phrase "Je t'aime" ("I love you") as an exemplification of the speech-act theory he wants to put in place of Austin's or Searle's. Derrida originally presented his analysis of this phrase in two seminars given in December 1992 at the École des Hautes Études in Paris. He presented it again as one seminar in spring 1993 at the University of California at Irvine, in an English translation that he improvised on the spot. It has yet to be published.

The center of Derrida's argument is the claim that "Je t'aime" is a performative, not a constative, utterance. This is true even though the locution seems to be set up as an assertion of fact: "It is the fact that I love you. Make what you will of that fact." "Je t'aime" is a performative locution in part because the one to whom it is spoken has absolutely no way to verify that what I claim is a fact. You must take it on faith that I am telling you the truth. Another way to put this is to say that my locution "Je t'aime" is always implicitly, even sometimes explicitly, accompanied by something like "I swear to you that what I say is true." The swearing is an explicit performative. Derrida goes so far as to assert that all performative language is testimony, bearing witness, and vice versa. Testifying is exemplary of performative speech acts. It is a way of doing things with words. Uttering "Je t'aime" is in turn an exemplary case of bearing witness. Why is this? Derrida's thought about this question depends on several basic presuppositions, which I will enumerate here.

First presupposition: Though I have direct access to what I am thinking and feeling (however much I may be fooling myself or however much my self-awareness may be distorted by primary masochism or by my unconscious motivations), no one else does. The presumption of the isolation of the separate ego is fundamental here. Derrida refers to Husserl's fifth Cartesian Meditation as the crucial text for this. Derrida states:

> This act of faith is required by love, just as by all witnessing insofar as witnessing is a question of what takes place or is experienced within someone, some singular existence (*ego* or *Dasein*) there where the other cannot in any way have a direct, intuitive, and original [*originaire*] access. The other will never be on my side and will never have an intuitive, original access, in person, to the phenomenality for which I am origin of the world. In order to describe this zone which remains basically that of the secret and of absolute singularity, the secret and singularity of what is absolutely proper to me and of which I cannot expropriate myself, one of the best routes to follow would be that of the Fifth of Husserl's *Cartesian Meditations*. Husserl recalls there what is at once an axiom and an absolute evidence, that is to say, that the ego which has an intuitive, immediate, and original phenomenological access, in person, to the present phenomenality of its own experiences and of all that is proper to it can never have access other than an indirect one, appresentative and analogical [*apprésentatif ou analogique*], to

the experiences of the other, of the alter ego, which will never themselves, in person, appear to the ego, and of which the constitution within me requires such embarrassing procedures for transcendental phenomenology. . . . The irreducible alterity [*L'irréductible altérité*], which is also the irreducible singularity and therefore the irreducible secret, is the condition of love and of the declaration of love as witness and not as proof [*comme témoignage et non comme preuve*].[28]

The second presupposition is this: the fact that you have absolutely no way to find out or to be certain one way or the other about my state of mind, though nothing could be more important, both makes "Je t'aime" possible and at the same time always undermines it with the possibility that I may be lying, or joking, or citing someone else. Its possibility depends on its impossibility, according to an aporia encountered above in this chapter, in my discussion of the more general theory of iterability in *Limited Inc*. In the following passage, Derrida expresses how in this new context the impossibility of knowing is both a catastrophe for knowledge and at the same time absolutely essential, a piece of good luck for it. The possibility that saying "Je t'aime" might be a felicitous performative, a successful way to do things with words, depends on this lucky catastrophe:

As I often do, I insist on the fact that here menace and chance [*chance*] are indissociable, and on the fact that what makes possible is also what puts in danger. I retain here the word "chance," which well testifies at once to good and to evil, to the condition of possibility that allows testimony to happen, which makes the event of witnessing possible but at the same time makes it risk losing itself or degenerating into non-singularity and into truth of the constative type of the "what," of the pointer, of the proof, of the sign, of the archive, etc. The word "chance" testifies admirably to this; it is good luck [*il tombe bien*], since it expresses a happy chance, a possibility, a good probability in order to allow testimony to follow [*pour que le témoignage survienne*], in order that there is such a thing [*pour qu'il y en ait*], and also what brings about a fall, descent, decadence, or a falling due as forfeiture, fall, or decay [*et aussi ce qui fait tomber, la chute, la décadence ou l'échéance comme déchéance*]. There is a falling-due of testimony that renders indissociable in the body of the event this condition of possibility and this corruptibility.

Third presupposition: Like the Declaration of Independence, "Je t'aime" creates the event it names. What Derrida means here sounds scandalous: You do not fall in love until you say "Je t'aime." The question of the relation of language to passion, affect, or pain has an important place in twentieth-century thought, even in Anglo-American philosophy. The question is seen as in one way or another exemplary of the opposition between constative and performative language. When I express one passion or another, love or anger, or articulate my pain, do my words do no more than name something that already exists, or do my words create what they name, performatively? Wittgenstein's interminable reflections about the impossibility of a private language and about the problems of expressing my private pain, a pain that only I can feel or know; Austin's essay "Pretending," which takes off from the claim, made by another philosopher, that you are not angry until you express anger; and Proust's claim that lies, for example his lie to Albertine that he no longer loves her and wants to break with her, have a way of coming true just because we have said them out loud—here are three examples (to be discussed in Chapters 4 and 5 below) of the problematic that Derrida takes up in his own way in his claim, based explicitly on the human wisdom of Proust and of other great French novelists, that you are not in love until you say "Je t'aime." Saying "Je t'aime" is therefore for Derrida an exemplary case of his special kind of performative utterance, the kind that is ungrounded but creates its own grounds in the act of being proffered:

> "Je t'aime" is not a description; it is the production of an event by means of which, claiming not to lie, claiming to speak the truth (the "Je t'aime" is always true, deemed to be true, immediately true, and . . . [it has an] extraordinary allure of indubitability . . .), I tend to affect the other, to touch the other, literally or not, to give the other or to promise the other the love that I speak to him or her. . . . This performative declaration creates an event in manifesting, in attesting to that of which it speaks, in bearing witness to it; and that to which

it testifies is not elsewhere, but here and now, nearly merging [*se con-fondant*] with the act that consists in saying it, which has caused more than one to say [*ce qui a pu faire dire à plus d'un*], from Stendhal to Gide or to Proust (I can't remember), that one begins truly to love af-ter or at the earliest from the moment when love is declared and not before that [*qu'on commence veritablement à aimer après que ou au plus tôt au moment où l'amour est déclaré et non plus tôt*].

Fourth presupposition: A felicitous utterance of "Je t'aime," even if it is written in a letter, or spoken over the telephone, or sent by fax or e-mail, requires something more than words. It requires a breath, a gesture, a touch or the insinuation of a touch, something bodily that incarnates it in the here and now:

> I tend to affect the other, to touch the other, literally or not, to give the other or to promise him or her the love that I speak to him or her. In touching the other, by a certain caress in the words, even by a body to body engagement, of the body given or promised, even if this were be-yond all present contact, in a letter, or on the telephone or in the fac-simile of a fax. . . . This also implies that the enunciation is not effec-tive [*ne s'en puise pas*] in what is strictly speaking the enunciation, in a purely discursive manifestation, I mean verbal (lexical or syntactic); the body, intonation, and gesture are necessary, were it a breath, a look, not necessarily a caress, but in any case something singular and singu-larly sensible which makes it the case that the verbal speech alone does not suffice to a testimony, which signifies that the act or the gesture of witnessing, in a declaration of love, does not reduce itself to language, or to that in language which belongs to lexico-grammatical verbality.

This particular seminar contained a final insinuating ironic joke. It is impossible to be sure that Derrida, in merely citing "Je t'aime" in his seminar, as he repeats the phrase over and over, more or less acting it out, is not also using it to seduce each member of his large audience. The uncertainty goes both ways:

> This also means, other ineffaceable face of the same truth, that the ci-tation of "Je t'aime," a citation whose possibility remains implicit in the iterability itself that is the condition of every "Je t'aime," can, in certain conditions, to be sure, far from turning away from the "Je t'aime,"

therefore have certain seductive effects, certain seductive bonuses [*certains effets de séduction, certaines primes de séduction*], which it is also perhaps necessary to guard oneself against.

It is necessary to guard oneself from this danger, the danger of committing a strange case of sexual harassment with a whole lecture hall full of seventy or eighty students and faculty of all ages and both sexes, but Derrida cannot, by his own analysis, or even by Austin's, guard himself from doing this, since all mention is to some degree use and even the most deliberately constative statement has an element of the performative, and vice versa. I cannot say or write "Je t'aime" without to some degree using it.

I have allowed myself to quote abundantly here partly because this admirable seminar has not yet been published, much less translated, and partly to guard myself, of course, from doing anything more than mentioning by citation what Derrida says. Citing the phrase in French is another protection. Surely I am not really saying "I love you" to my readers when I cite Derrida's French phrase, which he used, by the way, even in the English version of the seminar in order to call attention to what is idiomatic and untranslatable in the French phrase. You can say "Je t'aime" only in French, the true language of love. This is most obvious in the way, in French, the object of the declaration is given in the second-person singular, an impossibility in English, unless you say something archaic like "I love thee," which is not likely to be too effective these days. Nevertheless, by appropriating Derrida's words to my own purposes, I too have not eluded turning mention into use. By taking "Je t'aime" as paradigmatic for the ethical situation in general, I have committed an ethical act of my own and have solicited my readers to understand in a certain way the new ethics and politics Derrida proposes.

§ 3 Paul de Man

The terminology of speech-act theory appeared in Paul de Man's work as an explicit target of interrogation at least as early as "Rhetoric of Persuasion (Nietzsche)," an essay of 1975 reprinted as chapter 6 of *Allegories of Reading*.[1] That interrogation continued throughout the rest of de Man's writing career. Like Jacques Derrida's speech-act theory, de Man's is a radical revision and putting in question of the apparent certainties of J. L. Austin's *How to Do Things with Words*, not to speak of John Searle's appropriation of Austin. I say "apparent certainties" of Austin's theory because Austin is a slippery fellow, an ironic writer if there ever was one, as I have shown above in Chapter 1. De Man's deviation from Austin differs in important ways from Derrida's. It would be an error to stress the differences too much, since there are many similarities, too; but even so, their speech-act theories seem quite different, certainly quite different in "tone." For example, irony (which is by no means incompatible with being serious) is a somewhat less prevalent mode in Derrida's work than it is in de Man's. Both in *Limited Inc* and more elaborately in Derrida's later work, Derrida's appropriation of speech-act theory moves—for example in the last pages of "Psyche: The Invention of the Other"[2]—toward a new notion of responsibility that is presented without irony. Speech acts are a response, a saying yes, to a demand or command that comes from the other, from what Derrida calls the wholly other, "le tout autre." Such por-

tentous terms as "the wholly other," along with the overt justification of what is being written by an appeal to a demand from some
radically other other that commands respect, are, at least so it
seems, entirely foreign to de Man's thought. De Man's revision or
"deconstruction" of Austin takes a different tack. He works soberly
within rhetorical or linguistic terminology that, at least initially, de-
rives from Nietzsche. Nietzsche, of course, can never exactly be described as "sober," nor as promoting sobriety (in spite of his own
abstinence from alcohol and distaste for the Germans as beer drink-
ers). Nietzsche is, rather, a philosopher who uses philosophical argumentation to demonstrate its impossibility. De Man was a sober
man, too, but still there is a certain ironic wildness in his sobriety,
as I shall show, and as his readers know. He reaches surprising or
even scandalous affirmations through a process of apparently inde-
fectible reasoning.

Beginning with the impossibility of distinguishing clearly between constative and performative utterances, though the whole enterprise of speech-act theory depends on this distinction, de Man is
led again and again, whenever he employs speech-act terminology,
up to a margin of unintelligibility that reflects back over his whole
enterprise. This, he argues, makes it forever uncertain whether it is
possible to ascertain what has been done with words and who or
what should be held responsible for it, or even if it is possible to do
anything with words at all. Consideration of the performative dimension of language is, for de Man, a way of encountering not "the
wholly other" but the limits of knowledge, a kind of impenetrable
penumbra of unknowability that surrounds all the clarity of en-
lightened reasoning, as darkness surrounds the bright circle of light
cast by the desk lamp in a study where a scholar sits late at night
bent over his book. Reading, for de Man, only makes that surrounding darkness darker, brings it, paradoxically, into the light.

"Rhetoric of Persuasion (Nietzsche)" is one example of such a
reading. De Man's reading is put under the aegis of the question of
"the relationship between philosophical and literary discourse" (*AR*,
119). De Man's essay is primarily a reading of section 516 of Nietzsche's so-called *The Will to Power* (*Der Wille zur Macht*), with at-

tention to related texts in Nietzsche. De Man focuses on Nietzsche's use, in section 516 and elsewhere, of the verb *setzen* ("posit") and its cognates *aussetzen* and *voraussetzen*, as opposed to *erkennen* ("know"). Variants of that word "posit" exist elsewhere in de Man, for example in the later essay "Shelley Disfigured," of which more later. De Man correctly sees that Nietzsche's opposition corresponds to Austin's distinction between performative and constative utterances: "The difference between performative and constative language (which Nietzsche anticipates)," says de Man, "is undecidable" (*AR*, 130).

Nietzsche "deconstructs" the principle of contradiction, or, in another formulation, of noncontradiction (*A* is self-identical; *A* cannot be both *A* and non-*A* at the same time), a basic tenet of logical reasoning since Aristotle: "According to Aristotle," says Nietzsche, in a passage cited by de Man (*AR*, 122), "the law of contradiction is the most certain of all principles." The deconstruction of this certainty achieves its end by showing that the identity principle is a matter of *setzen*, not of *erkennen*. The law is an unwarranted positing not based on any certain knowledge. The entire airy fabric of logical reasoning is based on a blind performative: "The language of identity and logic asserts itself in the imperative mode [That is, you must obey the law of noncontradiction.—JHM] and thus recognizes its own activity as the positing of entities. Logic consists of positional speech acts" (*AR*, 124). This seems clear enough. It gives the mastery that comes from clear knowledge, even if it is negative knowledge. *Erkennen* has been swallowed up in *setzen*. The whole field of speaking, thinking, and writing has become a kind of pan-performative act: "This would allow for the reassuring conviction that it is legitimate to do just about anything with words, as long as we know that a rigorous mind, fully aware of the misleading power of tropes, pulls the strings" (*AR*, 131).

With the help of some other passages in Nietzsche, especially section 477 of *The Will to Power*, however, de Man performs the sort of additional twist on this achieved knowledge that readers of his work come to expect. It is always worth remembering, though, what he says—citing Nietzsche's "On Truth and Lie in an Extra-

Moral Sense" ("Über Wahrheit und Lüge im aussermoralische Sinn")—in another essay, "Rhetoric of Tropes (Nietzsche)," about the person "who does not learn from experience and always again falls in the same trap" (*AR*, 118). Readers of de Man, or readers in general, may be like Linus and the football in the "Peanuts" cartoons, falling again and again for the same trick. In de Man's essays the irresistible trick is the illusion of an apparently achieved clear knowledge that is just about to be undone.

The further twist depends on the radical separation of the cognitive from the performative dimensions of language that is a basic presupposition of de Man's speech-act theory. It is not that performative and constative utterances can be sharply distinguished. They cannot. All utterances are a mixture of the two. But insofar as an utterance is performative, it is outside the realm of the knowable. This means that all acts of *Setzung*, far from being the region of a possible mastery, are a region of radical ignorance and intellectual weakness: "Performative language is not less ambivalent in its referential function than the language of constatation" (*AR*, 127). The referential function of performative language presumably means the ability to do something with words and at the same time to know what that doing is. It turns out that this is impossible: "The first passage (section 516) on identity showed that constative language is in fact performative, but the second passage (section 477) asserts that the possibility for language to perform is just as fictional as the possibility for language to assert" (*AR*, 129). This is expressed a couple of sentences later in a figure: "What seems to lead to an established priority of 'setzen' over 'erkennen,' of language as action over language as truth, never quite reaches its mark. It under- or overshoots it and, in so doing, it reveals that the target which one long since assumed to have been eliminated has merely been displaced" (*AR*, 130).

De Man, as usual, draws the most far-reaching consequences from this double impossibility and this double ignorance. The reassuring conviction that it is legitimate to do just about anything with words, so long as we know that a rigorous mind, fully aware of the misleading power of tropes, pulls the strings, is undone by the fact that neither we nor the rigorous mind can know any such things: "But if it turns out that this same mind does not even know whether it is doing or not doing something, then there are considerable grounds for suspicion that it does not know *what* it is doing" (*AR*, 131). This reminds me of something de Man said in a seminar at Yale. A speech act, he commented, makes something happen all right, but it is never what is intended or what is predicted beforehand. You aim at a bear and some innocent bird falls out of the sky.

His discovery by way of Nietzsche of this inability to know what one is doing leads de Man to another example of the kind of climactic, mind-twisting, generalizing affirmation that I have elsewhere described as the allergenic element in his work.[3] De Man has earned the affirmation by his close reading of Nietzsche, but the Nietzschean scaffolding is at this moment thrown away, and the affirmation hangs in the air alone, validated primarily by de Man's own say-so and expressed in his own special vocabulary:

> Considered as persuasion, rhetoric is performative but when considered as a system of tropes, it deconstructs its own performance. Rhetoric is a *text* in that it allows for two incompatible, mutually self-destructive points of view, and therefore puts an insurmountable obstacle in the way of any reading or understanding. The aporia between performative and constative language is merely a version of the aporia between trope and persuasion that both generates and paralyzes rhetoric and thus gives it the appearance of a history. (*AR*, 131)

An aporia is a blind alley, a dead end marked "No through street." The aporia in this case is both an absolute obstacle to knowledge and an absolute obstacle to doing, or at least to a doing that knows it is doing and knows what it is doing.

De Man's essay returns elegantly to its beginning by observing that though the question of the relation of literature and philosophy in Nietzsche (and, by implication, the question of this relation generally, not just in Nietzsche) has not been answered, at least we have "a somewhat more reliable point of 'reference' from which to ask the question" (*AR*, 131). The point of reference, however, is a recognition that "the deconstruction of metaphysics, or 'philosophy,' is an impossibility to the precise extent that it is 'literary'" (*AR*, 131). Here is another impossibility, though perhaps one in which philosophy should rejoice. The deconstruction of metaphysics (the phrase is surely an allusion to Derrida) sounds as if it would be a good thing, but the tool that might be expected to perform that salutary act, namely rhetoric or literature, turns out to be unable, to lack power, to be entirely too weak, to do what it is supposed to be able to do. This would leave metaphysics—which here is shorthand for one region of what de Man was later to call aesthetic ideology—happily intact, destined to repeat its errors interminably, however valiant the efforts to "deconstruct" it.

"Rhetoric of Persuasion (Nietzsche)" establishes the program for all de Man's later investigation of speech acts, for example in "Promises (*Social Contract*)," in "Excuses (*Confessions*)," "Shelley Disfigured," "Pascal's Allegory of Persuasion," and "The Concept of Irony." Each of these is an intricate essay that would demand an elaborate exegesis even if the goal were simply to establish the theory of speech acts in the essay. Though de Man's speech-act theory remains consistent with itself and does not "progress," a gradual shift occurs away from focus on the predicaments of consciousness in relation to performative utterances to the ability of language to act performatively on its own, without any intervention from consciousness or intentionality at all. De Man still focuses in his speech-act theory on the way "performative rhetoric and cognitive rhetoric, the rhetoric of tropes, fail to converge" (*AR*, 300), but he pays more attention to how this happens independently of the conscious, willing, and feeling mind, on how it happens as a mechanical fact of language. "Promises (*Social Contract*)" ends with the assertion that the unfulfillable and deceitful promise of political amelioration "does not occur at the discretion of the writer . . . language itself dissociates the cognition from the act. *Die Sprache verspricht (sich)*" (*AR*, 276, 279). The intricate reading of the episode of "the purloined ribbon" from Rousseau's *Confessions* in "Excuses (*Confessions*)" (*AR*, 278–301) occurs in layers, each disqualifying the one before by going it one better or by going beyond it, penetrating more deeply into the text. The reading in terms of a desire to possess, in a metaphorical system of exchange and substitution, is replaced by a reading in terms of desire for the pleasurable shame felt at self-exposure, though this motivational structure is still seen as falling within the circuit of metaphorical displacement and therefore as open to understanding. These two readings are in turn radically disrupted through the assertion that Rousseau, by his own testimony, excused himself not with strategies of substitution fueled by desire but with the first sound that happened to come onto his tongue: "Rousseau was making whatever noise happened to come into his head; he was saying nothing at all, least of all someone's name" (*AR*, 292). The culmination of this constantly self-canceling reading process, built on Rousseau's assertion that the name Marion just came into his head as an excuse ("I excused myself upon the first thing that offered itself" [*Je m'excusai sur le premier objet qui s'offrit*] [*AR*, 288]), is the assertion that excuses and other speech acts are purely mechanical, like grammar. The emphasis here is on "random" interruption, disjunction, disruption, what de Man calls, in a fine phrase, "the almost imperceptible crack of the purely gratuitous" (*AR*, 291). In the end, however, or all along, this disruption is distributed throughout, like irony in an ironic text, as a "permanent parabasis."

Excuses, de Man concludes, are performed by language itself, not by the willing, intending subject. This means that, like speech acts in general, excuses are closed to cognition and understanding, though these remained triumphantly operative at the end of the two earlier stages of the reading. A "complete disjunction" exists "between Rousseau's desires and interests and the selection of this particular name" (*AR*, 288). De Man generalizes this in the development that follows: "There can be no use of language that is not, within a certain perspective, thus radically formal, i.e. mechanical, no matter how deeply this aspect may be concealed by aesthetic, formalistic delusions. . . . The deconstruction of the figural dimension is a process that takes place independently of any desire; as such it is not unconscious but mechanical, systematic in its performance but arbitrary in its principle, like a grammar" (*AR*, 294,

298). As a result, the affective accompaniments of a speech act such as an excuse are generated by the performative utterance, not assuaged by it. Just as "in the plays of Kleist, the verdict repeats the crime it condemns" (*AR*, 245), so "excuses generate the very guilt they exonerate, though always in excess or by default. At the end of the *Rêverie* there is a lot more guilt around than we had at the start" (*AR*, 299). If this guilt, moreover, is in principle open to cognition, the excuse that both exonerates and generates it is blind, beyond understanding, a matter of what Friedrich Schlegel called *Unverständlichkeit* ("incomprehensibility"):

> Since guilt, in this description, is a cognitive and excuse a performative function of language, we are restating the disjunction of the performative from the cognitive: any speech act produces an excess of cognition, but it can never hope to know the process of its own production (the only thing worth knowing). Just as the text can never stop apologizing for the suppression of guilt that it performs, there is never enough knowledge available to account for the delusion of knowing. (*AR*, 299–300)

In "Shelley Disfigured"[4] de Man gives this radical theory of speech acts' unknowability one more twist by seeing language itself, in its aboriginal and then endlessly iterated appearance, as the product of a senseless self-positing that is entirely independent of human consciousness. The use of the term "positing," however, shows the continuity of de Man's speech-act theory from the relatively early "Rhetoric of Persuasion (Nietzsche)" on. The positing in Shelley's *The Triumph of Life* is a recurrent "single, and therefore violent, act of power achieved by the positional power of language considered by and in itself" (*RR*, 116). This senseless, violent positing, performed by language acting on its own, without intervention by any subjectivity, is then obliterated, forgotten, half-erased by a second positing that without warrant ascribes meaning to what language has posited:

> How can a positional act, which relates to nothing that comes before and after, become inscribed in a sequential narrative? How does a speech act become a trope, a catachresis which then engenders in its

turn the narrative sequence of an allegory? It can only be because we impose, in our turn, on the senseless power of positional language the authority of sense and of meaning. But this is radically inconsistent: language posits and language means (since it articulates) but language cannot posit meaning; it can only reiterate (or reflect) it in its reconfirmed falsehood. Nor does the knowledge of this impossibility make it less impossible. This impossible position is precisely figure, the trope, metaphor as violent—and not as dark—light, a deadly Apollo. . . . Considered performatively, figuration (as question [De Man is thinking of the iterated "Why?" "Why?" "Why?" that echoes through *The Triumph of Life.*—JHM]) performs the erasure of the positing power of language. (*RR,* 117–18)

The reader is perhaps beginning to get the hang of de Man's acerb rigor, though it may be a hanging matter to think you have got the hang of it. Language, on its own, without any help from man or woman, from his or her subjectivity and its intentions, posits itself, in a violent and senseless act of positing. This positing is a speech act, but of a most anomalous kind, since it is detached from the ego with its conscious intentions. The latter was, for J. L. Austin, as he is usually interpreted at least, the necessary agent of felicitous speech acts, as when someone says, "I promise."[5] *Die Sprache verspricht,* "Language promises," but it does so in a violent, senseless, mechanical way, without any consciousness of what it is doing. Language therefore also *verspricht sich* in one meaning of this verb as a reflexive: to make a slip of the tongue, to say the wrong thing. Language makes a slip of the tongue. When I make a slip of the tongue, I say what I did not mean to say. My tongue speaks for me, senselessly, as, for de Man, language speaks on its own. Only in a secondary unwarranted positing do I ascribe meaning to language in an act that necessarily forgets or erases the violence and senselessness of the original performative positing. This is "the emergence of an articulated language of cognition by the erasure, the forgetting of the events this language in fact performed" (*RR,* 118).

The erasure is only partial, however, since the new act of positing that confers sense and meaning on what is without them is also violent: "The initial violence of position can only be half erased, since the erasure is accomplished by a device of language that never ceases to partake of the very violence against which it is directed" (*RR*, 118–19). The sequence is then ready to begin again with another violent act of self-positing by language, followed by its recuperation into meaning, the setting up of a system of tropes, and the allegorizing of their unreadability. A pervasive irony, however, suspends that allegory's clarity of meaning all along its narrative line.

The initial violence, though it engenders history and has material force, is outside of time, punctual, instantaneous. It happens in the blink of an eye, as the sun in Shelley's *The Triumph of Life* "sprang forth." The first violent positing is immediately covered over by the second act of positing that confers meaning on what is a senseless act of power. The second positing generates ideologies that are not events, that in a sense do not happen. De Man affirms that though Kant's writing was an event, the long misreading of Kant initiated by Schiller was a series of non-events: "In the whole reception of Kant from then until now, nothing has happened, only regression, nothing has happened at all."[6] In "Shelley Disfigured," as in previous essays, though by a somewhat different route, de Man comes by way of his own special investigation of speech acts as senseless positing back up once more to the borders of unknowability.

I ask now a question that is not at all innocent. Much hangs on the answer. Does de Man's own work have a performative component? At first it would seem not. His work is presented in the sober constative mode of a reading that is either true or not true to the text it reads. Its cognitive truth or falsity ought to be open to objective validation. Either Raymond Geuss is right about Hegel or de Man is. De Man's "Reply to Raymond Geuss" is for the most part a carefully reasoned and documented attempt to show that Geuss (and the traditional canonical reading of Hegel) have got Hegel wrong, while de Man has got him right.[7]

Nevertheless, it is easy to show that de Man's work, like any text, but in this case in particular ways, has a crucial performative component. One way is in a characteristic locution that appears many times in different forms in de Man's writings. This is the phrase "what we call," as in "what we call ideology" in a celebrated definition in "The Resistance to Theory,"[8] or as in the last words of "Pascal's Allegory of Persuasion": "what we call allegory."[9] To denominate is a positional speech act, a catachresis, as when we call a baby "Andrew" or "Mary." The "we" in de Man's formulations is both an authorial "we" (he really means *he* calls it allegory) and at the same time an indicator of the collective, conventional, fictional character of the denomination. *We* call it ideology, but that is not really its proper name. It has no proper name, except by agreed-upon convention.

The performative dimension of de Man's work is, however, more pervasive than this. He iterates the "warning" he finds in *The Triumph of Life* not just as "mention" but as "use." De Man, or rather de Man's text, is warning the reader, though it also warns her that she cannot heed the warning:

> "The Triumph of Life" warns us that nothing, whether deed, word, thought, or text, ever happens in relation, positive or negative, to anything that precedes, follows, or exists elsewhere, but only as a random event whose power, like the power of death, is due to the randomness of its occurrence. It also warns us why and how these events then have to be reintegrated in a historical and aesthetic system of recuperation that repeats itself regardless of the exposure of its fallacy. (*RR*, 122)

Many other such performative statements can be found in de Man's writings. His entire work might be defined as a warning. This happens, however, most decisively and strategically through a characteristic and often repeated move that is a performative utterance disguised as a constative one. This move is the shift from periphrastic statements that claim only to mime constatively in slightly different language, but with many citations, what a given text says and means to statements of universal generality that emerge from the reading but that are now claimed to apply to all texts at all times.

De Man's work is full of such, strictly speaking, unwarranted displacements of register. They are unwarranted because nothing in the text de Man is reading, which has its own unique particularity and historical overdetermination, justifies leaping to all-or-nothing generalizations. A paradigmatic example of this leap is the way the sentence "The paradigm for all texts consists of a figure (or a system of figures) and its deconstruction" (*AR*, 205) erupts suddenly from a reading of Rousseau's *Julie*. Insofar as this sentence is a continuation of the account of what Rousseau's text says, it is constative. Insofar as it can be detached from that context and made to apply universally, as many accounts of de Man's "theories" have done with such statements, then it is an implicit performative. That performative takes the form of a covert addendum or tail: "I declare that this applies universally, though this declaration of the principle's independence from its source in reading cannot be justified constatively or cognitively on the authority of the text I have been reading. I know it because I know it or rather because language knows it, not because the text I am reading knows it as a universal."

"*Die Sprache verspricht (sich)*; to the extent that is necessarily misleading, language just as necessarily conveys the promise of its own truth" (*AR*, 277) is another salient example of such a leap, as are most of the other climactic aphorisms that are characteristic border utterances in de Man's work. That many of these are covert prosopopoeias, personifying language as if it were a conscious being capable of acting on its own, making promises or slips of the tongue, "generating" allegories or "history" (*AR*, 277), being "implacable" (*AR*, 275) or "mad" (*RR*, 122), "dissociating" (*AR*, 277), and so on, only confirms the performative aspect of such locutions. The "madness of words" is unstoppable because it is a madness of words, not a madness of those who use words. The users may remain indefectibly sane, though their words are mad. It is impossible to put words in an asylum, or to psychoanalyze them, or to cure them with drugs. If they are mad, they remain mad. Of Rousseau's making political promises in the *Social Contract* in spite of the fact that he has said such promises are aberrant and groundless, de Man says: "This model is a fact of language over which Rousseau himself has no control. Just as any other reader, he is bound to misread his text as a promise of political change. The error is not within the reader; language itself dissociates the cognition from the act" (*AR*, 277).

A prosopopoeia is radically performative. It ascribes a name, a face, or a voice to the absent, the inanimate, or the dead. Language as such, prior to being illegitimately animated and given a soul by the ascription of meaning, is, as de Man himself says in "Shelley Disfigured" and elsewhere, inanimate, dead, sheer materiality. De Man's performatives animate language by an "implacable" necessity forcing him to do what he elsewhere clearly recognizes as aberrant—for example in "Autobiography as De-Facement" or in "Anthropomorphism and Trope in the Lyric" (*RR*, 67–81; 239–62)—thereby at the same time confirming his theory and disqualifying its claims to mastery. De Man's project might be defined as a radical attempt to suspend or do without the category of the self-conscious, deliberately intending subject or ego as the agent of either cognitive statements or speech acts. The personality denied in one place, however, reappears in another, that is, in the performative ascribing of personality and agency to language itself.

As might have been expected, however, de Man has been there already. He has foreseen and forestalled any such reproach to him for doing what he says is fallacious. Speaking of such prosopopoeias in "Hegel on the Sublime," de Man says: "If we say that language speaks, that the grammatical subject of a proposition is language rather than a self, we are not fallaciously anthropomorphizing language but rigorously grammatizing the self. The self is deprived of any locutionary power; to all intents and purposes it may as well be mute."[10] Maybe so, but to say "language speaks" looks like a prosopopoeia to me. Of course what de Man means is that it is a catachrestic prosopopoeia that knows it is a personification of something that is not living, that disqualifies itself by an open irony: "Language *speaks*" (!). It is a catachresis because no language other than some personifying term or other exists to name the autonomous activity of language. Moreover, de Man stresses the reciprocal of this personification, namely the depersonification of the self, its rigorous grammatizing. To that I would answer that the disqualifying irony in "Language speaks" may or may not be detected by a given person. Heidegger, for example, who notoriously said "Die Sprache spricht [Language speaks]," appears to have meant it pretty literally, though even so, he meant it perhaps without actually thinking of language as a person or wanting his readers to do so. It is difficult, however, perhaps impossible, to resist the beguiling enchantment of a prosopopoeia.

The final consequence of recognizing the performative aspect of de Man's own texts is the most disquieting. His statement that the cognitive and performative aspects of any text "cannot be distinguished or reconciled" (*AR*, 276) must apply to his own texts, too, however silent he may be about what this implies. The warning in "Shelley Disfigured" also warns us that we cannot heed the warning expressed by *The Triumph of Life*. "Promises (*Social Contract*)" states this unhappy predicament on a level of totalization that would make it apply to de Man's texts as much as to any others:

> A text is defined by the necessity of considering a statement [such as this one we are in the act of reading—JHM], at the same time, as performative and constative, and the logical tension between figure and grammar [which it has been the thrust of the earlier part of the essay to identify in Rousseau's *Social Contract*—JHM] is repeated in the impossibility of distinguishing between two linguistic functions which are not necessarily compatible. It seems that as soon as a text knows what it states, it can only act deceptively, like the thieving lawmaker in the *Social Contract*, and if a text does not act, it cannot state what it knows. The distinction between a text as narrative and a text as theory also belongs in this field of tension. (*AR*, 270)

As de Man makes clear on the next page, narrative is performative while theory is constative. Any text—this essay by de Man, for example, or my essay here on de Man that you are at this moment reading—is both constative and performative through and through, though it is impossible to distinguish between the two operations and though we cannot know for sure whether they are compatible, though we surely suspect they are not. To know that they are not necessarily compatible and that we cannot ever know for sure whether they are in a given case is enough to ruin the project of reconciling them.

The tension between the two functions means that the performative aspect of the text makes it produce deceptive, illusory knowledge, or the illusion of knowledge. This illusion takes the form of a performative narrative, such as the clear narrative story each de Man essay tells. The text must act, that is, must tell a story, in order to state what it knows, but this narrative statement is necessarily deceptive, like a thieving lawgiver who passes laws to take things illicitly for himself. A text, such as de Man's essay, neither knows for sure what it knows nor knows what it is doing nor even knows whether it knows anything or is doing anything or not. Its doing is radically incompatible with its knowing, so if it does something, that something is always more or less than what the original knowing seemed to promise. The text always overshoots or undershoots the target it aims at: "It always produces a little more or a little less than the original, theoretical input" (*AR*, 271). *Die Sprache verspricht (sich)*.

The investigation of de Man's speech-act theory has brought "us" repeatedly up to the borders of the unintelligible. De Man speaks or writes in the name of that unintelligibility. It authorizes him to say what he says. That authority, however, does not, it goes without saying, authorize him to say anything in particular that can be verified as cognitively valid or not. Rather, it undermines and disqualifies anything that is said in its name. As related to the unintelligible or "based on it," no statement is either true or false, though it may be performatively effective in unforeseen and unknowable ways.

Are de Man's writings an event in the sense that, as he says in "Kant and Schiller," Kant's *Critique of Judgment* was an event? Yes. I declare that I believe this to be the case. Can we know what sort of event it was, its meaning and consequences? No, by de Man's own testimony. Have de Man's writings been, as he declared was inevitable, recuperated, written back into aesthetic ideology? Yes. Is my own chapter here an example of that? I cannot in principle answer that question and must leave it to my readers to decide, though I must warn them that their decision will be performative, not constative.

§ 4 Passion Performative

Derrida, Wittgenstein, Austin

> An entire epoch of so-called literature, if not all of it, cannot survive a certain technological regime of telecommunications (in this respect the political regime is secondary). Neither can philosophy, or psychoanalysis. Or love letters. . . .
>
> Refound here the American student with whom we had coffee last Saturday, the one who was looking for a thesis subject (comparative literature). I suggested to her something on the telephone in the literature of the 20th century (and beyond), starting with, for example, the telephone lady in Proust or the figure of the American operator, and then asking the question of the effects of the most advanced telematics [*la télématique la plus avancée*] on whatever would still remain of literature. I spoke to her about microprocessors and computer terminals, she seemed somewhat disgusted [*elle avait l'air un peu dégoutée*]. She told me that she still loved literature (me too, I answered her, *mais si, mais si*). Curious to know what she understood by this.
>
> —Jacques Derrida, "Envois," in *The Post Card*

In these final chapters I want to show with one example—a reading of several interrelated passages in Proust's *À la recherche du temps perdu*, including one about telephone operators—how a prudent, circumspect, suitably refined awareness of speech-act theories may be helpful or even perhaps indispensable in interpreting literature.

The comment Derrida makes through his protagonist in *The Post Card* in the passage I have taken as epigraph[1] for this chapter is truly frightening, at least to a lover of literature like me or like the protagonist's hapless interlocutor, the American graduate student in comparative literature who was looking for a dissertation topic. The comment arouses in me (by an efficacious performative effect) the passions of anxiety, fear, disgust, disbelief, and perhaps a little secret desire to see what it would be like to live beyond the end of literature, love letters, philosophy, and psychoanalysis. It would be like living beyond the end of the world.

Derrida's curt and even insolent words in *The Post Card* may indeed generate such passions in most readers. We passionately and instinctively resist the statement. How could a change in something so superficial, mechanical, and contingent as the dominant means of preservation and dissemination, the change from a manuscript and print culture to a digital culture, bring to an end things that seem so universal in any civilized society as literature, philosophy, psychoanalysis, and love letters? Surely these will survive any change in the regime of telecommunications? Surely I can write love letters by e-mail! Surely I can compose and transmit literature or philosophy with a computer connected to the Internet just as well as I can with handwriting or a typewriter or through the printed book? How is psychoanalysis, based as it is on face-to-face interlocution (it's called the "talking cure"), tied to the regime of print, and how is it to be brought to an end by a shift to digital culture? Preposterous!

The scholar Avital Ronell, by the way, has written on the telephone in modern literature, though no doubt not as a response to any direct solicitation from Derrida. Both Proust on the telephone and Derrida's *The Post Card* figure in Ronell's admirable work *The Telephone Book*, the format of which anticipates the emerging regime of telecommunications. Laurence Rickels has also written brilliantly on the telephone in modern literature, psychoanalysis, and culture generally, as has Friedrich Kittler.[2]

Implausible though Derrida's claim may be, he means it: the change in "regime of telecommunications" will not simply transform but absolutely bring to an end literature, philosophy, psychoanalysis, and even love letters. It will do this by a kind of death-dealing performative fiat: "Let there be no more love letters!" How in the world could this be? My reading of Proust will try, among other things, to give an answer. Insofar as Derrida's words generate the passions of fear, anxiety, disgust, incredulity, and secret desire, those words are a "felicitous" performative utterance in yet another way. They do what they say and help bring about the end of literature, love letters, and so on, just as saying "Je t'aime," as Derrida argued in the seminar discussed above in Chapter 2, not only creates love in the speaker but may generate belief and reciprocal love in the addressee, the one to whom the words are spoken.

In spite of all Derrida's love for literature, his writings, for example *Glas*, or *The Post Card* itself, have certainly contributed to the end of literature as we have known it in a particular historical epoch and culture, say the last two or two and a half centuries in Europe and America. The concept of literature in the West has been inextricably tied to Cartesian notions of selfhood, to the regime of print, to Western-style democracies and notions of the nation-state, and to the right to free speech within such democracies. "Literature" in that sense began fairly recently, in the late seventeenth or early eighteenth century, and in one place, Western Europe. It could come to an end, and that would not be the end of civilization. In fact, if Derrida is right—and I believe he is—the new regime of telecommunications is bringing literature to an end by transforming all those factors that were its preconditions or its concomitants. If de Man is right to say that language acts performatively on its own, then the material embodiment of that language is not irrelevant. A change in embodiment, such as that in which we are now participating, will produce corresponding changes in the way words (and, I should add, other sign systems, including graphic ones such as cinema) act on their own to do unforeseen things.

One of Derrida's main points in *The Post Card* is that the new regime of telecommunications breaks down the inside/outside dichotomies that presided over the old print culture. The new regime is ironically allegorized by Derrida with somewhat obsolete forms: not only with the many telephone conversations the protagonist or protagonists have with their beloved or beloveds but also with an old-fashioned remnant of the rapidly disappearing culture of handwriting, print, and the postal system: the postcard. The postcard anticipates the publicity and openness of the new communications regimes. These are causing much anxiety these days about the loss of "privacy." A postcard is open for anyone to read, just as e-mail today is by no means sealed or private. If an example of either happens to fall under my eye, I can make myself or am magically made into its recipient, as Derrida asserts in regard to postcards and letters not only in *The Post Card* but also in the admirable essay called "Telepathy."[3] The postcard or e-mail message, if it falls under my eye, is meant for me, or I take it as meant for me, whoever its addressee may be. This certainly happens when I read the passage from *The Post Card* I have cited as an epigraph for this chapter. The bad news the speaker conveyed to the graduate student, news of the end of literature, philosophy, psychoanalysis, and love letters, is also conveyed to me. I become the recipient of the bad news. The passions that the protagonist's comment aroused in the graduate student are also aroused in me.

Passionate Speech Acts

What is the relation between speech acts and passion? We ordinarily celebrate or deplore the power literary works have to generate strong feelings. Just how do they do so? The word "passion" has both a passive and an active sense. The passive sense emerges when we speak of "the Passion of Christ," referring to his suffering unto death on the cross. Passion as passive endurance, as suffering, tends to be associated with the ultimate passion of the death throe. The active sense of "passion" is exemplified in such statements as "I have a passion for mountain climbing," or more poignantly, "He loves her passionately." Passion is concupiscent and intentional. It wants to possess or transform its object. It tends to be hyperbolic, as with Bradley Headstone's passion for Lizzie Hexam in Dickens's *Our Mutual Friend*. It motivates action, even dangerous, irrational, or self-destructive action, as with the passion for reaching the top of Mount Everest or for sailing alone around the world. A curious passage in the *Calendar of State Papers Relating to Scotland*, written by one Nicholas White after he visited Mary Queen of Scots during her nineteen-year captivity in England, affirms that Mary's "pretty Scotch speech," along with her "searching wit, clouded with mildness," might instigate someone to attempt to free her: "Glory joined to gain might stir others to adventure much for her sake; then joy is a lively impetuous passion, and carrieth persuasions to the heart, which moveth all the rest."[4] Meeting Mary Stuart face to face, according to White, stirred the passion of joy.

The problem of passion, however, is not just the often undecidable distinction between passive and active but also the problem of the inside/outside opposition, or, to put it in terms of the distinction between constative and performative utterances, the problem of whether the outward expression of passion, in words or other signs, simply reports, constatively, an emotion that already exists inwardly, or whether the outer expression creates, performatively, the inner passion. Do I first feel love and then say "I love you," or does saying "I love you" bring about the passionate state of being in love?

That we regard this as a question, perhaps an unanswerable question, depends on our accepting in some form or to some degree the assumption that Husserl expressed most overtly and apodictically in the fifth of the *Cartesian Meditations*:[5] that I have in principle no direct access, and no verifiable indirect access either, to the ego of another person, to his or her thoughts, feelings, memories, hopes, sensations, passions. If I had such direct access, there would be no problem, or the problem would be fundamentally different. I have shown in Chapter 2 how Derrida's admirable investigation of the performative force of the locution "Je t'aime" explicitly presupposes the Husserlian opacity of the other ego. In another essay,[6] I have shown how this presupposition determines Derrida's argument in "Passions" that literature hides unfathomable secrets, for example the answer to the question of whether Baudelaire's protagonist in "Counterfeit Money" gave a counterfeit coin or a real coin to the beggar. Derrida's name for the unfathomable secret is *le tout autre*, the wholly other, that is, an otherness that in no way can be known or assimilated into some version of "the same." It is this otherness in literature, Derrida argues, that "impassions us." Derrida means by this that the unfathomable secret in each literary work has the strange performative effect of arousing our passion. This passion, as Derrida expresses it, takes the form of an irresistible but wholly unfulfillable sense of obligation.[7] In hiding an impenetrable secret, a work of literature is strictly parallel to a love affair: my sense that my beloved hides an unrevealable secret, that she is unfathomably mysterious, arouses in me the passions of love and desire for the beloved when she says (or does not say) "Je t'aime," just as the secrets literature hides arouse my desire to find out those secrets. A similar secret impassions the religious person when he or she prays to God, as Derrida asserts at one moment in "Sauf le nom (Post-Scriptum)."[8] Here is what Derrida says about the way the secret in literature impassions us with the call of the other:

> There is in literature, in the *exemplary* secret of literature, a chance of saying everything without touching upon the secret. When all hypotheses are permitted, groundless and ad infinitum, about the meaning of a text, or the final intentions of an author, whose person is no more represented than nonrepresented by a character or by a narrator, by a poetic or fictional sentence, which detaches itself from its presumed source and thus remains *locked away* [*au secret*], when there is no longer even any sense in making decisions about some secret behind the surface of a textual manifestation (and it is this situation which I would call text or trace), when it is the call [*appel*] of this secret, however, which points back to the other or to something else [*à l'autre ou à autre chose*], when it is this itself which keeps our passion aroused, and holds us to the other, then the secret impassions us.[9]

Wittgenstein's Pain

Ludwig Wittgenstein's prolonged meditation on the expression of the passions extends from book to book of his published writings. It is a topic, for example, in *The Blue and Brown Books*, in *Philosophical Investigations*, in *Remarks on the Philosophy of Psychology*,[10] and so on. These meditations center on the location, expressibility, and openness to knowledge of the pain of another, as well as on the way the solitude of pain raises the question of private language, another topic of prolonged meditation by Wittgenstein. On the one hand, a private language is a contradiction in terms, as Wittgenstein shows again and again from different perspectives. As he says, "the very nature of the investigation . . . compels us to travel over a wide field of thought criss-cross in every direction,"[11] and he certainly does that. On the other hand, how could I speak otherwise than in a private language about something so unique and incommunicable as my own private pain, pain that I alone can feel? Gerard Manley Hopkins, in an eloquent passage in the "Commentary on the Spiritual Exercises of St. Ignatius Loyola," one of the greatest expressions of this insight, poses this problem not in terms of pain but in terms of something even more enduring, that is, my persistent, singular, and unique "taste of myself." This taste is a kind of basic bodily passion (in the passive sense of endurance) of self-awareness, my "feeling of myself":

> And this [my isolation] is much more true when we consider the mind; when I consider my selfbeing, my consciousness and feeling of myself, that taste of myself, of *I* and *me* above and in all things, which is more distinctive than the taste of ale or alum, more distinctive than the smell of walnutleaf or camphor, and is incommunicable by any means to another man (as when I was a child I used to ask myself: What must it be to be someone else?). Nothing else in nature comes near this unspeakable stress of pitch, distinctiveness, and selving, this selfbeing of my own. Nothing explains it or resembles it. . . . Searching nature I taste *self* but at one tankard, that of my own being. The development, refinement, condensation of nothing shews any sign of being able to match this to me or give me another taste of it, a taste even resembling it.[12]

When Hopkins says the distinctiveness of his self-taste is "unspeakable," the word must be taken literally. No way exists to speak his self-taste, to express it in words. This is because there are no literal words for distinctive or private inner feelings. At the same time no figural language works to express them, either, because "nothing . . . resembles" his self-taste. The striking figures here (taste of ale or alum, smell of walnutleaf or camphor) must be defined as catachreses. They name inadequately something that has neither any literal name nor any similarity to any other thing. It is wholly other. Nevertheless, the goal of poetry for Hopkins, like the goal of narrative for Proust, is to find some way to speak this unspeakable, this wholly other of my private emotions. Examples of this attempt are Hopkins's "The Wreck of the Deutschland" and his so-called "terrible sonnets," his "sonnets of desolation."

Wittgenstein expresses the incommunicability of private experience less hyperbolically but in a no less apodictic way: "The essential thing about private experience is really not that each person possesses his own exemplar, but that nobody knows whether other people also have *this* or something else. The assumption would thus be possible—though unverifiable—that one section of mankind had one sensation of red and another section another."[13] It would be unverifiable because no way exists to get the evidence from both sides out on the table where it can be compared. My sensation of red, the passion it impassions me with, is incommunicable by any means to another man (or woman). Pain is passion as something suffered. How can I know that the other is in pain? How can I know the pain of another? What is the relation of pain to the body?[14] To consciousness? Is there such a thing as "unconscious pain"? What do we mean when we say "My pain is located *here*" (pointing to a place on my body)? Do animals have emotions, or are emotions purely human and ascribed only in figure to a cat or a dog, as when I say, "The angry dog attacked me" or "The cat purred with satisfaction." There would be much to say about this topic in Wittgenstein, partly because he had so much to say about it, returning to it again and again as to an obscure pain that he could not quite locate or rid himself of. Here is one example, from *The Blue Book*, of Wittgenstein's expression of this nagging pain:

> We are [in being led to think that "everything that we can know and say about the world {rests} upon personal experience" means that "it is all 'subjective'"] up against a trouble caused by our way of expression.
>
> Another such trouble, closely akin, is expressed in the sentence: "I can only know that *I* have personal experiences, not that anyone else has."—Shall we then call it an unnecessary hypothesis that anyone else has personal experiences?—But is it an hypothesis at all? For how can I even make the hypothesis if it transcends all possible experience? How could such a hypothesis be backed by meaning? (Is it not like paper money, not backed by gold?)—It doesn't help if anyone tells us that, though we don't know whether the other person has pains, we

certainly believe it when, for instance, we pity him. Certainly we shouldn't pity him if we didn't believe that he had pains, but is this a philosophical, a metaphysical belief? Does a realist pity me more than an idealist or a solipsist?—In fact the solipsist asks: "How *can* we believe that the other has pain; what does it mean to believe this? How can the expression of such a supposition make sense?"[15]

If Husserl or Derrida or, as I shall show, Proust accepts the complete otherness of the other and proceeds to draw consequences or, in the case of Proust, to investigate the problem by dramatizing its complexities in a narrative, Wittgenstein cannot rest satisfied with an apodictic formulation (e.g., "the other is wholly other"), but goes on asking questions and experimenting with new sentences from ordinary language that might allow a movement beyond this aporia. The aporia lies in the fact that we cannot know the pain of the other and yet behave as though we could, for example by manifesting the passion of pity in response to the other's pain. Wittgenstein had one of the most restless and inventive minds among the great philosophers. His inventiveness went partly into the thinking up of brilliant examples. If Wittgenstein was nagged by the pain of the other's inaccessibility, he kept nagging away at the problem, coming at it from different directions, crisscross, as though he hoped he might suddenly find the way out. In the passage just cited, as in general, Wittgenstein tends to assume that an apparent impasse in philosophical thinking is not so much a conceptual problem as a problem in "expression," that is, a problem in the way the issue is formulated in language.

"Expression" is a key word in Wittgenstein. It is used with the full force of its root as meaning a kind of blow or stamp. This notion of the force in language is even more evident in the German equivalent: *Ausdruck,* literally, "pressure outward" or "thrust outward." *Ausdruck* must often have been in Wittgenstein's bilingual mind. *Druck* in German means, among other things, "print," or "printing," the blow of the inked type on paper. If we have no direct access at all to the bodily feelings or mind of the other and can only hypothetically infer his or her pain—or not even hypothetically, since a genuine hypothesis must be verifiable as true or false, which is not possible in this case—it follows that our response to the other's pain, our passion of pity in response to the other's presumed pain, is a matter of belief. That is a way of saying that this response involves in implicit performative utterance, not a cognitive or constative statement. "I believe the other is in pain," just as I believe the other loves me when she says, "Je t'aime."

One escape from this impasse is to say—recalling Derrida and, as I shall show, Austin—not that pain or any other passion in the other is hidden away somewhere and then expressed, but that the expression is the passion or is indistinguishable from the passion (two very different things, and that is the problem). Wittgenstein states this eloquently, with some help from William James, in a much later passage in *The Blue and Brown Books*, this time from *The Brown Book*:

> You will find that the justifications for calling something an expression of doubt, conviction, etc., largely, though of course not wholly, consist in descriptions of gestures, the play of facial expressions, and even the tone of voice. Remember at this point that the personal experiences of an emotion must in part be strictly localized experiences; for if I frown in anger I feel the muscular tension of the frown in my forehead, and if I weep, the sensations around my eyes are obviously part, and an important part, of what I feel. This is, I think, what William James meant when he said that a man doesn't cry because he is sad but that he is sad because he cries. The reason why this point is often not understood, is that we think of the utterance of an emotion as though it were some artificial device to let others know that we have it. Now there is no sharp line between such "artificial devices" and what one might call the natural expressions of emotion. Cf. in this respect: a) weeping, b) raising one's voice when one is angry, c) writing an angry letter, d) ringing the bell for a servant you wish to scold.[16]

This seems clear enough and plausible enough. Wittgenstein is forcibly rejecting the notion that emotions are hidden away somewhere in a purely subjective realm, as Hopkins's formulations might suggest if it were not for the strongly bodily figures of taste and smell he uses. "I taste myself," "I smell myself," even though no one else can perform the same act of tasting or smelling. Each person's feeling of self is, for Hopkins, strongly incarnated. For Wittgenstein, here at least, emotions are incarnated too, whether in the muscular feeling of frowning when I am angry or in the sensations that go along with crying when I am sad, though in paragraph 331 of the *Philosophical Investigations* Wittgenstein denies that a man is necessarily aware of such things: "There is no ground for assuming that a man feels the facial movements that go with his expression, for example, or the alterations in his breathing that are characteristic of some emotion. Even if he feels them as soon as his attention is drawn towards them."[17]

Emotions, for Wittgenstein in the passage I have cited from *The Brown Book*, are also incarnated in what I say or write when I am angry or sad. The words, like the frowns or the tears, are not signs for something that remains sequestered off at a distance but an inextricable part of the emotion. The problem lies in that locution "part of." The careful reader will see the equivocation present in Wittgenstein's expressions: "largely, though of course not wholly," and in "obviously part, and an important part, of what I feel." The justifications for calling something an *expression* of doubt or conviction consist largely, though of course not wholly, in descriptions of gestures, the play of facial expressions, and so on, that go along with the expression in words. The frown is part, an important part, of what I feel. What about the rest of the emotion? Where is it located? What is it made of? How could we come to know it in another person? Just what is the relation between the part we can see, hear, or understand as spoken language, gesture, or facial expression and the part we can neither see, hear, nor read from the outside? The difficulty and perhaps the impossibility of answering these questions satisfactorily within the enclosure of his thought keeps Wittgenstein returning and returning to this topic, for example in the lengthy sections on pain in the *Philosophical Investigations*.

Another equivocation, however, perhaps equally undecidable, occurs in the passage I have cited and at least implicitly throughout Wittgenstein's analyses. Is the "expression" of an emotion, whether by words or by signs such as weeping or frowning, related to the emotion cognitively or performatively? Wittgenstein does not use this distinction, and that may have been part of the reason he could not solve the problem of the accessibility of the pain of another to his satisfaction. On the one hand, he remains caught in the terminology of "expression," a cognitive term. Tears and frowns, along with certain words, "express" the emotion, make it knowable, even though they are inseparable from the emotion, not signs of it at a distance from it. On the other hand, William James's famous assertion that crying makes us sad, which Wittgenstein accepted in his own way, gives to tears a performative power to make us sad. The tears generate the emotion rather than just being the cognitive part of it: "a man doesn't cry because he is sad . . . he is sad because he cries." Though the passion is certainly a different one, this assertion seems very similar to Derrida's argument that a person is not in love until he or she says "Je t'aime." The utterance or the outer sign is a speech act or a sign act that creates the thing it names.

How many emotions are there? How would you be sure that you had collected and labeled them all? Is there a different emotion for every name? Is "gratitude," for example, the name of a distinct emotion, different from every other, for example "thankfulness"? Are there different emotions for those who speak a different language, as the bilingual Wittgenstein, who must often have had occasion to reflect about this, suggests: "In which cases would you say that a word of a foreign language corresponded to our 'perhaps'?—to our expressions of doubt, trust, certainty?"[18] Does this not suggest that the names of emotions are performative, that we feel gratitude because there is a word "gratitude"? This might suggest that *Dankbarkeit* and *Erkenntlichkeit*, German words for gratitude, generate different emotions. Do those who speak exclusively German never experience gratitude, only *Dankbarkeit*?

The dismaying number of different words in different languages for (apparently) different emotions is a little like the dismaying number of different active verbs (the third power of ten, says Austin, you will remember) that can be used in performative utterances. Each performs a different action. Each is open to a different analysis. In a similar way (but what is the force of "similar" here?), gratitude may not be the same emotion as thankfulness or a sense

of obligation, as when someone says, "I am much obliged to you."
Do these distinctions name different somethings already there or
create them by naming them? The latter hypothesis seems absurd,
as absurd as saying I am sad because I cry, angry because I frown,
or fall in love only when I say "Je t'aime," but how could you dis-
prove these hypotheses? How could you be sure one way or the
other? J. L. Austin, the reader will recall, asserts that the increase in
discriminatory power in language through the centuries has created
the distinctions named by refined modern language. It may have
been Wittgenstein's failure to possess the distinction between constative and performative utterances that Austin was to make a few
years later (at Oxford rather than at Cambridge) that kept him
from breaking out of the impasse indicated in his phrases "largely,
though of course not wholly," and "part, and an important part, of
what I feel."

Wittgenstein's choice of the word "perhaps" as an example of a
word whose translation may perhaps be dubious seems arbitrary,
just one example chosen at random. Moreover, it hardly seems the
name of an emotion, like "doubt," "trust," "certainty," or "gratitude." It is, however, highly significant. To say "perhaps," *veilleicht*,
or *peut-être* is in a peculiar way, different for each language, to express uncertainty. Each word expresses in its language a strange
combination of just those emotions of doubt, trust, and certainty
that Wittgenstein goes on to name after raising the question·about
the translation of "perhaps." What can one say of the emotion appropriately corresponding to the locution "perhaps"? Someone asks,
"Is that a goldfinch?" or "Is that person really angry and not just
pretending?" or "Is that a tornado on the horizon?" or "Am I expe-
riencing the first symptoms of a fatal heart attack?" I answer "perhaps." It is neither doubt, nor trust, nor certainty, but somewhere
amidst them all, a neither/nor or both/and, a neuter or neutral.
"Perhaps" expresses a passion oriented toward the future moment
that will, it is hoped or feared, settle the matter one way or another
in a definitive event. "Perhaps" keeps the game going, keeps life
open. As long as I can say "perhaps," I am still alive, still waiting for
something unexpected, whereas if I know for sure, then the future

is entirely programmed and predictable, not really a human life anymore, or at any rate not worth living. The human ability to say "perhaps" is perhaps a sign of a distinctively human way to be related to time, that is, by putting off indefinitely the last word of certainty. "Perhaps" defines human temporality as such, even though it is oriented, we all "know," toward the future definitive event of death that will come sooner or later to all, though luckily we do not, at least not usually, know just when. That perhaps is what Hamlet means when he says, "The readiness is all." "Perhaps" is a way of saying "Yes, I am ready," ready even for death, when that event comes.

Jacques Derrida says something closely related to this in two places where he discusses "perhaps" in various languages. One is in *Politics of Friendship*, apropos of what Nietzsche calls "this dangerous perhaps."[19] The other is in a paragraph in a quite recent essay, "Comme si c'était possible, 'within such limits,'" which refers back to *Politics of Friendship*. What Derrida says in "Comme si c'était possible" resonates with passages in "Psyche: The Invention of the Other":

> Have I not elsewhere tried [He means in *Politics of Friendship*.—JHM] to analyze at once the possibility and the necessity of this "perhaps"? Its promise and its fatality, its implication in all experience, at the approach of *that* which comes, of (this) (the other) *which* comes from the future and brings about what one calls an event [*à l'approche de ce qui vient, de (ce) (l'autre) qui vient de l'avenir et donne lieu à ce qu'on appelle un événement*]? But this experience of the "perhaps" would be *at once* that of the possible *and* of the impossible, of the possible *as* impossible. It arrives *as* the coming of the impossible, there where a "perhaps" deprives us of every assurance and leaves the future to the future. . . . The "perhaps" keeps the question alive, it assures it, perhaps, survival [*il en assure, peut-être, la-survie*]. What would a "perhaps" mean then, at the disarticulated junction [*à la jointure désarticulée*] of the possible and the impossible. Of possible *as* impossible.[20]

The possible would be on the side of the constative, on the side of something that can be predicted to happen, with certain knowledge. The impossible is on the side of the performative, of the un-

predictable and unknowable that is inaugurated by the sort of radically initiatory and anomalous performative exemplified by saying
"Je t'aime" or by the United States Declaration of Independence.

Austin's Anger

J. L. Austin possessed the distinction between constative and
performative utterances all right. He invented it, in a revolutionary
inaugural move. That, however, did not solve the problem indicated in Wittgenstein's "largely, though of course not wholly," as
what I have said so far about Wittgenstein might have implied
would be the case. This is made clear in two essays by Austin that
are to a considerable degree about the expression of anger: "Other
Minds" and "Pretending."[21]

Though an example is an example, chosen somewhat at random
from among many, any one of which, at least implicitly, would
have worked just as well, the passions or excessive emotions chosen
by a given philosopher or novelist as exemplary of emotions in general are clearly symptomatic. The careful reader will have noted
that the English (or Austrian) philosophers go in for violent, un-
pleasant feelings or emotions (pain, anger), while the French (Derrida, Proust) prefer the passion of love (by no means always pleasant, as Proust abundantly shows). That seems almost too good to
be true, since it fits the stereotypes of the various countries: maso-
chistic Austrians, irascible English, amorous French. Certainly the
choice of anger as paradigmatic fits with the zany violence that runs
through all Austin's examples in *How to Do Things with Words*.

In "Other Minds" and "Pretending," Austin makes and analyzes
a long series of subtle distinctions concerning usage in ordinary
language, for example the difference between "He was pretending
to play chess" and "He was pretending that he was playing chess."
In both essays, as in *How to Do Things with Words*, no firm conclusions are drawn. The enterprise at the beginning is said to be
peripheral, not central, and the essays, like the lecture series, end
by saying all the work is yet to be done. In a somewhat similar way,
Austin begins "A Plea for Excuses" by asking the reader to excuse

him for not talking about what the title promises, thereby, as Derrida observes,[22] creating a "performative contradiction," since in asking us to excuse him for not talking about excuses he is talking about excuses and performatively uttering a plea to be excused. The contradiction is itself a felicitous performative.

"Other Minds" begins with another excuse or plea to be pardoned. Austin says he mostly agrees with what John Wisdom says in *Other Minds* but has something to say about peripheral issues: "At best I can hope only to make a contribution to one part of the problem, where it seems that a little more industry still might be of service. I could only wish it was a more central part. In fact, however, I did find myself unable to approach the centre while still bogged down on the periphery" (*PP*, 76). There is that figure of "bogging down" again, so crucial to *How to Do Things with Words*! No careful reader of Austin can doubt that it is both good and bad to be bogged down on the edge. It is bad because it forbids further movement, good because it means that you are protected from reaching the center of the swamp, a kind of deadly black hole that all Austin's work approached and at the same time vigorously resisted.

"Pretending" begins with another performative, another apology or demand to be forgiven. The instigation this time is a paper by one Errol Bedford, also in *Proceedings of the Aristotlean Society*. Bedford has argued that being angry consists entirely in behaving as if one were angry. In Austin's paraphrase: "There is no specific feeling that angry men as such feel, nor do we, to be angry, have to feel any feeling at all" (*PP*, 253). Austin apologizes for being concerned not with this thesis (though the essay *is* indirectly concerned with it throughout, and persuasively, even contemptuously, demolishes Bedford's thesis) but with something peripheral, something that comes up quite incidentally in Bedford's argument, namely the question of what it might mean to *pretend* to be angry, or to pretend in general: "With this thesis [that being angry consists entirely of behaving angrily] I am not concerned, but only with some remarks that he makes, quite incidentally, about pretending (and I realize it is hard on him to pick these out for intensive criticism)" (*PP*, 253).

"Other Minds" ends by affirming that to suppose the question "How do I know that Tom is angry?" is meant to mean "How do I introspect Tom's feelings?" "is simply barking our way up the wrong gum tree" (*PP*, 116), though just which gum tree we ought to bark our way up is left to a considerable degree open.

"Pretending" ends by asking "What, finally, is the importance of all this about pretending?" The answer is that "although I am not sure importance is important: truth is," and that while the "clarification of pretending" may not be important, "the assignment to it of its proper place within the family of related concepts must find some place, if only a humble one" (*PP*, 271). A final strange footnote reports an unlikely dream, though who but an ordinary-language philosopher knows what sort of dreams ordinary-language philosophers ordinarily have? The twisted, dreamlike echo of Shakespeare, moreover, is characteristic of Austin: "I dreamt," says Austin, "a line that would make a motto for a sober philosophy: *Neither a be-all nor an end-all be*" (*PP*, 271).

Why this resistance to ending conclusively? Why this penchant in Austin for remaining bogged down on the periphery? Two possibilities come to mind, both different from the "perhaps" that for Derrida keeps questioning open to the possible impossibility of an "event," the coming of the unforeseen and unforeseeable other. The second hypothesis I propose for Austin, however, is perhaps closely related to Derrida's "perhaps." Here is the first possibility: Ordinary-language philosophy, it could be argued, is a language game, a serious enough game, but one whose rules penalize those who bring the game to an end. Those "win the game" and are rewarded who can carry on a given line of investigation the longest without coming to a conclusion. They do this by thinking up ever-new nuances in ordinary language (e.g., the difference between pretending to play chess and pretending that I am playing chess [I'm not saying there is no difference!]) and ever-new comic little stories or situations in which such and such a locution would plausibly be used. A good example of the latter comes near the beginning of "Pretending": "Now he goes further, let us say he bites the carpet: and we will picture the scene with sympathy—the carpet innocent, the bite untentative and vicious, the damage grave. Now he has gone too far, overstepped the limit between pretence and reality, and we cannot any longer say 'He is pretending to be angry' but must say 'He is really angry'" (*PP*, 254). Austin is matchlessly brilliant in keeping the ball rolling, so to speak, in these ways.

The second possible explanation for Austin's resistance to being a be-all or end-all is this: He may be reluctant ever to reach the undesired conclusion toward which his thinking is nevertheless remorselessly tending. Such reluctance would give more than a conventional or institutional reason for staying bogged down on the periphery for as long as possible. Austin wants to stay away from the center that nevertheless exerts a centripetal attraction and secretly motivates all the moves in his particular ordinary-language game. It may be this whiff or soupçon of grave menace, a mortal danger bravely resisted but nevertheless constantly flirted with, that gives Austin's work, after all, its great value. He is like a great bullfighter who lives within a hairbreadth of death.

Just what is this center that both attracts and repels Austin, as an abyss attracts the dizzy man who hovers on its brink? It can, I think, be named. It has two facets. The first is the fear that the language for emotions may be predominantly performative, not constative. It really is the case that we fall in love only when we say "Je t'aime." Preexisting emotions have nothing to do with it. The other facet is the fear that it may be impossible ever to know for sure whether the other is angry or loves me. The two fears are aspects of the same fear. Only so long as the game continues in a "perhaps" that forbids premature closure and keeps open the hope for a breakthrough event transforming the fear into a happy certainty can the philosopher playing the ordinary-language game keep bogged down on the periphery. Only by prolonging the game can he or she stay away from the center that generates such excessive anxiety.

The reader will note that this fear is closely related to the aporia I identified in my chapter on Austin as central to *How to Do Things with Words*. This is the aporia between the need to invoke conscious intention as a prerequisite to a felicitous performative utterance and the recognition that unless we say "My word is my bond" and disconnect the performative's efficacity from intention, the performative (promise, act of proffering love, etc.) is moved back into an inaccessible, unverifiable, and wavering realm. How can we ever know for sure whether someone is "sincere" or not? Such uncertainty would give support to bigamists, welshers on bets, and Don Juans who say "Je t'aime" only as a cynical aid to seduction, without really loving. In the essays I am discussing, as in *How to Do Things with Words*, the highest issues are at stake: no less than the possibility of securing morality, law, and order on a firm foundation. A passion for law and order always lies somewhat covertly behind Austin's lighthearted jokes about how we can be sure that little bird is a goldfinch or how we can know that man is angry unless he takes a ferocious bite out of the carpet.

Though "Other Minds" precedes *How to Do Things with Words* by a decade, and though it focuses on the question of how we can know another man is angry, it already contains in embryo, an embryo that was to produce Austin's biggest chicken, the distinction between performative and constative language. In a footnote, for example, the expressions "I know" and "I promise" are contrasted:

> It is the use of the expressions "I know" and "I promise" (first person singular, present indicative tense) alone that is being considered. "If I knew, I can't have been wrong" or "If she knows she can't be wrong" are not worrying in the way that "If I ('you') know I ('you') can't be wrong" is worrying. Or again, "I promise" is quite different from "he promises": if I say "I promise," I don't *say* I promise, I *promise*, just as if he says he promises, he doesn't say he says he promises, he promises: whereas if I say "he promises," I do (only) say he *says* he promises—in the other sense of "promise," the "sense" in which *I* say *I* promise, only *he* can say he promises. I *describe* his promising, but I *do* my own promising and he must do *his* own. (*PP*, 98–99)

The problem, as you can see, is that if I say "I promise," evidently I can know whether I really mean it or am just pretending to promise, whereas if the other says "I promise," this does not tell me anything about his or her intention to keep the promise. In this uncertainty lies the attraction of saying "My word is my bond." Whatever is in my mind or his or her mind when one of us says "I promise," the words commit the one who speaks to whatever he or she promises. The intention is irrelevant.

The problem with this is that it leads to the sort of conclusion that Paul de Man reached by his intransigent rigor of thinking this out, namely the conclusion that language acts mechanically, performatively, on its own, often against the wishes or intentions of the one who speaks. *Die Sprache verspricht (sich)*; language promises and at the same time contradicts itself, misspeaks, makes a slip of the tongue. Austin wanted at all costs to avoid reaching de Man's somewhat scandalous conclusion, though it was the center of the swamp on whose periphery he remained bogged down.

Austin comes closest to this center in a remarkable sequence in "Other Minds" contrasting the locution "I promise (to do so and so)" with the locution "I know (that is a goldfinch or that he or she is angry)." It would appear that the contrast between the two locutions more or less corresponds to the opposition between performative and constative utterance. To say "I promise" is to promise. It is a way of doing things with words. To say "I know (that is a goldfinch or that he or she is angry)" appears to be constative. It looks like a description or a statement of fact that is verifiable as true or false. The verb "know" puts it in the realm of the cognitive. You might be mistaken, but what you know is either true or false. One of de Man's arguments is that performatives are not open to cognition, while constative statements *are* open to knowledge.

The sharpness of Austin's thinking, however, leads him to recognize, through careful discriminations and painstaking analyses, that "I promise" and "I know" are both forms of what he was later to call a performative utterance. The somewhat muted climax of Austin's argument comes in a paragraph in "Other Minds" that begins: "To suppose that 'I know' is a descriptive phrase, is only one example of the *descriptive fallacy*, so common in philosophy" (*PP*, 103). What the descriptive fallacy is we know from the beginning of *How to Do Things with Words*. It is the false assumption that all meaningful language is constative, either true or false. Well, if "I know so and so" is not descriptive, then what is it? The rest of the paragraph makes more or less clear, though does not exactly say in so many words, that "I know so and so" must therefore be a performative, that is, "not *describing* the action we are doing but *doing* it" (ibid.). To say "I know he is angry" is a declaration, not a statement of fact. It is closely akin, though not identical, to a declaration of belief. It is a positing through language, such as those positings Nietzsche described, the law of noncontradiction for example, not a representing of something otherwise known and verifiable.

It might almost be said that the other becomes angry because I say "I know he is angry." My testimony or bearing witness brings his anger into the social world where the word "anger" has a shared meaning. A parallel can be drawn with that pivotal clause in the Declaration of Independence: "We hold these truths to be self-evident." If the truths are self-evident, they speak for themselves. To say "we hold," however, is a performative positing or declaration, an assertion of belief or of allegiance. Even if I can verify that the bird is a goldfinch by examining its anatomy and plumage, or prove that the man is angry by measuring his blood pressure, to say "I know it" is as much a performative utterance as to say "Je t'aime." It creates the condition it names. This somewhat dismaying conclusion, however, the center of the swamp on the periphery of which Austin remained bogged down, was just what he wanted to avoid reaching at all costs, even at the cost of an interminable and inconclusive rumination.

This self-resistance is strikingly apparent in some ringing words of affirmation at the end of "Other Minds." The problem is that the evidence Austin has given in his careful teasing out of the implications of various ordinary-language expressions (e.g., "I know he is angry because he has taken a big bite out of the carpet") by no means leads unequivocally to such a consoling conclusion. Nevertheless, Austin needs to utter it as a kind of declaration of faith. It is not a constative utterance but a performative one, or a performative masking as a constative:

> It seems . . . that believing in other persons, in authority and testimony, is an essential part of the act of communicating, an act which we all constantly perform. It is as much an irreducible part of our experience as, say, giving promises, or playing competitive games, or

even sensing colored patches. We can state certain advantages of such performances, and we can elaborate rules of a kind for their "rational" conduct (as the Law Courts and historians and psychologists work out the rules for accepting testimony). But there is no "justification" for doing them as such. (*PP*, 115)

There is no justification for doing them because they cannot be verified or supported rationally. They are not open to knowledge. They are "performances" (Austin's use of the word anticipates the later coinage "performative") that are acts of "belief." We believe in the testimony of other persons all the time, for example when my beloved says "Je t'aime," and we had better believe them, since law, order, communication, felicitous marriages, and the happy working of society depend on such belief, even though that belief flies in the teeth of the evidence that we can never have sufficient grounds for such confidence.

§ 5 Marcel Proust

What contribution does Marcel Proust's work make to under-standing the relation of passions to performatives? The central and always excessive passion, though by no means the only passion, for him is love, erotic or familial, as it relates to death and lying, and also to illicit homosexual desire.

I have elsewhere identified the special problems in presenting a reading of Proust.[1] *À la recherche du temps perdu* is extremely long. Nevertheless, each page would merit a lengthy commentary, ten pages, let us say, of careful exegesis. That would produce a critical book thirty thousand pages long, clearly an impossibility, though it is an ironically attractive fantasy. The only expedient is to read se-lected passages, as Paul de Man, for example, did in "Reading (Proust)" in *Allegories of Reading*, or as Jacques Derrida did in a re-cent seminar on the episode of the death of Bergotte in the "La prisonnière" section of the *Recherche*. Nevertheless, the *Recherche* is so diverse and so shifting that no part can adequately stand for the whole. If the *Recherche* is like a fractal design in which each part re-peats the pattern of the whole (what is technically called "self-similarity"), it is like those most interesting fractals in which an el-ement of the aleatory or of the "perhaps" has been introduced into the generative formula. Each part embodies the whole or is even greater than the whole, just as the little patch of yellow wall in Ver-meer's *View of Delft* seems to the dying Bergotte, in that episode of the *Recherche* Derrida discussed, to concentrate in itself Vermeer's special genius and to be greater than the whole painting. Each part, however, mirrors the whole in its own unique way, so that synecdochic generalizations from part to whole are invalid. This possible impossibility cannot be escaped or finessed. The critic must live with it and choose the better part, that is, careful readings of small sections, sections almost infinitesimal in their relation to the enormous whole, without claiming that they are necessarily characteristic of the whole except as representations with a difference.

Another problem with writing on the *Recherche* is that it is by no means a finished text, as the English translation and the older Pléiade edition of 1954, in three volumes, might beguile a reader into thinking. Proust died when he was only part way through correcting and revising "La prisonnière." The rest is the posthumous creation of his editors working from drafts and notes. The new Pléiade edition in four volumes, however, in printing masses of "esquisses," or preliminary drafts (almost as many words as the main text in the case of volume two, for example), creates a disturbing new *Recherche*. It becomes a kind of hypertext before the fact or a palimpsest that consists of many layers and branching versions, none definitely superseded, each containing valuable and fascinating material that makes up part of the nontotalizable "whole." One could imagine a literal hypertext version with buttons allowing instant access to previous drafts and alternative versions. Such a computer-readable version might be truer to the actual nature of this text than the linear print version going word by word from the beginning to the end that the standard English translation, for example, for the most part presents, though it gives a few draft passages. That so much of what we have is dependent on the testimony or say-so of the editors who have deciphered Proust's notoriously difficult handwriting only compounds the difficulty.

A further problem is the intervening mass of distinguished criticism of Proust. As I have observed in *Black Holes*, practically every important French-language literary critic or theorist since Proust has written something important about him: Ramon Fernandez, Samuel Beckett, Georges Bataille, Georges Poulet, Maurice Blanchot, Emmanuel Lévinas, Gilles Deleuze, Roland Barthes, René

Girard, Jean-Pierre Richard, Gérard Genette, Paul de Man, Vincent Descombes, Julia Kristeva, and Jacques Derrida in that recent seminar. One of Walter Benjamin's important essays in *Illuminations* is about Proust. A Proust critic of today is right to be intimidated by these august predecessors and to recognize how much he has to learn from this somewhat incoherent richness of commentary.

A final problem in reading Proust is the now widely recognized unreliability of the narrator or of the narrative voice. It has sometimes been thought that the "Then I foolishly thought so and so; later on [*plus tard*] I came to know better" structure of the narration is a signal that the "writing Marcel" now, as opposed to the "written Marcel" then, can be taken with confidence as speaking from a position of achieved wisdom, as speaking for Marcel Proust himself. More astute critics, Paul de Man for example, have argued convincingly that this is not the case, that the novel remains open-ended, never reaching a convergence of the author, the narrator, and the protagonist.[2] This means that readers are on their own, can never take at face value anything the narrator says, however persuasive it is. Readers must pass their own judgments—no easy task.

In such a shrewd situation, facing, with as much courage and clear-sightedness as can be mustered, all these obstacles to a felicitous reading, "one does what one can [*on fait ce qu'on peut*]," or "one has done one's possible," as the French lieutenant in Conrad's *Lord Jim* says of his actions in towing Jim's dangerously damaged ship, the *Patna*, back to port.[3] I have deliberately chosen passages in *À la recherche du temps perdu* that neither obviously contain performative utterances—promises, lies, and so on—nor are explicitly about such overtly performative speech acts, though many such passages exist in Proust's work. I have done this in order to demonstrate that speech-act theory is useful or even necessary in order to read justly even passages not overtly containing performatives.

Unknowable Françoise

I pluck the first passage early out of the long ruminative opening of chapter one of "The Guermantes Way," as though taking one apple out of a basket of apples. All three of my passages, as it happens, come from the same chapter, which may suggest some perhaps spurious connection among them. I say "perhaps spurious" because Proust's presentation is often discontinuous, juxtaposing passages or episodes frequently without much transition or other than fortuitous connection. My second passage, for example, was dragged in by the heels by Proust from a much earlier essay and inserted in the midst of another narrative. My first passage characteristically moves from a particular observation about the Proust family servant Françoise to generalizations asserted to be true for all persons at all times. We make this sort of change in register all the time without reflecting that it is a performative statement of conviction, not a constative statement that might be proved true or false. Just because something is true for one person does not make it true for everyone. The move Proust makes here is parallel to the move Paul de Man makes when he leaps from the reading of a single passage in Rousseau's *Julie* to posit the claim that "The paradigm for all texts consists of a figure (or a system of figures) and its deconstruction."[4] *All* texts?! How many texts would you need to study in order to justify that generalization? How many Françoises and other people of all types would you need to investigate in order to justify claiming that our relation to all of them is the same in just the way the narrator (let us call him "Marcel," since the narrator at one point invites the reader to do that) affirms? This, the reader will observe, is just my own problem in at least implicitly "holding," positing, or claiming that this particular apple is a fair sample of the whole basket of them.

In this passage Marcel reports that while their old servant Françoise had been treating him with respect and apparent affection, she had also been telling their neighbor Jupien that "I was not worth the price of a rope to hang me [*je ne valais pas la corde pour me pendre*]."[5] Marcel has mistakenly assumed that Françoise and people in general are transparent. Their words and behavior are unambiguously valid signs of what is going on in their minds and feelings: "When Françoise, in the evening, was nice to me, and asked my permission to sit in my room, it seemed to me that her face became transparent and that I could see the kindness and honesty [*la bonté et la franchise*] that lay beneath" (E2: 63–64; F2: 366). Marcel is "appalled" by the revelation that this is not the case. It leads him to ask if such duplicity is true in general: "Was it the same with all one's social relations? And into what depths of despair might this not some day plunge me, if it were the same with love? That was the future's secret [*C'était le secret de l'avenir*]" (E2: 64; F2: 366). This is a characteristic proleptic gesture by the narrator, speaking now in the present of the narration about the hero's anxiety and ignorance then: "Little did I know then. Now I know. The future has revealed its secret." The reference is presumably to all the suffering his inability to know his beloved Albertine's real feelings, propensities, and secret behavior were to cause him. These are narrated in the fourth and fifth of the six main sections of this immense novel.

Those sufferings exemplify with a vengeance the law that Proust has Marcel enunciate somewhat later in "The Guermantes Way," apropos of Robert de Saint-Loup's ignorance of the real nature of his mistress, Rachel: "He was ignorant of almost all these infidelities. One could have told him of them without shaking his confidence in Rachel. For it is a charming law of nature, which manifests itself in the heart of the most complex social organisms, that we live in perfect ignorance of those we love [*Il ignorait presque toutes ces infidélités. On aurait pu les lui apprendre sans ébranler sa confiance en Rachel; car c'est une charmante loi de nature qui se manifeste au sein des sociétés les plus complex, qu'on vive dans l'ignorance parfaite de ce qu'on aime*]" (E2: 291–92; F2: 578). This admirably intransigent passage is echoed by the much later passage that contrasts Swann's ignorance of Odette's many lovers with Charlus's ability to recite their names as accurately as a schoolboy can name the kings of France (E3: 303; F3: 804). It is echoed as well by the narrator's long, unsuccessful attempt to know Albertine. He can never know for sure, even after her death, whether or not she betrayed him in lesbian love affairs. He can know only when he no longer loves her and so no longer cares. Someone could get Robert to *apprendre*, to take in, to grasp, Rachel's infidelities without budging his confidence in her. His naive belief is a performative act that goes against knowledge. It is a matter of faith, not altered by knowledge, just as the religious believer's faith in the creationist account in Genesis remains untouched by the evidence of the age of the earth and of our evolution from lower animals. Confidence and apprehension are separate spheres that do not touch except at some uncrossable frontier. It is a "charming" law of nature that love and knowledge are incompatible. This law transcends history. It is true of any time and place, in any culture. It is a law of nature, like the law of gravity, not a law of one particular culture. It is as true in complex societies like Marcel's Paris as in more "primitive" ones. We have no hope of "evolving" beyond this sad universal law. "Charming" in Proust's formulation must be taken literally. This law charms the lover into ignorance, as a snake charms its prey or as a magical charm makes something invisible. Poetry is a charm, charming. "Carmen" in Latin means a lyric poem. Originally it was a name for a magic abracadabra performed by language, in short, for a species of speech act. All speech acts that work, that are felicitous, are charming. They work magically, like a charm.

The bottom line in what Marcel says is the dismaying, even terrifying, proposition, posited as achieved truth, that just because you love someone, feel toward him or her the passion that would lead you to say "Je t'aime" and mean it, you are condemned to a total ignorance of that person. Robert de Saint-Loup is condemned to be ignorant of Rachel's real nature and life just because he is so infatuated with her. Passion, particularly the passion of love—the paradigmatic passion for Proust as pain is for Wittgenstein and anger for Austin—is antipathetic to knowledge. The more you love, the less you know. Excessive love means total ignorance. I shall return later to Saint-Loup's grotesque misreading of Rachel.

In the passage about Françoise's hypocrisy, Marcel moves rapidly to an absolute generalization on the basis of this single bit of evidence. No doubt what he says is also based on his larger experience of the many human beings he has met in society, not to speak of the long history of such generalizations in French moral and aphoristic writing and in historical memoirs and letters, such as those by his grandmother's beloved Madame de Sévigné. These associations make Proust's law of ignorance more believable, though his formulation has its own unique absolutism. For Proust (or at least for Marcel), as for Husserl in his fifth Cartesian meditation or for Derrida in his meditation on "Je t'aime," we have no direct access whatsoever to the mind and heart of another. We can only guess at it by what Husserl calls, in a barbarous and ambiguous formula, "'appresentation' (analogical apperception)."[6] The formula is barbarous because it is rebarbative. It is ambiguous because each word takes away what it gives, in the double or antithetical prefixes: "ana-" and "ap-." An "appresentation" is not the same thing as a "presentation," nor is "apperception" the same as "perception." Each is indirect, shadowy, a matter of yes-and-no, of perhaps. To appresent or apperceive by analogy doubles the perhaps. An analogy is not logical but "beside," "according to," or "against" logic, depending on which valence of "ana-" you take. The mind and feelings, the self-awareness, of the other may or may not be analogous to my own. Here is another case of "perhaps," since the interiority of the other can never be presented directly, only "appresented," presented without being presented. It is a matter of faith, a performative positing, not a verifiable knowledge.

Marcel compares knowing another to the way we "compose" the external world in perception. Here is another word with the "pose" root. "Pose" is one of the signatures of the performative. The performative has many signatures—counterfeit and genuine ones, aliases, pseudonyms, and sobriquets—as Austin knew. It takes a sharp eye to track this shape-changer down and unmask him. It takes courage, also, to countersign these signatures and thereby say, in effect, "Yes; I declare this to be a performative." "All reality," says Marcel,

> is perhaps equally dissimilar from what we believe ourselves to be directly perceiving and which we compose [*nous composons*] with the aid of ideas that do not reveal themselves but are none the less efficacious, just as the trees, the sun and the sky would not be the same as what we see if they were apprehended [*connus*] by creatures having eyes differently constituted from ours, or else endowed for that purpose with organs other than eyes which would furnish equivalents of trees and sky and sun, though not visual ones. (E2: 64; F2: 366)

Marcel must say "perhaps" here because even perception is always a matter of *peut-être*, never a matter of certain knowledge. "Perhaps" is another alias of the performative.

"Ideas that do not reveal themselves but are none the less efficacious [*mais sont agissantes*]" is a perfect definition of ideology as described by Louis Althusser or by Paul de Man.[7] It is only because they do not reveal themselves that they are efficacious, just as it is only because we are unaware of the uniqueness of the sense organs we happen to have that we are mistakenly led to believe that the world of sun, sky, and trees we perceive is the real and only world. Our sense organs are sensitive in a certain way to certain frequencies of light and sound, though not to others. A cat has infrared vision and so "sees" the world quite differently from the way human beings do. A cat "sees," for example, the heat radiated by a mouse behind the wainscot and so can see through walls. The similarity or analogy claimed in Marcel's "just as" is as slippery and untrustworthy, of course, as is "analogical" in Husserl's "'appresentation (analogical apperception)." We posit a similarity but have no way to prove it. We are just as blinded in our apperception of people as we are in our perception of the inanimate world. Marcel goes on to assert as much in the climax of this little sequence:

> At any rate I realised [*compris*] the impossibility of obtaining any direct and certain knowledge of whether Françoise loved or hated me. And thus it was she who first gave me the idea that a person does not, as I had imagined, stand motionless and clear before our eyes with his merits, his defects, his plans, his intentions with regard to ourselves (like a garden at which we gaze through a railing with all its borders spread out before us), but is a shadow [*une ombre*] which we can never penetrate, of which there can be no such thing as direct knowledge, with respect to which we form countless beliefs, based upon words and sometimes actions, neither of which can give us anything but inadequate and as it proves contradictory information—a shadow behind which we can alternately imagine, with equal justification, that there burns the flame of hatred and of love. (E2: 64–65; F2: 366–67)

All the suffering of Marcel's long affair with Albertine is contained proleptically in this sad and remorselessly demystifying passage. The key words here are "shadow," "beliefs," and "imagine." The other is not open to inspection, like a garden laid out before our eyes, but is a species of black hole, a "shadow" which we can never penetrate, of which we can never have direct knowledge. It is, however, a black hole that emits enigmatic, inadequate, and contradictory signs in the form of words and actions, just as an invisible object casts a shadow showing that something is there but giving little satisfactory evidence of what that something is. These signs, as a result, are open to a multitude of unverifiable interpretations. Since those interpretations can never be checked directly against the hidden object that casts the shadow, anything we say about that object (the mind and feelings of the other) is not a constative statement of fact but a statement of belief, a form of testimony, a performative utterance: "I hold that Françoise loves me," or "I hold that Françoise hates me." Proust's word for the projection of love or hate, either one equally justified and unjustified by the shadowy evidence, is "imagine": "un ombre où nous pouvons tour à tour imaginer avec autant de vraisemblance que brillent la haine et l'amour" (F2: 367). Did Françoise love Marcel, or did she think he was not worth the price of the rope to hang him? There is absolutely no way to tell for sure. Either is a plausible hypothesis that we can imagine to be true.

This assumption that the other is an impenetrable shadow, a shadow that emits contradictory signs open to endlessly varied contradictory hypotheses, all equally unverifiable, all equally fueled by one emotional need or another, is the presupposition of all Marcel's presentation of human life. I shall now read two examples of that and show how performatives are somewhat obliquely essential to both.

"Granny! Granny!"

The first example is a spectacular case of the episodic structure of *Recherche*. In the midst of an account of his visit to his friend Robert de Saint-Loup in the latter's barracks at Doncières, Marcel interpolates an account of a telephone call from his grandmother.

Parts of this episode are taken almost word for word from "Journées de lecture" (Reading days), an essay that Proust had published in *Le figaro* in 1907, more than a decade before the completion of the first chapter of "The Guermantes Way." The episode was inserted into the latter at printer's proof stage in 1919, like a small gem in a larger piece of jewelry.[8] In the *Figaro* essay Proust observes that we read only because we cannot always be telephoning. That observation becomes the occasion for a reflection on what is strange about talking to someone on the telephone. In "Journées de lecture" the telephone call is made to a female friend, "the friend we want to talk to [*l'amie à qui nous avions le désir de parler*]" (CSB, 528), while in the *Recherche* it is made to Marcel's grandmother. The passage prepares for the death of the grandmother, the climax of the first chapter of "The Guermantes Way."

Proust's meditation on the telephone constitutes one of the first great and still most penetrating reflections on the strangeness of this new medium. It is also one of the earliest profound considerations of the effects of new electronic communications media on human life. These effects result from the performative power not of any particular enunciation but of the medium in which enunciations are made. Cinema, phonograph, radio, television, VCRs, and now e-mail and the Internet have, it could be argued, simply augmented a hundredfold the powers of communication at a distance that were first made possible in the nineteenth century by the telephone and telegraph and that were anticipated in their own quite different ways by handwriting, printing, and the postal system. The augmentation, however, has at each stage crossed a certain threshold and has markedly transformed human life.

In analyzing his grandmother's telephone call, Marcel stresses the double performative that is necessary to make the call work, as well as the spooky magic of the telephone that brings the distant near. "Habit," he says, rapidly tends "to divest of their mystery the sacred forces [*les forces sacrées*]) with which we are in contact" and makes us simply impatient if it takes too much time to put the call through (E2: 133–34; F2: 431). The first performative utterance is to speak into the telephone and invoke the operator's power. The second performative is effected by the operators who complete the call. Marcel compares this to a magic of act of conjuration. It is like something in *The Arabian Nights* or in a fairy tale. A wish must be "expressed," turned into a speech act, if it is to be efficacious, just as an emotion or passion does not make anything happen until it is externalized in signs of some sort. When we have expressed a wish, the sorceress then fulfills that wish, if she decides to do so: "And we are like the person in the fairy-tale for whom a sorceress, at his express wish, conjures up, in a supernatural light, his grandmother or his betrothed in the act of turning over a book, of shedding tears, of gathering flowers, close by the spectator and yet very far away [*tout près du spectateur et pourtant très loin*], in the place where she actually is at the moment" (E2: 134; F2: 431). Television and webcams today do just that, for example in video conferencing. In the early days of the telephone, it is important to remember, automatic dialing did not yet exist, and "operator's assistance" was needed in one way or another for all calls, even if only to perform the invisible act of inserting plugs into the right sockets to make the connection in response to the caller's request: "Please connect me to so and so."

Not only is this double performative, the first invocation ratified by the second, something magical, a multiple act of conjuration; it is also, for Marcel, a sacred mystery that puts the caller in touch with the underworld, the world of the dead. Laurence Rickels has demonstrated in various essays how widespread was the assumption, in the early days of the telephone, that this technological device was a way of raising the dead and communicating with them.[9] Mary Baker Eddy's order that a telephone be put in her coffin so she could communicate from the other world after her death is only one example among many of this strange confidence or mystification. People thought they could hear the voices of the dead speaking somewhere off at a distance, an infinite distance, through the crackle of static characteristic of early telephones, as of early recording devices such as gramophone records. This belief that the dead speak through such devices persisted even up to the time of the first magnetic tape recordings during World War II.

As Rickels shows, most often those who thought they heard the voices of the dead speaking on the telephone or on tape recordings believed it was their mothers speaking. Though Marcel talks to his grandmother, not his mother, the biographical facts that one may suppose were behind this fiction were Marcel Proust's telephone conversations with his mother in 1896, when he was living apart from her in Fontainebleau while working on *Jean Santeuil.* Proust's feelings about his mother, one may surmise, particularly about his mother's death, were so painful that he needed, in writing the *Recherche*, to displace them onto a fictitious Marcel's feelings for his fictitious grandmother, both when he talks to her on the telephone and when, later in the same chapter, she dies. Proust's grandmother died in 1889, when Proust was 18, his mother in 1905, when he was 34. After his mother's death, he wrote, "My life has henceforth lost its only goal, its only pleasure and comfort, its only love, its only consolation [*Ma vie a désormais perdu son seul but, sa seule douceur, son seul amour, sa seule consolation*]."[10]

What Proust says of the telephone operators of his day, in its exuberant multiplication of classical and Christian figures for the operators' power as mediums of the unseen, is one of the most powerful expressions of the early sense that the telephone wields a species of sacred magic, white or black. Marcel poses a puissant "perspective by incongruity," breaking our habituation to what is so taken for granted by most people today as a mere technological device that we do not notice how remarkable it is, how thoroughly it has transformed human life. This transformation is even more radical now that so many people have "cell phones" and can speak to anyone anywhere in the world from more or less anywhere. Marcel suspends that familiarity by hyperbolically comparing the telephone to various forms of magic and contact with the supernatural, with ghosts and the dead, just as later, in *Ulysses*, James Joyce was to think of the network of telephone lines as like so many umbilical cords tying us ultimately back to Eve, our great progenitor:[11]

> We need only, so that the miracle may be accomplished, apply our lips to the magic orifice and invoke [*appeler*]—occasionally for rather longer

than seems to us necessary, I admit—the Vigilant Virgins to whose voices we listen every day without ever coming to know their faces, and who are our guardian angels in the dizzy realm of darkness whose portals they so jealously guard; the All-Powerful [*les Toutes-Puissantes*] by whose intervention the absent rise up at our side, without our being permitted to set eyes on them; the Danaids of the unseen who incessantly empty and fill and transmit to one another the urns of sound; the ironic Furies who, just as we were murmuring a confidence to a loved one, in the hope that no one could hear us, cry brutally, "I'm listening! [*J'écoute*]"; the ever-irritable handmaidens of the Mystery, the umbrageous priestesses of the Invisible, the Young Ladies of the Telephone [*les Demoiselles du téléphone*]. (E2: 134; F2: 431–32)

A passage of an ironic and disturbing power! Marcel (or Proust, in the passage from *Le figaro* here transposed) multiplies contradictory epithets for *les Demoiselles du téléphone*: guardian angels, Vigilant Virgins, the All-Powerful, Danaids, ironic Furies (a little later he adds "Daughters of the Night," "Messengers of the Word," and "capricious Guardians" [E2: 137; F2: 435]), as though he were hoping one at least of these epithets would succeed in invoking them to respond. To call them, respectfully, Vigilant Virgins is quite different from calling them Danaids. The Danaids were the 50 daughters of Danaus, descendants of that Io who was raped by Zeus and then tormented by the gadfly sent by jealous Hera. The Danaids were condemned in Hades to pour water perpetually into an urn with no bottom as punishment for having murdered their bridegrooms on their wedding nights at their father's command. The Furies were scarcely less terrible. They were fearsome winged goddesses who pursued and punished doers of unavenged crimes. Marcel's Furies punish through their sense of irony, interrupting confidential murmurings on the telephone to a beloved or to an intimate family member by saying "J'écoute," though just what crime that avenges in Marcel's case is not clear. Perhaps it is the crime of believing in intimate, private communication. Such reciprocity would be a transgression of the law that says each subjectivity remains solitary even while whatever outward signs it emits are promiscuously exposed.

It is as though Marcel were trying one by one a whole series of epithets for the operators, like a man praying to many gods in succession in the hope that at least one might hear and answer. Such a man might in effect be saying: "Hello? Is anyone there?" The epithets Marcel chooses, however, are hardly respectful, though they express fear and awe. They also strongly sexualize or make a matter of gender difference the encounter with the telephone. Not only are the operators—as well as the grandmother in the *Recherche* and the "friend" or "betrothed" in the *Figaro* version—women, but getting the operators to put the call through requires both courting them respectfully while keeping one's guard up against them as dangerous and capricious females, willful and hard to please, according to the stereotype that says women are always fickle. If I were an operator I would not like to be invoked as a Danaid, ironic Fury, capricious guardian, or "Daughter of the Night," though "Vigilant Virgin" might be acceptable!

One thing, as Marcel indicates, that disappears with the telephone is the sense of privacy we used to associate with being safe within the home. The telephone brings the outside in, breaks down the inside/outside dichotomy, and endangers the possibility of private communication. Proust does here for the telephone operator what Henry James did some years earlier for the telegraph operator in his short story "In the Cage." Both make of the "operator" someone who is a "housebreaker," potentially listening in or reading our most intimate communications by a species of "wiretap" that means we can never be sure we are alone with our beloveds. These operators are all-powerful. They make it possible for us to do things with words.[12] Proust's operators come to know everything about us. They are omniscient as well as all-powerful. One of the widespread fears about the Internet today is that it means everything most secret and private about us will become common knowledge.

One spectacular and disquieting way the telephone dissolves borders and brings the outside inside is by transporting the distant and giving it a spooky and spurious nearness. As soon as the call has been put through, we wait with ears glued to the apparatus listening to a dark aural space, like the "ombre" that hides the other person, a shadowy space filled with ghosts. The first thing we hear is a tiny sound, almost no sound at all, a small inarticulate hum or buzz or, not even that, an expectant clearing of the aural space, what Proust calls "an abstract sound [*un bruit abstrait*]." This is "the sound of distance overcome," the indication that the possibility of speaking at a distance has been opened up. That is what "telephone" means: speaking at a distance, as "television" means a perhaps even more magical "seeing at a distance." The latter is anticipated here in what Marcel says about the sorceress who conjures up a vision of one's grandmother or betrothed. Only when this abstract sound-no-sound has sounded do we hear at last the voice of the beloved: "As soon as our call has rung out, in the darkness filled with apparitions to which out ears alone are unsealed [*dans la nuit pleine d'apparitions sur laquelle nos oreilles s'ouvrent seules*], a tiny sound, an abstract sound—the sound of distance overcome—and the voice of the dear one speaks to us. It is she, it is her voice that is speaking, that is there [*qui est là*]. But how far away it is! [*Mais comme elle est loin!*]" (E2: 134–35; F2: 432). The voice one hears on the telephone is as close as that apparatus but at the same time, paradoxically, infinitely far away. It is an unnatural fabrication of the technology, as we speak today of a "computer artifact." What we hear is a kind of voice we would never hear in face-to-face talk. It brings the distant close as distant.

A little earlier in the passage, speaking in general of the power of the telephone (and using the masculine gender this time), Marcel stresses how the telephone brings close not just the voice of the loved one but the whole world in which he lives. The sentence is a good example of those long, run-on sentences, precariously maintaining their balance within many suspensions of syntax, for which Proust is famous:

> Like all of us nowadays, I found too slow for my liking, in its abrupt changes, the admirable sorcery [*féerie*] whereby a few moments are enough to bring before us, invisible but present, the person to whom we wish to speak, and who, while still sitting at his table, in the town in which he lives (in my grandmother's case, Paris), under another sky than ours, in weather that is not necessarily the same, in the midst of

circumstances and preoccupations of which we know nothing and of
which he is about to inform us, finds himself suddenly transported
hundreds of miles (he and all his surroundings in which he remains
immured [*lui et toute l'ambiance où il reste plongé*] within reach of our
ear, at the precise moment which our fancy has ordained [*au moment
où notre caprice l'a ordonné*]. (E2: 134; F2: 431)

Caprice is here given a performative power like "imagination" in
the first passage from the *Recherche* discussed above. Caprice or-
dains or invokes, just as imagination supposes or poses that the
other hates us or loves us.

In the transposition of the passage in "Journées de lecture" to the
Recherche, Proust omits a paragraph that elaborates on how we can
hear, on the telephone, not just the voice of the person at the other
end of the line but all the ambient sounds coming in his window:
the bicycle horn in the street, the song of a passerby, the distant
fanfare of a marching regiment. Just as a poet evokes a character's
milieu to make him real, so these ambient sounds reconstitute the
environment of the distant voice, bringing that distant world
strangely to life for us. This carrying over of the milieu justifies
saying, as Marcel does in the *Recherche*, that the one we speak to
on the telephone is magically transported hundreds of miles with
all his surroundings into a strange proximity to the listening ear
(CSB, 528–29).

More is endangered by the telephone, however, than just the security of private communication, the safety of my murmured words
of affection to my beloved or to my grandmother. More is shattered
than just the traditional boundaries between inside and outside,
here and there, close and distant, our habitual experience of space.
Marcel's experience of hearing his grandmother's voice on the telephone transforms his sense of what she is as a person. It does this
by estranging her voice from its normal association with her face
and body:

After a few seconds of silence, suddenly I heard that voice which I
mistakenly thought I knew so well; for always until then, every time

that my grandmother had talked to me, I had been accustomed to follow what she said on the open score of her face [*la partition ouverte de
son visage*], in which the eyes figured so largely; but her voice itself I
was hearing this afternoon for the first time. And because that voice
appeared to me to have altered in its proportions from the moment
that it was a whole, and reached me thus alone and without the ac-
companiment of her face and features, I discovered for the first time
how sweet that voice was; perhaps indeed it had never been so sweet
as it was now, for my grandmother, thinking of me as being far away
and unhappy, felt that she might abandon herself to an outpouring of
tenderness which, in accordance with her principles of upbringing,
she usually restrained and kept hidden. . . . I noticed in it [her voice]
for the first time the sorrows that had cracked it [*les chagrins qui
l'avaient fêlée*] in the course of a lifetime. (E2: 135–36; F2: 433)[13]

Marcel has two grandmothers. One he experiences when he is
face to face with her, and can read her face as though it were the
written or printed score of which her voice is the music as performed. The other is his "telephone-grandmother." A new regime
of telecommunications produces a new sense of selfhood, a new
experience both of myself and of others. The introduction of a new
technology, while it still overlaps with the old, provides inadvertently, by allowing Marcel to juxtapose the two grandmothers, a
striking confirmation of Marcel's assertion that we superimpose
upon or project into the dark and forever impenetrable shadow
that is another person this or that set of assumptions about what is
really there, what I have just called a "sense" of that person. It also
provides a way to understand what Derrida means when he says
that new regime of telecommunications will put an end to literature, philosophy, psychoanalysis, and love letters. All four of those
activities have depended on the assumption of a relatively stable
selfhood in me and in the other person, however problematic that
stability may have been. This relative stability was a feature of print
and manuscript culture. It was preserved only so long as print and
manuscript culture more or less exclusively dominated our ways of
communicating with others at a distance. With the introduction of
the telephone and then all those other far-seeing and far-hearing

devices that have transformed our lives today, it became possible, for a time, while the new technologies were still strange enough to be noticed, while they overlapped with the old print culture, to glimpse their role in new projections of selfhood. These projections seem to many people still today more shifting and unstable, more openly artificial, more "constructed" and "virtual" than, let us say, the self communicated in a love letter.

Proust's telephone passage registers a moment of that recognition. The telephone constructs a new grandmother by processes built into the medium and beyond our control. Is it not the case that each of us is a different person in succession in writing a letter, talking on the telephone, or composing an e-mail, just as we are different in interpersonal relations carried on in different languages? Do we not feel that the person is different in each case who writes to us a letter in longhand, or telephones us, or e-mails us? The other is what the medium makes her or him, not a fixed self, whether hidden or open, as Marcel still tends to presuppose in assuming that Françoise must either love him or hate him. Though the single unequivocal truth about Françoise's feelings may be eternally hidden, it still exists in the "shadow" behind the signs she makes in the open. Marcel's telephone experience points toward a different and even more disturbing hypothesis, namely that the self may be performatively created by the medium in which it expresses itself.

The great European epistolary novels of the seventeenth and eighteenth centuries, for example, explore, whether deliberately or not, the sort of self one becomes when writing a letter. The reduction in importance of the epistolary novel in the nineteenth century testifies, one might guess, to a resistance to, or outliving of, the notion that handwriting makes the self, in a species of speech act. Characters in novels by Balzac, Dickens, Trollope, and Hardy, though they write letters that are often given verbatim and embedded in the narration, for the most part speak for themselves, or are described by the narrator, or are dramatized by the narrator in indirect discourse—all variant ways to presume the existence of a self outside the words for it. That self is recorded or described by the narrator's words, not constituted by them, according to the conventions of "realism" in nineteenth-century fiction. This is the case however much nineteenth- and twentieth-century novels may in other ways put in question the assumption that each of us has a unitary and perduring self.

One last and even more disquieting feature of Marcel's telephone call from his grandmother remains to be identified. This is the way talking to someone on the telephone is a premonition of the death of that person. The voice on the telephone is not just that of a different grandmother. It is the voice of someone who is already virtually dead. This terrifying experience is prepared for by those hyperbolic and exuberantly, but defensively, comic epithets for the telephone operators as mediums, as "Danaids of the invisible," as guardian angels, as powers that open communication for the living with the underworld of shades, apparitions, specters, and ghosts.

Marcel experiences just what this means when he actually gets through to his grandmother. Marcel begins by saying that the experience of closeness and distance in talking to his grandmother on the telephone leads him to suspect that even if the person is right there before us we may be just as far away from him or her as when telephoning. The telephone person is generalized to become paradigmatic of the real person, whether close or far away: "I felt more clearly the illusoriness [*ce qu'il y a de décevant*] in the appearance of the most tender proximity, and at what a distance we may be from the persons we love at the moment when it seems that we have only to stretch out our hands to seize and hold them" (E2: 135; F2: 432). The most tender proximity is an illusion. We are always at an immense distance even from those we are touching and embracing. This means, as the passage goes on to specify, that it is as though our most proximate beloved were already dead. We are surrounded by ghosts and apparitions and walking dead, however alive they may appear: "A real presence, perhaps, that voice that seemed so near—in actual separation! But a premonition also of an eternal separation! Many were the times, as I listened thus without seeing her who spoke to me from so far away, when it seemed to me that the voice was crying [*clamait*] to me

from the depths out of which one does not rise again [*il m'a sem-
blé que cette voix clamait des profondeurs d'où l'on ne remonte pas*]"
(E2: 135; F2: 432).

"Real presence [*présence réele*]"—that is the technical theological term used to describe the actual presence of Christ's body and
blood in the consecrated wafer and wine of the Host. The Real
Presence is a guarantee, like the Incarnation itself, of the embodiment of supernatural spirit in an earthly form. Similarly, hearing
his grandmother's voice seems to Marcel to guarantee her spiritual
existence. It guarantees that presence, however, as something already dead, as a voice calling from the depths of death. The biblical "De profundis clamavi" is echoed in "clamait des profondeurs."

   That the telephone, by dispensing with the bodily presence of
the person and resurrecting him or her as a ghostly voice, presages
the real death of that person is reinforced later in the passage, when
the connection is suddenly broken. Marcel is left with a lifeless apparatus pressed against his ear, "vainly repeating 'Granny! Granny!'
[*Grand-mère, grand-mère*] as Orpheus, left alone, repeats the name
of his dead wife" (E2: 137; F2: 434). Even when he can still hear her
he has beside him only a specter, not a bodily presence: "'Granny!'
I cried to her, 'Granny!' and I longed to kiss her, but I had beside
me only the voice, a phantom as impalpable [*fantôme aussi impalpable*] as the one that would perhaps come back to visit me when
my grandmother was dead" (ibid.). It is difficult to be sure what
Marcel means when he says earlier that hearing his grandmother's
voice on the telephone anticipates "the anxiety that was one day to
wring my heart when a voice would thus return (alone and attached
no longer to a body which I was never to see again [*seule, et ne ten-
ant plus à un corps que je ne devais jamais revoir*]), to murmur in my
ear words I longed to kiss as they issued from lips for ever turned to
dust" (E2: 135; F2: 432). Does he mean an actual ghostly auditory
apparition or rather (as is possible) some form of recording, for example a gramophone record? One fulfillment of that terrible experience is now in any case so commonplace that we take it entirely
for granted, though it was novel then. I mean various recording devices ("ricordo" means memorial, souvenir, remembrance, in Ital-

ian): phonograph recordings on wax or plastic, then magnetic tape, now radios and CDs that allow us to hear voices or the music-making of the dead, as I am at this moment (8:38 a.m., January 24, 1999) hearing by way of a CD audio player in my computer Glenn Gould back in the 1960s playing Bach's *The Well-Tempered Clavier* with fingers now forever turned to dust.

These new technological devices are a resurrection of the dead, but that troubling power is also a permanent transformation of the living. It makes the living already dead, makes them living dead. The full title of the *Recherche*, after all, is *À la recherche du temps perdu*. The immense novel is a "research," a quasi-scientific investigation of how to resurrect lost time, as those recordings of Glenn Gould do. When we read the *Recherche* today, moreover, we are as it were hearing Proust's dead voice preserved by the old technological device of printing. Whether there are any actual recordings of his voice I do not know, but of course it would have been possible. Joyce, in a wonderfully comic passage in *Ulysses*, has Bloom imagine a use of the gramophone to resurrect the dead. Joyce's irony may be juxtaposed to Marcel's anguish about hearing a voice that issued from lips now forever turned to dust:

> Besides how could you remember everybody? Eyes, walk, voice. Well, the voice, yes: gramophone. Have a gramophone in every grave or keep it in the house. After dinner on a Sunday. Put on poor old great-grandfather Kraahraark! Hellohellohello amawfullyglad kraark awfullygladaseeragain hellohello amarawf kopthsth. Remind you of the voice like the photograph reminds you of the face. Otherwise you couldn't remember the face after fifteen years, say.[14]

A final ironic motif appears in the last sentence of this episode. Marcel says the operators tried in vain to reopen the connection: "Untiringly though they invoked, as was their custom, the venerable inventor of printing and the young prince, collector of Impressionist paintings and driver of motor-cars (who was Captain de Borodino's nephew), Guttenberg and Wagram left their supplications unanswered, and I came away, feeling that the Invisible would continue to turn a deaf ear [*sentant que l'Invisible sollicité resterait*

sourd]" (E2: 137; F2: 435). What in the world are Guttenberg, the
long-dead inventor of printing, and Wagram, Proust's contempo-
rary who collected impressionist paintings and motorcars and was
killed in World War I in October 1918, doing here as the objects of
unsuccessful invocations? It turns out that Guttenberg and Wagram were at that time the names of central telephone stations in
Paris, personified here by Proust as the people for whom they were
named. The Guttenberg central was so-called for no better reason
than that it was located on the rue de Guttenberg. The name associated with the printing press, the technological device that was being displaced by the telephone, must be invoked to make the telephone system work. The accidental and ironic juxtaposition of two
incompatible regimes of telecommunications, each the creator of
different senses of self and other, did not escape Proust's notice.

Rachel When from the Lord

I turn now to the third of my examples from the *Recherche* showing how speech acts work in literature by way of the passions that
power them. Each of these examples is a separate and to some degree detachable anecdote, episode, or little narrative, a bead strung
on the potentially endless sequence of such units, some short, some
long, that make up the *Recherche*. It is potentially endless because
the number of such anecdotes, already large, will be extended as
long as Marcel is still alive and has new experiences, that is, as long
as the gap between the writing Marcel and the written Marcel still
exists. That gap is the definition of still being alive. The sequence is
also potentially endless because each episode can be dilated interminably. As Mark Calkins has shown in a brilliant dissertation on
Proust, dilation and delay are the chief characteristics of Proust's
narration.[15] Both features can be defined as a putting off or holding off of death. Proust dilates and delays, stealing with each invention a moment more of life, just as Scheherazade in the *Arabian
Nights*, so frequently referred to in the *Recherche*, told story after
story, thereby avoiding execution.

This third episode (E2: 157–75; F2: 453–70) can be quickly summarized. Marcel and his aristocratic friend Robert de Saint-Loup make a visit to a suburb of Paris where Robert keeps his mistress, Rachel, whom he deeply loves and who causes him much jealous suffering. Robert wants Marcel to meet Rachel and to admire her sensitivity and beauty. It is a splendid early spring day. The shabby little village is crowded with pear and cherry trees in bloom. Marcel waits to admire these while Robert goes to fetch his mistress. When he sees her, Marcel instantly recognizes her to be "Rachel when from the Lord," a prostitute he had last seen in a brothel he used to frequent. She was a person anyone was able to buy for twenty francs. Now Robert showers expensive presents on her in order to keep in her good favor. He is prepared to sacrifice everything to his infatuation. Marcel reflects on this discrepancy, hiding from Saint-Loup the real history of the woman the latter so loves by pretending to be moved by the beauty of the pear trees in bloom.

All three then take the train back to Paris, where they dine together and where Rachel causes Robert great anguish by making eyes at a waiter. Though neither Marcel nor the reader knows it at this point, Rachel is a gifted actress. When Marcel sees her on the stage he comes to understand somewhat why Saint-Loup has become infatuated with her and "the nature of the illusion of which Saint-Loup was a victim" (E2: 177; F2: 472). Seen close up she is nothing much, a thin freckled face, but seen at a distance, on the stage, as Saint-Loup had first seen her, she is transformed into someone radiant and mysterious. Seeing her first this way, Saint-Loup "had asked himself how he might approach her, how get to know her, a whole miraculous world had opened up in his imagination [*en lui s'était ouvert tout un domaine merveilleux*]—the world in which she lived—from which emanated an exquisite radiance [*des radiations délicieuses*] but into which he could never penetrate" (E2: 178; F2: 472).

No more than that happens in this sequence. The genius, however, is in the detail—both the detail of Marcel's reflections and the detail of the language he uses to describe Rachel and the scene in which he now again meets her. The passage concerns the passion of erotic desire, what Marcel calls "the general malady called love [*l'affection générale appelée amour*]" (E2: 158; F2: 454), its creative power, its ability to project behind the face of the beloved a fictitious person.

Marcel's name for this power is, once more, "imagination." His terminology throughout the passage has to do with value, the relative "worth" of the two Rachels, the cheap twenty-franc prostitute, "nothing more nor less than a little whore [*une simple petite grue*]" (E2: 164; F2: 459), that Marcel knows and the glorious, radiant, unattainable woman, sensitive, intelligent, and tender, to whom Robert de Saint-Loup gives a necklace costing thirty thousand francs and who seems worth all the world to him. The two valuations follow from the way Rachel's "little scrap of a face" has been approached initially:

> I realised then how much a human imagination can put behind a little scrap of a face, such as this woman's was, if it is the imagination that has come to know it first; and conversely into what wretched elements, crudely material and utterly valueless, something that had been the inspiration of countless dreams [*rêveries*] might be decomposed if, on the contrary, it had been perceived in the opposite manner, by the most casual and trivial acquaintance. (E2: 161; F2: 457)

This citation anticipates a great passage much later in the *Recherche* when Marcel, in Venice—a city he always associated with Ruskin—suddenly sees that beautiful place he so loves "decomposed" into a worthless heap of stones, something crudely material and utterly valueless.[16] This present passage, like the later one, and like countless other passages in the *Recherche*, seems to oppose a mystified view, generated by passion and leading to a performative "reading into" of trivial signs, in this case Rachel's face, to the demystified view that sees the signs as no more than crudely material, not valid signs for anything, that is, sees them truly as what they are. Here the two views are not the innocent Marcel as against the Marcel who has learned from experience ("Then I thought . . . ; later I came to learn"), but two simultaneous perspectives by different persons on the same object, or rather person. That Saint-Loup's infatuation with Rachel is a performative "reading into," expressed in his language about her intelligence and sensitivity, is reinforced throughout the passage.

Saint-Loup's misreading starts when he makes the big mistake of "imagining her as a mysterious being, interesting to know [*curieux à connaître*], difficult to seize and to hold" (E2: 161; F2: 457). This is a surface/depth error, the assumption that there must be something hidden and secret behind a visible superficies taken as a sign. Proust has Marcel compare this more than once to the projection of a deity behind an icon, altar, or veil. Rachel's remarks seem to Saint-Loup "quite Pythian" (E2: 159; F2: 455), that is, as if uttered by an oracle through whom the God Apollo speaks. Her personality is enclosed in her body as if "mysteriously enshrined as in a tabernacle" (E2: 160; F2: 456). She, or rather what he can see of her, especially her face, is "the object that occupied incessantly his toiling imagination, whom he felt that he would never really know, as to whom he asked himself what could be her secret self, behind the veil of eyes and flesh [*derrière le voile des regards et de la chair*]" (E2: 160; F2: 456).

So far so good. The passage seems unequivocally to demystify Saint-Loup's projection, propelled by the passion of love, into an imaginary place behind Rachel's eyes and face, a sanctum of inaccessible complexities like those the religious believer imagines behind the icons of his god. This mistake is set against Marcel's disillusioned recognition of what is really there: just so much female flesh with nothing mysterious behind it, flesh that can be bought for twenty francs. Things are not quite so simple here, however, as a more complete and scrupulous reading will show and as the reader will not be surprised to learn. Let me look a little more closely at the "rhetoric," in the sense of tropological integument, in the passage.

The reader may begin by reflecting that Marcel is not exactly a disinterested spectator of Rachel. He is hardly able to see her dispassionately as just what she is. He has displayed much homosocial affection for Saint-Loup, for example when he visits him at his army barracks at Doncières. Saint-Loup turns out ultimately, toward the end of this immense novel, to be homosexual or bisexual. He betrays his wife, Gilberte, Marcel's first great love, in homosexual liaisons. Marcel's affection for Saint-Loup is the place in the novel where Marcel Proust's presumed homosexuality surfaces most overtly. Covert suggestions are present; for example, all Marcel's beloveds have transposed male names (Gilberte, Albertine, Andrée), not to mention that the supposedly straight Marcel, as a recorder of the mores of his Third French Republic society, is fascinated by homosexuality, a theme treated obsessively in "Sodom and Gomorrah" and elsewhere. *À la recherche du temps perdu* is one of the first great novels about the role of homosexuality in modern bourgeois European society. A curious scene adjacent to the one I am reading shows the amazed (and still innocent)[17] Marcel witnessing Saint-Loup's beating of a man who has accosted him on the street with an invitation to a homosexual tryst (E2: 186–87; F2: 480–81). Marcel has every reason to be jealous of his friend Saint-Loup's extravagant love for Rachel.

The sequence I am reading begins with Marcel's ecstatic admiration of the fruit trees in bloom in the shabby suburb—cherry and pear trees, especially pear. In the Middle Ages, as Proust may conceivably have known, pear trees are a symbol of lust, as in Chaucer's tale of January and May, *The Franklin's Tale*. These trees are personified in Marcel's descriptions, first as women, then, rather unexpectedly, as men, and finally as angels, whereas the "clusters of young lilacs," "light and pliant in their fresh mauve frocks [*souples et légères, dans leurs fraîche toilette mauve*]" (E2: 159; F2: 455) are straightforwardly maidens. The pear and cherry trees in the little gardens are first personified as "newcomers, arrived overnight [*nouvelles venues arrivées de la veille*], whose beautiful white garments [*les belles robes blanches*] could be seen through the railings along the garden paths" (E2: 159; F2: 455). By the next page, however, one particularly beautiful pear tree alone in a meadow is personified as possibly male. At least that is the choice made by the translators: "There had nevertheless arisen, punctual at the trysting place like all its band of brothers [*comme toute la bande de ses compagnons*], a great white pear-tree which waved smilingly in the sun's face" (E2: 160; F2: 455). Finally, as they leave the little suburb Marcel sees yet another pear tree, this time personifying it as an angel. All angels, the reader will remember, are masculine, messengers of the Lord: "We cut across the village. Its houses were sordid. But by each of the most wretched, of those that looked as though they had been scorched and branded by a rain of brimstone, a mysterious traveller [*un mysterieux voyageur*] halting for a day in the accursed city, a resplendent angel stood erect, stretching over it the dazzling protection of his widespread wings of innocence [*ses ailes d'innocence en fleurs*]: it was a pear tree in blossom" (E2: 163; F2: 459).

Why all this attention on my part to Marcel's prosopopoeias? Are they anything more than examples of Marcel's "poetic" way of seeing things and embellishing them with extravagant language? This language, it might seem, need not be taken all that seriously nor interrogated all that deeply. The passage just quoted gives the clue that something more is at stake in its transformation of the little suburb into Sodom and Gomorrah. The latter cities are destroyed by God in Genesis 19 by a rain of fire and brimstone. Lot is saved because he has welcomed two mysterious strangers, actually angels, into his house, offering them hospitality. The reader will remember that Lot's wife is turned to a pillar of salt when she, Orpheus-like, disobeys the angelic prohibition and turns to look back at the home city she was fleeing with Lot in obedience to the angels' warning. Jacques Derrida, in an admirable recent seminar on hospitality, has read in detail the marvelous story of Lot's hospitality to the disguised angels.

The whole Proust episode I am reading is permeated by biblical references, allusions, and echoes. Rachel, after all, is not just any name. It suggests that this character is Jewish. Certainly she is a Dreyfusard. She weeps to think of Dreyfus's suffering in his prison cell on Devil's Island (E2: 167; F2: 462). Rachel was of course the name of that one of Jacob's wives he most loved. Jacob served Rachel's father for seven years in order to earn the right to marry her. Jacob is at first fooled by Laban into marrying her elder sister Leah, just as Robert de Saint-Loup is fooled into thinking his Rachel is something she is not: "And it came to pass in the morning, behold, it was Leah: and he [Jacob] said to Laban [father of Leah and Rachel], What is this thou hast done unto me? Did I not serve

with thee for Rachel? Wherefore then hast thou beguiled me?"
(Gen. 29:25). Laban then also gives Rachel to Joseph as a wife,
though Joseph has to serve Laban yet another seven years to earn
her. Those Old Testament patriarchs were unashamedly polyan-
drous, polygamist, and even in a certain sense incestuous, as in Jacob's simultaneous marriage to two sisters. In England from 1835 to
1907 it was illegal even to marry one's deceased wife's sister, let
alone to marry them both at once.[18] While Leah was bearing Jacob
four sons, Rachel was at first barren. She finally conceived: "And
God remembered Rachel, and God hearkened to her, and opened
her womb. And she conceived and bare a son" (Gen. 30:22–23).
Rachel is a distant type of the virgin Mary. God miraculously
opened her womb, just as God impregnated the virgin Mary, or
rather the Holy Ghost did in the form of a dove, accompanied by
the angel Gabriel as messenger of the Annunciation. Gabriel spoke
a miraculous performative utterance if there ever was one: "And the
angel said unto her, Fear not, Mary: for thou hast found favor with
God. And, behold, thou shalt conceive in thy womb, and bring
forth a son, and shalt call his name Jesus," to which Mary answered, in a self-fashioning speech act in response to his speech act:
"Behold the handmaid of the Lord" (Luke 1:30–31, 38). Rachel's
first son was Joseph. Joseph was not Jacob's male heir that counted
most in the long genealogy that leads through the house of David
down to Jesus himself. The genealogy of Jesus at the beginning of
Matthew lists "Judas" as the son of Jacob who established the line.
Presumably this is the fourth son of Leah, "Judah" in the Old Testament. Joseph, nevertheless, with his coat of many colors (Gen.
37), receives much attention in Genesis. Joseph is of course also the
name of Mary's husband, cuckolded before their marriage by God
or rather by the Holy Ghost in the form of a dove. "C'est le pi-
geon, Joseph," Joyce has Stephen Dedalus in *Ulysses* imagine Mary
as saying to her husband in explanation of her pregnancy. Joseph
has asked, "*Que vous a mis dans cette fichue position?* [What has put
you in this deuced situation?]"[19] All the names of Jacob's sons by
his various wives are "motivated." The names' meanings are highlighted in the text of Genesis. Rachel calls her firstborn "Joseph,"

meaning "Adding," as a magic proleptic optative indicating her hope to add still more sons now that she has proved not barren: "And she called his name Joseph; and said, The Lord shall add to me another son" (Gen. 30:24).

This whole tangled background is imported into the reader's understanding of Saint-Loup's relations to his mistress by the name that Proust chose to give her, just as a network of meanings was injected into biblical history by the symbolic names that Jacob's wives gave their sons. Whatever is gained by the allusions to a celebrated French actress known simply as "Rachel" or "Mlle Rachel,"[20] Proust could, after all, have called Saint-Loup's mistress anything he liked, in the exercise of that godlike prerogative of naming his creatures that constitutes one aspect of the writer's magic performative power: "I name thee 'Rachel.'" This power is disquietingly revealed when the reader discovers from the drafts that Proust originally called Robert de Saint-Loup "Montargis." "What was his real name?" the reader naively asks.

Why, then, does Marcel call Rachel "Rachel when from the Lord [*Rachel quand du Seigneur*]"? That does not have a biblical precedent, at least not in so many words, though the unapprised reader may think it refers to the fact that God finally hearkened to Rachel's prayers and opened her womb, so that she conceived and bore Joseph. The reference, however, is actually to the first words of the most famous aria in a nineteenth-century opera by Joseph (Jacques François Fromental Élie) Halévy (1799–1862), *La juive* (1835), with a libretto by Eugène Scribe. This opera was still performed in Proust's day, though it is rarely heard now. (The only recording I could find of this aria was made by Enrico Caruso on September 14, 1920, almost at the end of his career, though I have heard on Public Radio part of a more recent recording of the whole opera.) The heroine of the opera bears the biblical name "Rachel," with all its connotations. Joseph Halévy, a member of a prominent nineteenth-century Jewish family,[21] may have been attracted to Scribe's libretto by the fact that its heroine bore the name of the biblical Joseph's mother.

It is easy to see why the opera is little performed these days, though it is included in Ernest Newman's *More Stories of Famous Operas* of 1943.[22] *La juive* treats the sensitive subject of anti-Semitism and is outrageously melodramatic, to say the least. The action takes place in Constance in 1414. It dramatizes the persecution of the Jews by a certain Cardinal de Brogni and the authorities of the Holy Roman Empire. Rachel and her father, Eleazar, a rich goldsmith, are condemned to death because Rachel has become the beloved of a gentile, Leopold, prince of the empire. She lies to save Leopold. Rachel, however, is not really a Jewess, daughter of Eleazar. She is the lost daughter of Cardinal de Brogni. That daughter the Jews had saved years before from a fire that had burned Brogni's palace in Rome to the ground and killed his mistress, Rachel's mother. Eleazar and Rachel, having refused to save themselves by abjuring the Jewish faith, are led up the scaffold to be plunged into a cauldron of boiling water in the public square of Constance. (I kid you not!) As Rachel mounts the scaffold first, Eleazar whispers to the Cardinal that Rachel, at that moment being pushed into the cauldron, is really Brogni's lost daughter. Eleazar then goes triumphantly to his own death by the same hideous means of execution. You see what I mean by melodramatic!

The most famous aria in this opera, "Rachel quand du Seigneur" ("Rachel when from the Lord"), is sung at the end of the fourth act by Eleazar as he meditates on the conflict between his desire to save his beloved adopted daughter and his hatred of Christians and unwillingness to abjure his faith even to save Rachel. Apparently the aria was written not by Scribe but by Adolphe Nourrit, the leading French tenor of the period. Nourrit persuaded Halévy that the fourth act needed a dramatic climax and, reportedly, supplied the words for the famous aria that resulted:

> Rachel! quand du Seigneur la grâce tutélaire
> A mes tremblantes mains confia ton berceau,
> J'avais à ton bonheur voué ma vie entière.
> O Rachel! . . . et c'est moi que te livre au bourreau!

> Rachel! when from the Lord the guardian grace confided your cradle to my trembling hands, I have devoted my entire life to your happiness. Oh Rachel! . . . and it is I who delivers you to the executioner![23]

At first Eleazar decides to save Rachel, but when he hears the cries of hatred from the crowd outside he determines to sacrifice both her and himself to their faith. Proust's allusion to this celebrated aria from *La juive* carries of course one more reference to the theme of anti-Semitism associated with the Dreyfus case, a central motif in all this part of the *Recherche*. It connects Rachel, the twenty-franc prostitute Marcel had first encountered in a brothel, with the heroic Rachel of Halévy's opera. Though Marcel never actually sleeps with Rachel, the madame repeatedly offers her to him and goes along with Marcel's witty name for her, though not understanding it. Calling the whore Rachel a gift from God savagely ironizes the way she is offered to him and to all comers by the procuress (for this episode see E1: 619–22; F1: 565–68). Moreover, just as the Rachel of the opera is revealed to be not the Jewish daughter of the hated Eleazar but actually the daughter of a cardinal of the Church, so Proust's Rachel is transformed from the lowly prostitute to the beloved mistress of the aristocrat Robert de Saint-Loup: "In this woman I recognised instantaneously 'Rachel when from the Lord,' she who, but a few years since (women change their situation so rapidly in that world, when they do change) used to say to the procuress [*la maquerelle*]: 'Tomorrow evening, then, if you want me for someone, you'll send round for me, won't you?'" (E2: 160; F2: 456).

I have mentioned that the power of naming, whether Proust's naming of his characters or Jacob's wives' naming of their sons, exemplifies one salient performative utterance: "I name thee... (so and so)." Marcel's spontaneous, witty, allusive invention of the sobriquet "Rachel when from the Lord," metonymy for the aria and for the whole opera, is a striking example within the novel itself of naming as a sovereign speech act making or remaking the one who is named. The reader will remember Austin's use of the figure of christening to name what is happening in his invention of a new nomenclature for speech acts: performative, constative, illocutionary, perlocutionary, behabitive, and so on.

One more reference functions powerfully in the complex integument of displacement woven into the episode of Marcel's meeting Saint-Loup's mistress. This is an allusion to perhaps the most famous prostitute of all, certainly the most famous in biblical and Christian tradition, Mary Magdalen. The invocation of Mary Magdalen is the telos toward which all the personifications of the pear trees have been tending. When Marcel recognizes that the mistress Saint-Loup has invested with so much mystery and value is no more than "Rachel when from the Lord," he is greatly moved: "It was not 'Rachel when from the Lord,' who seemed to me of little significance, it was the power of the human imagination, the illusion on which were based the pains of love [*les douleurs de l'amour*], that I found very great" (E2: 162–63; F2: 458). In order to hide the true source of his emotion from Robert, Marcel turns to the pear and cheery trees, "so that he might think it was their beauty that had touched me. And it did touch me in somewhat the same way; it also brought close to me things of the kind which we not only see with our eyes but feel also in our hearts" (E2: 163; F2: 458). The distinction here is between the clear and distinct, but cold, knowledge that comes from seeing and that other kind of non-knowing knowledge that is generated by passion. The latter is "knowledge" that we "feel also in our hearts [*qu'on se sent dans son coeur*]." The examples here are Saint-Loup's creation of a Rachel who does not exist and Marcel's transformation, through metaphor's performative power, of the pear trees into angels. Just as Saint-Loup had been mistaken about Rachel, so had Marcel been mistaken about the pear trees. These two similar mistakes, however, mistakes though they are, nevertheless—according to a paradigm explored later in the *Recherche*[24]—give the mistaken, mystified one access to a realm of beauty that is lost in a past that never was, though it is treasured as a "memory," a memory without memory, and hoped for in a future that always remains future, the "recompense which we strive to earn" (E2: 163; F2: 459). All works of the imagination—love, music, literature, art—however illusory in fetishizing this or that embodiment of beauty, give us a glimpse of this lost paradise, or rather these lost paradises, since they are multiple and incommensurate, each in its own separate and sequestered place in the capacious realm of the imagination. This multiple and unattainable beauty is allegorized by means of catachreses that employ the illusions of love as well as by the fictitious, factitious creations of poetry. These are used to name something unknown, unknowable, and unnamable in any literal words. The passage possesses great beauty, though it describes a speech act that both is "felicitous" and is at the same time seen as a mistake:

> In likening those trees that I had seen in the garden to strange deities [*des dieux étrangers*],[25] had I not been mistaken like Magdalen when, in another garden, on a day whose anniversary was soon to come [Easter], she saw a human form and "supposed it was the gardener." Treasurers of our memories of the golden age, keepers of the promise that reality is not what we suppose, that the splendor of poetry, the wonderful radiance of innocence may shine in it and may be the recompense which we strive to earn [*mériter*], were they not, these great white creatures, miraculously bowed over that shade so propitious for rest, for angling or for reading, were they not rather angels [*n'était-ce plutôt des anges*]? (E2: 163; F2: 458–59)

The reference is to that moving episode in the Gospel according to St. John (20:11–18) in which Mary Magdalen, the sinner whom Jesus cured of her devils and whom he loved, comes to the tomb of the crucified Jesus, finds the sepulcher empty and guarded by two angels in white. She then mistakes the risen Jesus standing in the garden for the gardener. When Jesus speaks to her, she suddenly recognizes him and hails him as "Master":

> She turned herself back, and saw Jesus standing, and knew not that it was Jesus. Jesus saith unto her, Woman, why weepest thou? whom seekest thou? She, supposing him to be the gardener, saith unto him, Sir, if thou have borne him hence, tell me where thou hast laid him, and I will take him away. Jesus said unto her, Mary. She turned herself, and saith unto him, Rabboni, which is to say, Master. Jesus saith unto her, Touch me not; for I am not yet ascended to my Father; but go to my brethren, and say unto them, I ascend unto my Father, and your Father; and to my God, and your God. Mary Magdalene came and told the disciplines that she had seen the Lord, and that he had spoken these things unto her. (John 20:14–18)

Mary Magdalen first turns away from the empty sepulcher and then turns again when she recognizes the "gardener" as Jesus. These turnings mime the reversals of conversion and of spiritual insight. Each of these turnings is a trope (that is what "trope" means: "a turning"), a redefinition of meanings by performative language, as when Jesus salutes Mary by her name, and she names him "Master." The turnings mime also the reversals of Marcel's evaluation of his transformation of the pear trees into angels, and Saint-Loup's transformation of Rachel into a person of infinite worth. First Marcel says the pear trees were just pear trees, not angels at all, just as Rachel was really "Rachel when from the Lord," but then he says they were really angels, and Rachel really Robert's Rachel, just as the gardener turned out to be Jesus and just as Mary Magdalen, according to tradition a prostitute, becomes a saint. A further complexity in Proust's allusion here is that the biblical passage is perhaps mediated by Letter XII of Ruskin's *Fors Clavigera*, which we know Proust read and in which Mary Magdalen's meeting with Jesus is discussed.[26]

Jesus' "Touch me not," "Noli me tangere," contrasts strikingly with another episode a few verses further on, also recorded only in John, namely the story of "Doubting Thomas," that is, Thomas Didymus (meaning "twin"), who was invited by Jesus to touch the nail holes in the risen Jesus' hands and to thrust his hand in the wound in Jesus' side. Thomas apparently did not touch Jesus, but believed on the strength of Jesus' words. The risen Christ is both tangible and intangible, embodied and disembodied, like a ghost or apparition:

> But he [Thomas Didymus] said unto them, Except I shall see in his hands the print of the nails, and put my finger into the print of the nails, and thrust my hand into his side, I will not believe. . . . Then saith he to Thomas, Reach hither thy finger, and behold my hands; and reach hither thy hand, and thrust it into my side: and be not faithless, but believing. And Thomas answered and said unto him, My Lord and my God. Jesus saith unto him, Thomas, because thou hast seen me, thou hast believed: blessed are they that have not seen, and yet have believed. (John 20:25, 27–29)

Seeing is believing, but the truest faith is to believe without seeing. Faith is precisely that: belief in things unseen.

The passage in Proust, when it is put back in its biblical context, is a passionate celebration of the human imagination for its power to reach a hidden truth, accessible not to reason but to performative speech acts. This is exemplified not only in Marcel's transformation of the pear trees into angels but even in Saint-Loup's transformation of "Rachel when from the Lord" into his beloved mistress.

As is known by anyone who has traced the evolution and per-mutations of the legends of Mary Magdalen down through the centuries, Mary Magdalen has been the focus of an activity of "imagination" as intense as that Saint-Loup lavished on Rachel. As opposed to the Virgin Mary, Mary Magdalen was a sinner, a re-pentant prostitute, therefore someone with whom mere mortal sinners could more easily identify themselves. Moreover, without sound scriptural authority, Christians early and late have conflated the various Marys in the gospels and made them into a single Mary (though not in the Eastern Church, where each Mary has a sepa-rate saint's day). Believers have then invented a whole circumstan-tial life story for Mary Magdalen, exemplified saliently and most familiarly in the version of her life in Jacobus de Voraigne's *The Golden Legend: Readings on the Saints*. A "legend" means, etymo-logically, something to read, but also an act of reading. There are, however, many other versions besides the *Legenda Aurea* one, ver-sions both literary and graphic, including even a fanciful apoc-ryphal version in which Mary Magdalen is the mother of a daugh-ter, Sarah, fathered by Jesus, who became the original mother of the line of Merovingian kings when Mary Magdalen and Sarah fled Palestine for Marseilles.[27] The transformation of Mary Mag-dalen into a Christian saint parallels the transformation of Rachel into Saint-Loup's beloved mistress and exemplifies the same power of the linguistic imagination. Mary Magdalen's transformation was inaugurated by Jesus when he forgave her sins, substituting, as Hegel states in a powerful passage in his early theological writings, Christian love for Judaic law and thereby inaugurating the new re-ligion as the cancellation and at the same time sublation or sublimation of the old, its *Aufhebung*. Mary Magdalen, for Hegel, comes just at the moment when Judaism was sublated into Christianity. She belongs simultaneously to both.[28]

The opposition in the episode of Marcel's meeting Saint-Loup's mistress and seeing that she is "Rachel when from the Lord" is not between Saint-Loup's "imagination" of a Rachel who is not there and Marcel's clear vision of what is there but between two forms of imagination that are nevertheless versions of the same power, fueled by emotion, and acting through performative positings: "The immobility of that thin face, like that of a sheet of paper subjected to the colossal pressure of two atmospheres, seemed to me to be held in equilibrium by two infinites which converged on her without meeting, for she held them apart. Looking at her, Robert and I, we did not both see her from the same side of the mystery [*nous ne la voyions pas du même côté du mystère*]" (E2: 162; F2: 458). Here Marcel ends by endorsing the belief that Rachel is a mystery, as thin as a sheet of paper (inscribed perhaps with words or graphic signs to be read, though Marcel does not say so), just as a face is an expressive but enigmatic sign. Rachel's face remains impenetrable, unfathomable, unknowable, whatever infinite imaginative pressure from either side is put on it. She is therefore open to the two radically different and infinitely powerful acts of imagination, one performed by Saint-Loup, one by Marcel. These end by balancing in an equilibrium, equally ignorant of what Rachel "really is."

The signals of Marcel's performative power are all those allusions and references that make the episode a complex allegory in which nothing is just itself but is also a sign that stands for something else. Rachel is for Marcel the biblical Rachel, but also the heroine of Halévy's play, and also Mary Magdalen, and also Lot's wife; and the pear trees are turned into men, then into angels that visited Lot, and then into the angels that guarded Christ's tomb after the Resurrection, all by sovereign speech acts.

Behind Marcel's performative positings, registered in the text of his narration, stands Marcel Proust, the narrator's maker and the ultimate source, in lordly self-effacement, of all these metaphorical or allegorical transpositions effected by acts of language. *À la recherche du temps perdu* may seem to many readers to be a fictitious autobiography obeying the conventions of realism. If this were so, the figures Marcel uses would be mere embroidery, fanciful metaphors brought in to make the realist narrative more vivid and to demonstrate Marcel's psychology, his "poetic" gifts. On the contrary, this episode, like the *Recherche* in general, is allegorical through and through. It names one thing by means of another, demonstrating that "reality is not what we suppose." The meaning of the *Recherche* depends on the tropes or turnings that make pear trees into angels and make Rachel the whore into "Rachel when from the Lord" in Halévy's opera, and then into Robert's mysterious, unfathomable beloved, a deep enigma.

Coda

Allegory as Speech Act

Of what is the *Recherche* an allegory? I can, to conclude, now answer that question, especially in the context of what has been said in earlier chapters about speech acts in literature as theorized by Austin, Derrida, and de Man. The episode just analyzed, like the *Recherche* "as a whole," is an allegory of allegory, that is, of the activity whereby impassioned language posits transformations. To put this in de Manian terms, the episode is an allegory of reading and of the attempt to read reading, that is, to understand the activity that I have been calling speech acts in literature.

As the reader of de Man's essay on Proust will remember, de Man observes that if Proust's *Recherche* is an allegory of reading, then reading Reading, as de Man puts it, whether one is reading Proust or texts in general, is forever impossible.[1] This is so—to offer one possible explanation for this impossibility—because the attempt to read Reading only leads to further performative positings. The act of trying to understand repeats the enigmatic, unknowable event that is the object of anxious interrogation. These new positings, positings on positings, such as my words about Proust, following Proust's words about Marcel's words about his own and Saint-Loup's words about Rachel, are a way of doing things with words rather than the constative expression of achieved knowledge. They exemplify the incompatibility between knowing through or by words and doing things with words that is perpetually demon-strated, as this book has tried to show, by speech acts in literature.

What Austin calls "performative utterances," Derrida calls dec-larations of independence or inventions of the other, de Man calls reading as an act of positing that is at once a lying promise and a contradiction, and I have been calling speech acts in literature, with all the crisscross, contradictory, aporetic polyvalence of that "in." To "call" is to name. Naming is an initiatory performative ut-terance, a "calling." That calling is based or grounded on nothing but the call from the other that impassions me. This call, in the case of literary study, is mediated by a text or embodied in a text. This call I respond to in another calling, for example in writing an essay or a book. This constitutes another demand for response. It is a demand for which I, as the one who has first responded, must, and hereby do, take responsibility.

Reference Matter

Notes

Introduction

1. A full bibliography of articles and books on speech-act theory would be a book in itself. Even a listing of those that bear more or less directly on the relation of speech acts to literature would be extensive. See, for example, the bibliography appended to Sandy Petrey, *Speech Acts and Literary Theory* (New York: Routledge, 1990). Here, however, in chronological order, is a highly selective list of important works, beside Petrey's, that are in one way or another relevant to my enterprise in this volume. (Note that most of them are about speech acts and literary theory, not about how to use speech-act theory to interpret specific works of literature, nor examples of that, much less about the literary aspects of speech-act theory itself, all three of which are primary concerns of this book.) Émile Benveniste, "La philosophie analytique et le langage," in *Problèmes de linguistique générale* (Paris, Gallimard, 1966), 267–76, published in English as "Analytical Philosophy and Language," in *Problems of General Linguistics*, trans. M. E. Meeks (Coral Gables, Fla.: University of Miami Press, 1971), 1: 231–38; Richard Ohmann, "Speech Acts and the Definition of Literature," *Philosophy and Rhetoric* 4 (1971): 1–19; Kenneth Burke, "Words as Deeds," *Centrum* 3, no. 2 (1975): 147–68; Michael Hancher, "Understanding Poetic Speech Acts," *College English* 36 (1975): 632–39; James A. Fanto, "Speech-Act Theory and Its Applications to the Study of Literature," in *The Sign: Semiotics Around the World,* ed. R. W. Bailey, L. Matejka, and P. Steiner (Ann Arbor: Michigan Slavic Publications, 1978), 280–304; Mary Louise Pratt, *Toward a Speech-Act Theory of Liter-*

ary Discourse (Bloomington: Indiana University Press, 1977); Stanley Cavell, "Austin and Examples," in *The Claim of Reason* (Oxford: Clarendon, 1979), 49–64; Shoshana Felman, *Le scandale du corps parlant: Don Juan avec Austin; ou, la séduction en deux langues* (Paris: Seuil, 1980), published in English as *The Literary Speech Act: Don Juan with Austin, or Seduction in Two Languages*, trans. Catherine Porter (Ithaca, N.Y.: Cornell University Press, 1983); Stanley Fish, "How to Do Things with Austin and Searle: Speech-Act Theory and Literary Criticism," in *Is There a Text in This Class* (Cambridge, Mass.: Harvard University Press, 1980), 197–245; and Barbara Johnson, "Poetry and Performative Language: Mallarmé and Austin," in *The Critical Difference* (Baltimore: The Johns Hopkins University Press, 1980), 52–66. I thank John Barton for bibliographical help.

2. J. L. Austin, *How to Do Things with Words*, 2d ed., ed. J. O. Urmson and Marina Sbisà (Oxford: Oxford University Press, 1980), 109, henceforth *HT*. The pagination of the Harvard University Press edition of 1975 is the same.

3. The example and the phrase "some low type" are given in Austin's BBC talk, "Performative Utterances," printed in J. L. Austin, *Philosophical Papers*, 3d ed., ed. J. O. Urmson and G. J. Warnock (Oxford: Oxford University Press, 1979), 239–40. See also *HT*, 23, 117. The BBC talk is an elegant abbreviated version, often using the same words and adducing the same examples, of the whole first part of *How to Do Things with Words*. It is the thing to read if you want to get a quick idea of what Austin's doctrine was. In giving this example, Austin once says "the *Mr. Stalin*" (*HT*, 23). He obviously found this example funny, as do we, but it also sticks in the mind as a prime example of a speech act and of speech acts' general precariousness. Many of Austin's examples are comic, but that does not make them less serious, or does it? At the least, one can say the examples are undermined by being ironic.

Chapter 1

1. Some of these titles are real, some imaginary, my own inventions. For a discussion of real "how-to" books, especially those sinister and disquieting ones published in the United States by a certain Loompanics Unlimited, see Scott Stossel, "Bound to Be Bad: True Crime Meets How-To," *New Yorker*, Oct. 12, 1998, 92–96. Among the books published by Loompanics, Stossel lists *How to Sneak into the Movies, How to Launder*

Money, How to Legally Obtain a Second Citizenship and Passport—And Why You Want To, How to Collect Illegal Debts, How to Disappear Completely and Never Be Found, and *How to Steal Food from the Supermarket.*

2. J. L. Austin, *How to Do Things with Words,* 2d ed., ed. J. O. Urmson and Marina Sbisà (Oxford: Oxford University Press, 1980), 122, 132, henceforth *HT.*

3. The example and the definitions come from *Webster's New Collegiate Dictionary* (Springfield, Mass.: G. and C. Merriam, 1949), 401.

4. See Martin Heidegger, "Das Ding," in his *Vorträge und Aufsätze* (Pfullingen: Neske, 1967), 2: 47–50 and passim, published in English as "The Thing," in Martin Heidegger, *Poetry, Language, Thought,* trans. Albert Hofstadter (New York: Harper and Row, 1971), 165–82, see esp. 174–77 and passim.

5. Henry James, preface to *The Golden Bowl,* (reprint of the New York edition, New York: Augustus M. Kelley, 1971), 23: xxiv–xxv.

6. George Eliot, *Middlemarch,* ed. Rosemary Ashton (London: Penguin, 1994), 838.

7. In 1723, Alexander Pope published a satirical attack on Ambrose Philips, Lewis Theobald, and John Dennis, among others, entitled "Martinus Scriblerus peri Bathous: Or the Art of Sinking in Poetry."

8. Backflap statement from the paperback edition of J. L. Austin, *Philosophical Papers,* 3d ed., ed. J. O. Urmson and G. J. Warnock (Oxford: Oxford University Press, 1979), henceforth *PP.*

9. Austin's presentation of this example in "Performative Utterances" is characteristically witty and thought provoking: "Or again, suppose that somebody sticks up a notice, 'This bull is dangerous,' or simply 'Dangerous bull,' or simply 'Bull.' Does this necessarily differ from sticking up a notice, appropriately signed, saying 'You are hereby warned that this bull is dangerous'? It seems that the simple notice 'Bull' can do just the same job as the more elaborate formula. Of course the difference is that if we just stick up 'Bull' it would not be quite clear that it is a warning; it might be there just for interest or information, like 'Wallaby' on the cage at the zoo, or 'Ancient Monument.'" J. L. Austin, "Performative Utterances," in *PP,* 243.

10. Charles Dickens, *Great Expectations,* Norton Critical Edition, ed. Edgar Rosenberg (New York: W. W. Norton, 1999), 73–75.

11. Plato, *Protagoras,* trans. W. K. C. Guthrie, in *The Collected Dialogues,* ed. Edith Hamilton and Huntington Cairns, Bollingen Series LXXI (Princeton, N.J.: Princeton University Press, 1973), 351–52.

12. "That [the third *Critique*]," says de Man, "was an occurrence, something happened there, something occurred—[but] in the whole reception of Kant from then until now, nothing has happened, only regression, nothing has happened at all." Paul de Man, "Kant and Schiller," in *Aesthetic Ideology*, ed. Andrzej Warminski (Minneapolis: University of Minnesota Press, 1996), 134.

13. Paul de Man, "Conclusions: Walter Benjamin's 'The Task of the Translator,'" in *The Resistance to Theory* (Minneapolis: University of Minnesota Press, 1986), 96.

14. See M. H. Abrams, "Rationality and Imagination in Cultural History," *Critical Inquiry* 2, no. 3 (Spring 1976): 457–58, and J. Hillis Miller, "The Critic as Host," in *Theory Now and Then* (Durham, N.C.: Duke University Press, 1991), 143–70.

15. Paul de Man, "The Concept of Irony," in *Aesthetic Ideology*, 165.

16. Ibid., 184.

17. Schlegel says irony allows "den Schein des Verkehrten und Verrückten oder des Einfältigen und Dummen" ("the semblance of the absurd and of madness, of simplicity and foolishness") to shine through. Friedrich Schlegel, *Kritische Schriften* (Munich: Carl Hanser, 1964), 501–2; the English is from Friedrich Schlegel, "Dialogue on Poetry," in *Dialogue on Poetry and Literary Aphorisms*, trans. Ernst Behler and Roman Struc (University Park: The Pennsylvania State University Press, 1968), 86.

18. The Nixon example comes from J. R. Searle, "The Logical Status of Fictional Discourse," *New Literary History* (1975), 5: 324–25. Searle's article is amusingly discussed and played with at the very end of "Limited Inc a b c... ." See Jacques Derrida, *Limited Inc*, trans. Samuel Weber and Jeffrey Mehlman (Evanston, Ill.: Northwestern University Press, 1988), 106.

19. For these and other examples, as well as expositions of Searle's speech-act theory, see John R. Searle, *Speech Acts: An Essay in the Philosophy of Language* (London: Cambridge University Press, 1969); idem, *Expression and Meaning: Studies in the Theory of Speech Acts* (Cambridge, Eng.: Cambridge University Press, 1979); and idem, "Reiterating the Differences: A Reply to Derrida," *Glyph 1* (Baltimore: The Johns Hopkins University Press, 1977), 198–208. The last essay contains a footnote reference to other essays by Searle on speech acts. The essay in *Glyph 1* is the one to which Derrida is responding so aggressively in "Limited Inc a b c... ."

20. Jacques Derrida comments on the impossible/possible doubleness of signature in "Signature Event Context": "Effects of signature are the most common thing in the world. But the condition of possibility

of those effects is simultaneously, once again, the condition of their impossibility, of the impossibility of their rigorous purity. In order to function, that is, to be readable, a signature must have a repeatable, iterable, imitable form; it must be able to be detached from the present and singular intention of its production. It is its sameness which, by corrupting its identity and its singularity, divides its seal [*sceau*]." Derrida, *Limited Inc*, 20.

21. *HT*, 24, 34–35, 125–26; "A Plea for Excuses," passim (*PP*, 175–204); *HT*, 16, 30, 96, 107, 48, 31, 24, 101–2, 72, 20, 119, 95, 20, 119.

22. *HT*, 6, 37, 111, 101–2, 38, 84, 27, 9–10, 96.

23. Here is a more or less complete list: *HT*, 4, 7, 13, 19, 22, 24, 31, 33, 35, 36, 40, 41, 42, 57, 59, 65, 85, 88–89, 98–99, 122, 128, 130, 141, 153, 154, 155, 157.

24. Derrida, *Limited Inc*, 96–97.

Chapter 2

1. Jacques Derrida, *Limited Inc*, trans. Samuel Weber and Jeffrey Mehlman (Evanston, Ill.: Northwestern University Press, 1988), 133–34, henceforth *LI*. The translation of "Signature Event Context" (henceforth, following Derrida's usage, *Sec*) in this volume is by Jeffrey Mehlman and Samuel Weber. The other two translations—"Limited Inc a b c... " and "Afterword: Toward an Ethic of Discussion"—are entirely by Weber. For the French original of these essays, paradoxically gathered in a single volume only after the publication in English of *Limited Inc*, see *Limited Inc*, presentation and trans. Elisabeth Weber (Paris: Galilée, 1990), henceforth *LI/F*. Weber "presents" what was originally written in French, though "Limited Inc a b c... " and "Afterword: Toward an Ethic of Discussion" had never before been published in the French original. She translates into French the citations from Searle and others that Derrida left in English (since "Limited Inc a b c... " and "Afterword" were written in French but intended for translation into English).

2. Jacques Derrida, "Avances," in Serge Margel, *Le tombeau du dieu artisan* (Paris: Minuit, 1995), 7–43, esp. 15–27. "In order to be a promise," writes Derrida, "a promise *must be able* to be broken [*intenable*] and therefore be able *not to be* a promise (for a breakable promise is not a promise). Conclusion: one *will* never *state* [*constatera* jamais], any more than for the gift, *that there is or that there has been* [*qu'il y a ou qu'il y a eu*] a promise" (26, my translation).

3. Jacques Derrida, *Spectres de Marx* (Paris: Galilée, 1993), 60, published in English as *Specters of Marx*, trans. Peggy Kamuf (New York: Routledge, 1994), 30–31.

4. Ibid., French ed. p. 89, English ed. p. 51.

5. J. L. Austin, *How to Do Things with Words*, 2d ed., ed. J. O. Urmson and Marina Sbisà (Oxford: Oxford University Press, 1980), 3, henceforth *HT.*

6. J. L. Austin, *Philosophical Papers*, 3d ed., ed. J. O. Urmson and G. J. Warnock (Oxford: Oxford University Press, 1979), 233.

7. John R. Searle, "Reiterating the Differences: A Reply to Derrida," *Glyph 1* (Baltimore: The Johns Hopkins University Press, 1977), 198–208.

8. See John R. Searle, "The World Turned Upside Down," *New York Review of Books*, Oct. 27, 1983, 174–79.

9. Thomas Hardy, *Tess of the d'Urbervilles* (London: Penguin, 1998), 80.

10. Paul Celan, "Ashglory (Aschenglorie)," ll. 24–26, *Breathturn (Atemwende)*, bilingual ed., trans. Pierre Joris (Los Angeles: Sun and Moon, 1995), 178.

11. John R. Searle, *Intentionality: An Essay on the Philosophy of Mind* (Cambridge, Eng.: Cambridge University Press, 1983).

12. See Jacques Derrida: "Freud et la scène de l'écriture," in *L'écriture et la différance* (Paris: Seuil, 1967), 293–340, published in English as "Freud and the Scene of Writing," in *Writing and Difference*, trans. Alan Bass (Chicago: University of Chicago Press, 1978), 196–231. For some of Derrida's later essays on psychoanalysis, see, for example, "Fors: Les mots anglés de Nicolas Abraham et Maria Torok," in Nicolas Abraham and Maria Torok, *Cryptonymie: Le verbier de L'Homme au Loups* (Paris: Aubier Flammarion, 1976), 7–73, published in English as "Foreword: *Fors*: The Anglish Words of Nicolas Abraham and Maria Torok," trans. Barbara Johnson, in *The Wolf Man's Magic Word: A Cryptonymy* (Minneapolis: University of Minnesota Press, 1986), xi–xlviii; "Speculer—Sur 'Freud'" and "Le facteur de la vérité," in *La carte postale* (Paris: Aubier-Flammarion, 1980), 275–437, 439–524, published in English as "To Speculate—On Freud" and "Le facteur de la vérité," in *The Post Card*, trans. Alan Bass (Chicago: University of Chicago Press, 1987), 257–409, 411–96; *Mal d'archive: Une impression freudienne* (Paris: Galilée, 1995), published in English as *Archive Fever: A Freudian Impression*, trans. Eric Prenowitz (Chicago: University of Chicago Press, 1996).

13. The allusion is to Freud's *Jokes and Their Relation to the Unconscious* (*Der Witz und Seine Beziehung zum Unbewussten*, 1905).

14. *American Heritage Dictionary of the English Language*, ed. William Morris (New York: American Heritage, 1969), 288a.

15. Paul Robert, *Le petit Robert; Dictionnaire . . . de la langue Française* (Paris: Société du Nouveau Littré, 1976), 1608b, my translation.

16. Wallace Stevens, *The Collected Poems* (New York: Knopf, 1954), 76, ll. 1–9.

17. William K. Wimsatt, Jr., and Monroe C. Beardsley, "The Intentional Fallacy," in William K. Wimsatt, Jr., *The Verbal Icon: Studies in the Meaning of Poetry*, with two preliminary essays written in collaboration with Monroe C. Beardsley (Lexington: University of Kentucky Press, 1954), 3–18.

18. See my "Derrida's Literatures," in *Derrida and the Future of the Human(ities)*, ed. Tom Cohen (Cambridge, Eng.: Cambridge University Press, 2001).

19. Marcel Proust, *À la recherche du temps perdu*, ed. Jean-Yves Tadié, éd. de la Pléiade (Paris: Gallimard, 1988), 2: 526–27, published in English as *Remembrance of Things Past*, trans. C. K. Scott Moncrieff and Terence Kilmartin (New York: Vintage, 1982), 2: 236.

20. Jacques Derrida, *Otobiographies: L'enseignement de Nietzsche et la politique du nom propre* (Paris: Galilée, 1984), henceforth O/F. The seminar on Nietzsche, but not the "Declarations of Independence" preamble, was also presented later, in October 1979, at the University of Montreal, and then published in Jacques Derrida et al., *L'oreille de l'autre: Otobiographies, transferts, traductions*, ed. Claude Lévesque and Christie McDonald (Montreal: VLB Éditeur, 1982), published in English as "Otobiographies: The Teaching of Nietzsche and the Politics of the Proper Name," trans. Avital Ronell, in *The Ear of the Other: Otobiography, Transference, Translation*, all but "Otobiographies" trans. Peggy Kamuf (Lincoln: University of Nebraska Press, 1988), 1–38, henceforth O/E.

21. Jacques Derrida, "Declarations of Independence," trans. Tom Keenen and Tom Pepper, *New Political Science* 15 (1986): 7, henceforth DI/E.

22. See J. L. Austin, "A Plea for Excuses," in his *Philosophical Papers*, 175–204.

23. Paul de Man, *Aesthetic Ideology*, ed. Andrzej Warminski (Minneapolis: University of Minnesota Press, 1996), 165.

24. Stéphane Mallarmé, "Mimique," in his *Oeuvres complètes*, ed. Henri Mondor and G. Jean-Aubry, éd. de la Pléiade (Paris: Gallimard, 1945), 310: "Ici devançant, là remémorant, au futur, au passé, *sous une apparence fausse de présent.*" "Mimique" is cited and discussed in Jacques

Derrida, "La double séance," in *La dissémination* (Paris: Seuil, 1972), 199–317, esp. 239–40, published in English as "The Double Session," in *Dissemination*, trans. Barbara Johnson (Chicago: University of Chicago Press, 1981), 173–285, esp. 211.

25. Jacques Derrida, "Psyché: L'invention de l'autre," in *Psyché: Inventions de l'autre* (Paris: Galilée, 1987), 11–61, published in English as "Psyche: The Invention of the Other," trans. Catherine Porter, in *Reading de Man Reading*, ed. Lindsay Waters and Wlad Godzich (Minneapolis: University of Minnesota Press, 1989), 25–65.

26. Jacques Derrida, *Parages* (Paris: Galilée, 1986).

27. See David de Kanter Arndt, "The Declaration of Independence," in *Ground and Abyss: The Question of* Poiesis *in Heidegger, Arendt, Foucault, and Stevens* (Ann Arbor, Mich.: UMI Dissertation Services, 1998), microfilm, pp. 127–83. Arndt formulates his thesis as follows in the "Abstract": "The Declaration offers itself as an example of the revolutionary act of foundation it describes in the principle of revolution, but it can only justify its own act of foundation on the basis of the principle of revolution it itself lays down" (xi).

28. Jacques Derrida, seminar of December 2, 1992, given at École des Hautes Études, Paris, France, my translation, used by permission of the author, from a computer file in my possession. Further citations will be from this text. I thank Barbara Cohen and Peggy Kamuf for help with the translation. Since a computer file does not have fixed page numbers (because its format may be altered), I do not give page references. The discussion of "Je t'aime" continued in the seminar of December 9, 1992, but I make no citations from this continuation. Both seminars may be consulted in the Derrida Collection at the Critical Theory Archive in the library of the University of California at Irvine.

Chapter 3

1. Paul de Man, *Allegories of Reading* (New Haven, Conn.: Yale University Press, 1979), henceforth *AR*.

2. For these pages see Jacques Derrida, "Psyché: L'invention de l'autre," in *Psyché: Inventions de l'autre* (Paris: Galilée, 1987), 58–61, published in English as "Psyche: The Invention of the Other," trans. Catherine Porter, in *Reading de Man Reading*, ed. Lindsay Waters and Wlad Godzich (Minneapolis: University of Minnesota Press, 1989), 59–62. I discuss these pages in "Derrida's Literatures," in *Derrida and the Future*

of the Human(ities), ed. Tom Cohen (Cambridge, Eng.: Cambridge University Press, 2001).

3. In J. Hillis Miller, "Paul de Man as Allergen," in *Material Events* (Minneapolis: University of Minnesota Press, 2000), 183–204. I discuss de Man's theory and practice of irony in a longer version of this essay, with the same title. See chapter 10 of *Others* (Princeton, N.J.: Princeton University Press, 2001).

4. Paul de Man, *The Rhetoric of Romanticism* (New York: Columbia University Press, 1984), 93–123, henceforth *RR*.

5. Things are not quite this simple for Austin. Felicitous speech acts for him both require and must not require deliberate intention. This is a central crux in Austin's theory of how to do things with words, as I have shown in Chapter 1 above.

6. Paul de Man, "Kant and Schiller," in *Aesthetic Ideology*, ed. Andrzej Warminski (Minneapolis: University of Minnesota Press, 1996), 134.

7. Paul de Man, "Reply to Raymond Geuss," in *Aesthetic Ideology*, 185–92.

8. Paul de Man, "The Resistance to Theory," in *The Resistance to Theory* (Minneapolis: University of Minnesota Press, 1986), 11.

9. Paul de Man, "Pascal's Allegory of Persuasion," in *Aesthetic Ideology*, 69.

10. Paul de Man, "Hegel on the Sublime," in *Aesthetic Ideology*, 112.

Chapter 4

1. My epigraph is from Jacques Derrida, "Envois," in *The Post Card*, trans. Alan Bass (Chicago: University of Chicago Press, 1987), 197, 204; the French original is in *La carte postale* (Paris: Aubier-Flammarion, 1980), 212, 219.

2. See Avital Ronell, *The Telephone Book* (Lincoln: University of Nebraska Press, 1989); Laurence Rickels, "Kafka and Freud on the Telephone," *Modern Austrian Literature: Journal of the International Arthur Schnitzler Association* 22, nos. 3/4 (1989): 211–25; Laurence Rickels, *Aberrations of Mourning* (Detroit: Wayne State University Press, 1988), esp. chaps. 7 and 8; and Friedrich Kittler, *Essays: Literature, Media, Information Systems*, ed. John Johnston (Amsterdam: G+B Arts International, 1997), esp. 31–49.

3. See Jacques Derrida, "Télépathie," *Furor* 2 (Feb. 1981): 5–41, reprinted in Jacques Derrida, *Psyché: Inventions de l'autre* (Paris: Galilée,

1987), 237–70, published in English as "Telepathy," trans. Nicholas Royle, *Oxford Literary Review* 10, nos. 1–2 (1988): 3–41.

4. *Calendar of State Papers Relating to Scotland* (London: Longmans: 1858), 4: 300, cited in Jayne Elizabeth Lewis, "'All Mankind Are Her Scots': Mary Stuart and the Birth of Modern Britain," in *Literature and the Nation*, ed. Brook Thomas, *REAL: Yearbook of Research in English and American Literature*, vol. 14 (Tübingen: Gunter Narr Verlag, 1998), 59.

5. Edmund Husserl, *Cartesian Meditations: An Introduction to Phenomenology*, trans. Dorion Cairns (The Hague: Nijhoff, 1960), 89–151.

6. J. Hillis Miller, "Derrida's Literatures," in *Derrida and the Future of the Human(ities)*, ed. Tom Cohen (Cambridge, Eng.: Cambridge University Press, 2001).

7. Jacques Derrida, *Passions* (Paris: Galilée, 1993), 67–68, published in English as, "Passions: 'An Oblique Offering,'" trans. David Wood, in *On the Name*, ed. Thomas Dutoit (Stanford, Calif.: Stanford University Press, 1995), 29–30.

8. Jacques Derrida, "Sauf le nom," in *On the Name*, 56.

9. Derrida, *On the Name*, 29; in French, *Passions*, 67–68.

10. Ludwig Wittgenstein, *The Blue and Brown Books* (New York: Harper Torchbooks, Harper and Row, 1965); idem, *Philosophical Investigations*, trans. G. E. M. Anscombe (Oxford: Blackwell, 1968); idem, *Bemerkungen über die Philosophie der Psychologie / Remarks on the Philosophy of Psychology*, ed. G. E. M. Anscombe and G. G. von Wright, trans. G. E. M. Anscombe, 2 vols. (Chicago: University of Chicago Press, 1980).

11. Wittgenstein, *Philosophical Investigations*, vii.

12. Gerard Manley Hopkins, *Sermons and Devotional Writings*, ed. Christopher Devlin (London: Oxford University Press, 1959), 123.

13. Wittgenstein, *Philosophical Investigations*, 95 (English page).

14. For a distinguished book about pain and the body, see Elaine Scarry, *The Body in Pain: The Making and Unmaking of the World* (New York: Oxford University Press, 1985).

15. Wittgenstein, *Blue and Brown Books*, 48.

16. Ibid., 103.

17. Wittgenstein, *Philosophical Investigations*, 105 (English page).

18. Wittgenstein, *Blue and Brown Books*, 103.

19. Jacques Derrida, *Politiques de l'amitié* (Paris: Galilée, 1994), chaps. 2 and 3, pp. 43–92, esp. 46, 86, published in English as *Politics of Friendship*, trans. George Collins (London: Verso, 1997), chaps. 2 and 3, pp. 26–74, esp. 29, 67–68.

20. Jacques Derrida, "Comme si c'était possible, 'within such limits,'" in the section "Derrida with his replies," *Revue Internationale de Philosophie* 3 (Oct. 1998): 498–99, my translation.

21. J. L. Austin, *Philosophical Papers*, 3d. ed., ed. J. O. Urmson and G. J. Warnock (Oxford: Oxford University Press, 1979), 76–116, 253–71, henceforth *PP*. "Other Minds" was first published in *Proceedings of the Aristotelian Society* in 1946, that is, nine years before the presentation of *How to Do Things with Words* at Harvard in 1955. "Pretending" was first published in the 1957–58 *Supplementary 32* of *Proceedings of the Aristotelian Society*.

22. Derrida, "Comme si c'était possible, 'within such limits,'" 500–501.

Chapter 5

1. See J. Hillis Miller, *Black Holes* (Stanford, Calif.: Stanford University Press, 1999), 313–77, odd pages only.

2. See Paul de Man, "Reading (Proust)," in *Allegories of Reading* (New Haven, Conn.: Yale University Press, 1979), 78.

3. Joseph Conrad, *Lord Jim*, ed. Cedric Watts and Robert Hampson (London: Penguin, 1989), 146.

4. De Man, *Allegories of Reading*, 205.

5. Marcel Proust, *À la recherche du temps perdu*, ed. Jean-Yves Tadié, éd. de la Pléiade (Paris: Gallimard, 1989), 2: 366, published in English as *Remembrance of Things Past*, trans. C. K. Scott Moncrieff (New York: Vintage, 1982), 2: 63–64. Further references will be to the volume and page numbers of these texts, indicated by "F" and "E" respectively.

6. Edmund Husserl, *Cartesian Meditations: An Introduction to Phenomenology*, trans. Dorion Cairns (The Hague: Nijhoff, 1960), 108.

7. See Louis Althusser, "Ideology and Ideological State Apparatuses (Notes Towards an Investigation)," in *"Lenin and Philosophy" and Other Essays*, trans. Ben Brewster (New York: Monthly Review Press, 1972), 162: "Ideology is a 'representation' of the imaginary relationships of individuals to their real conditions of existence." Also see Paul de Man, "The Resistance to Theory," in *The Resistance to Theory* (Minneapolis: University of Minnesota Press, 1986), 11: "What we call ideology is precisely the confusion of linguistic with natural reality, of reference with phenomenalism."

8. Marcel Proust, "Journées de lecture," in his *"Contre Sainte-Beuve," précedé de "Pastiches et mélanges" et suivi de "Essais et articles,"* éd. de la

Pléiade (Paris: Gallimard, 1971), 527–33, henceforth *CSB*, all translations are mine. The passage about the telephone is on pp. 527–29. At the end of the brief essay Proust returns obliquely to essential elements or themes present in the telephone passage. He had intended, he says, to discuss "Snobbism and Posterity" apropos of the memoirs of Mme de Boigne, a late-eighteenth- and early-nineteenth-century court figure, but a swarm of ghostly figures from his memory, phantoms or specters, interposed and distracted him, as the swarm of shades importuned Ulysses in *The Odyssey* and had to be beaten back with his sword. Proust promises that in a sequel he will resist such distraction and that, if such an "indiscreet fantasy" interposes again, he will ask "her" not to cut off his communication with his reader, as though the interrupting "blocking idea [*idée de traverse*]" were an unhelpful telephone operator: "We're talking. Don't cut us off, Miss! [*Nous causons, ne nous coupez pas, mademoiselle!*]" (532–33). For the insertion of the passages about the telephone from the *Figaro* essay into the proofs of "The Guermantes Way," see *À la recherche du temps perdu*, 2: 1590.

9. See Laurence Rickels, "Kafka and Freud on the Telephone," *Modern Austrian Literature: Journal of the International Arthur Schnitzler Association* 22, nos. 3/4 (1989): 211–25; and Laurence Rickels, *Aberrations of Mourning* (Detroit: Wayne State University Press, 1988), esp. chaps. 7 and 8.

10. Cited in F1: cxxv, from Marcel Proust, *La correspondence*, 21 vols., ed. Philip Kolb (Paris: Plon, 1976–93), 5: 348, my translation.

11. Joyce even claims to know the telephone number of "Edenville." It is made primarily of ones and zeroes, like our present-day binary computer language: "The cords of all link back, strandentwining cable of all flesh. That is why mystic monks. Will you be as gods? Gaze in your omphalos. Hello. Kinch here. Put me on to Edenville. Aleph, alpha: nought, nought one." James Joyce, *Ulysses* (New York: Modern Library, n.d.), 39.

12. One name for a performative utterance Austin considered and then dismissed was "operative." See J. L. Austin, *How to Do Things with Words*, 2d ed., ed. J. O. Urmson and Marina Sbisà (Oxford: Oxford University Press, 1980), 7.

13. Marcel Proust said the same thing in a letter about the way the telephone changed his mother's voice and turned her, to his immense pain, into someone else. "It is no longer your voice [*Ce n'est plus ta voix*]," he wrote to her in a letter of 1896. In a letter to Antoine Bibesco, written six years later, in 1902, he describes how his mother's voice over the telephone was changed and aged: "And in the telephone [*dans le téléphone*],

suddenly I heard her poor broken voice, bruised [*meurtrie*], one forever other than the one I had always known, full of cracks and fissures; and it is in receiving in the earpiece the bloody and broken pieces of it that I have had for the first time the atrocious sensation [*la sensation atroce*] of what was forever broken in her." F2: 1589–90, cited from Proust, *Correspondence*, 2: 144 and 3: 182, my translation.

14. Joyce, *Ulysses*, 112. Brook Thomas cites and discusses this passage in his *James Joyce's "Ulysses": A Book of Many Happy Returns* (Baton Rouge: Louisiana State University Press, 1982), in a chapter called "History Repeating Itself with a Difference." See 149–50.

15. Mark Calkins, *À la recherche de l'unité perdue: Genre and Narrative in Proust* (Ann Arbor, Mich.: UMI Dissertation Services, 1998), microfilm.

16. See F4: 230–34; E3: 666–70. I have discussed this passage in *Black Holes*, 467–83, odd pages only.

17. Somewhat later in the chapter Marcel does not, apparently, understand the advances the Baron de Charlus makes to him when they leave Mme de Villeparisis's reception together, or rather when Charlus runs to catch up with him (F2: 581–92; E2: 294–306).

18. See Margaret Morganroth Gullette, "The Puzzling Case of the Deceased Wife's Sister: Nineteenth-Century England Deals with a Second-Chance Plot," *Representations* 31 (summer 1990): 142–66.

19. Joyce, *Ulysses*, 42.

20. A celebrated early-nineteenth-century tragedienne, born Elisa Félix (1820–58). This counts of course as another level of complexity within the name that Proust gives Saint-Loup's mistress. The portrait in my *Nouveau petit Larousse illustré* (Paris: Larousse, 1937), 1635, shows that the real actress named Rachel did have a long, narrow face. That Rachel lived far too early to have been Saint-Loup's mistress, however.

21. Daniel Halévy (1872–1962), grand nephew of Joseph Halévy, and author of a book about the early years of the Third French Republic, *La fin des notables* (*The End of the Notables*) (2 vols. Paris: B. Grasset, 1930, 1937), was Marcel Proust's schoolmate and friend. Daniel Halévy also wrote a book about the Dreyfus case, *Regards sur l'affaire Dreyfus* (Paris: Éditions de Fallois, 1994).

22. Ernest Newman, *More Stories of Famous Operas* (Philadelphia: Blakiston, 1946), 320–40.

23. Eugène Scribe, *Oeuvres complètes* (Paris: Furne; Aimé André, 1841), 2: 69, my translation. For the assertion that Adolphe Nourrit wrote these lines, see Newman, *More Stories of Famous Operas*, 322.

24. Proust explores this paradigm apropos of Vinteuil's septet and the creative power of Albertine's lies, in passages I have discussed elsewhere. See Miller, *Black Holes*, 407–39, odd pages only.

25. Proust means the two disguised angels to whom Lot offered hospitality (Gen. 19:1) as well as the two angels at the tomb of the risen Christ in John's account of the Resurrection (John 20:10).

26. For the claim for this connection see Julia Kristeva, *Le temps sensible: Proust et l'expérience littéraire* (Paris: Gallimard, 1994), 26.

27. See Jacobus de Voraigne, "Saint Mary Magdalen," in *The Golden Legend*, 2 vols., trans. William Granger Ryan (Princeton, N.J.: Princeton University Press, 1993), 1: 374–83; Marina Warner, *Alone of All Her Sex: The Myth and the Cult of the Virgin Mary* (New York: Vintage; Random House, 1983); Susan Haskins, *Mary Magdalen: Myth and Metaphor* (London: HarperCollins, 1993); Laurence Gardner, *Bloodline of the Holy Grail: The Hidden Lineage of Jesus Revealed* (New York: Barnes and Noble, 1997), esp. 66–73, 100–142; Margaret Starbird, *The Woman with the Alabaster Jar: Mary Magdalen and the Holy Grail* (Santa Fe, N.M.: Bear, 1993), esp. 26, 49–52, 60–62; Michael Baigent, Richard Keigh, and Henry Lincoln, *Holy Blood, Holy Grail* (New York: Dell, 1983), 330–47; and Ean Begg, *The Cult of the Black Virgin* (London: Penguin, 1996), 93–99. Linda Georgiana and Matthew Miller have helped me with these references, for which I thank them.

28. G. W. F. Hegel, "The Spirit of Christianity and Its Fate," in *Early Theological Writings*, trans. T. M. Knox (Philadelphia: University of Pennsylvania Press, 1971), 242–44.

Coda

1. Paul de Man, *Allegories of Reading* (New Haven, Conn.: Yale University Press, 1979), 77.

Index

À la recherche de l'unité perdue: Genre and Narrative in Proust (Calkins), 231n15

À la recherche du temps perdu (Proust), ix, 109–10, 155–56, 177–213, 214–15; characters: Albertine, 137, 181, 184, 202, 232n24; Andrée, 202; Bergotte, 177–78; Françoise, 179–85, 194; Gilberte, 201–2; Jupien, 180; Marcel, 179–213, 214; Marcel's grandmother, 185–98; Odette de Crécy, 181; Rachel, 181–82, 198–213, 214; Swann, Charles, 181

Abrams, Meyer, 36

Althusser, Louis, 184, 229n7a

American Heritage Dictionary, 99

"Anecdote of the Jar" (Stevens), 104–5

Apollo, 201

Arabian Nights, The, 187

Ariel, in *The Tempest*, 35

Aristotle, 79, 142

Arndt, David, 128, 226n27

Austin, J. L., ix, 1, 2–5, 6–62, 64, 66–67, 76, 79–81, 84, 86–91, 92, 95, 96, 97–99, 100, 102, 105, 110, 112, 116, 122, 125–26, 127, 128, 129, 131, 132, 133–34, 137, 140, 141, 148, 166–67, 169–76, 182, 183, 207, 214–15, 220n3, 221n9, 227n5; *How to Do Things with Words*, ix, 3–5, 6–62, 66, 68, 76, 102, 116, 125–26, 140, 169, 170, 172–73, 174; "Other Minds," ix, 169, 169, 170, 171, 173–76; "Performative Utterances," 11–12, 16, 19–20, 22, 58, 67, 220n3, 221n9; *Philosophical Papers*, 11; "Plea for Excuses, A," 41, 44, 54–55, 56, 132, 169–70; "Pretending," ix, 137, 169, 170, 171–72

Balzac, Honoré de, 194

Barthes, Roland, 178

Bataille, Georges, 178

Baudelaire, Charles, 159

Beardsley, Monroe C., 105–6

Beckett, Samuel, 178

Bedford, Errol, 170

Benjamin, Walter, 179

Beyond the Pleasure Principle (Freud), 97

Bibesco, Antoine, 230n13
Black Holes (Miller), 178
Blanchot, Maurice, 125, 178
Bloom, Harold, 42
Bloom, Leopold, in *Ulysses*, 197
Blue and Brown Books
    (Wittgenstein), ix, 160–68
Boigne, Mme de, 230n8
"Bound to Be Bad: True Crime
    Meets How-To" (Stossel), 220–
    21n1
Brogni, Cardinal de, in *La juive*,
    206–7

*Calendar of State Papers Relating to
    Scotland*, 158–59
Calkins, Mark, 198
Can You Forgive Her? (Trollope), 1
Carroll, Lewis, 27, 40
Cartesian Meditations (Husserl),
    135–36, 159, 183
Cavell, Stanley, 62
Celan, Paul, 85
Cervantes, Miguel de, 25
Charlus, Baron de, 181, 231n17
Chaucer, Geoffrey, 202
Clinton, Bill, 1
"Commentary of the Spiritual
    Exercises of St. Ignatius Loyola"
    (Hopkins), 161, 164–65
Confessions (Rousseau), 145–46
Conrad, Joseph, 179
"Counterfeit Money" (Baudelaire),
    159
Critique of Judgment (Kant), 26,
    154, 222n12

Danaids, 189
De Man, Paul, ix, 1, 2, 26, 32, 42,
    46, 61–62, 118, 140–54, 174, 177,
    179, 180, 184, 214–15, 222n12,
    229n7; *Allegories of Reading*, 140;

"Anthropomorphism and Trope
    in the Lyric," 152; "Autobiog-
    raphy as De-Facement," 152;
    "Concept of Irony, The," 42, 46,
    145; "Excuses (*Confessions*),"
    145–46; "Hegel on the Sublime,"
    152; "Kant and Schiller," 154,
    222n12; "Pascal's Allegory of
    Persuasion," 145, 150; "Promises
    (*Social Contract*)," 145, 153;
    "Reading (Proust)," 177; "Reply
    to Raymond Geuss," 149;
    "Resistance to Theory, The,"
    149–50, 229n7; "Rhetoric of
    Persuasion (Nietzsche)," 140,
    141–45, 148; "Rhetoric of Tropes
    (Nietzsche)," 143; "Shelley
    Disfigured," 142, 145, 147–49,
    152, 153
Declaration of Independence, The,
    112–28, 175
"Declaration of Independence,
    The," in *Ground and Abyss: The
    Question of* Poiesis *in Heidegger,
    Arendt, Foucault, and Stevens*
    (Arndt), 226n27
Declaration of the Rights of Man,
    113, 117
Dedalus, Stephen, in *Ulysses*, 204
Deleuze, Gilles, 178
Derrida, Jacques, ix, 1, 2, 29, 37, 43,
    59, 62, 63–139, 140, 155–60, 163,
    166, 168–9, 171, 177, 179, 183, 193,
    203, 214–15, 222–23n20, 223n2;
    "Afterword: Toward an Ethic of
    Discussion," 65, 69, 76–77, 77–
    78, 92, 129, 129–31; "Avances,"
    64, 223n2; "Comme si c'était
    possible," 168–70; "Declarations
    of Independence," 112–28;
    Dissemination, 123; "Envois,"
    155–58; "Freud and the Scene

of Writing," 94; *Glas*, 62; "Je
t'aime," 134–39, 159–60, 166,
167, 172, 173, 176, 182, 183;
Limited Inc, ix, 29, 63, 65–111,
128–34, 136, 140; "Limited Inc
a b c... ," 63, 69–70, 75, 88, 89,
94, 95, 107, 108; "Logique de la
vivante," 113–14; *On the Name*,
160; *Parages*, 125; *Passions*, 160;
Politics of Friendship, 168; *The
Post Card*, 92; "Psyche: The
Invention of the Other," 123,
140, 168; "Sauf le nom (Post-
Scriptum)," 160; "Signature
Event Context" (*Sec*)," 63, 66,
68, 69, 73, 74, 75, 76, 82–83,
86–87, 89, 90–91, 95, 98, 104,
105, 107, 111, 222–23n20; *Specters of Marx*, 64; "Telepathy,"
158
Descartes, René, 29, 60, 61, 87–88,
97–98
Descombes, Vincent, 179
"Dialogue on Poetry" (Schlegel),
222n17
Dickens, Charles, 18, 78, 107, 194
"Ding, Das" (Heidegger), 8
Donne, John, 25, 39, 40, 50
Dreyfus, Alfred, 203, 207

Ecce Homo (Nietzsche), 117
Eddy, Mary Baker, 187
Eleazar, in *La juive*, 206
Eliot, George, 10–11
Eliot, T. S., 35, 40, 49
Euripides, 25, 30–31, 35, 40, 51
*Expression and Meaning: Studies in
the Theory of Speech Acts* (Searle),
222n19

"Fable" (Ponge), 123–24
Ferdinand, in *The Tempest*, 35

Fernandez, Ramon, 178
Figaro, Le, 186, 189, 190
Fors Clavigera (Ruskin), 210
Franklin, Benjamin, 122
Franklin's Tale, The (Chaucer),
202
French lieutenant, in *Lord Jim*,
179
Freud, Sigmund, 29, 94, 224n13
Furies, 189

Genesis, 45, 182, 203, 232n25
Genette, Gérard, 179
Geuss, Raymond, 149
Gide, André, 138
Girard, René, 178–79
Golden Bowl, The (James), 9–11
*Golden Legend, The: Readings on the
Saints* (*Legenda Aurea*, Voraigne),
211
Graff, Gerald, 65, 129
Gray, John, in *Can You Forgive
Her?*, 1
Great Expectations (Dickens), 18

Halévy, Joseph, 205–7, 212–13
Hardy, Thomas, 79, 194
Headstone, Bradley, in *Our Mutual
Friend*, 158
Hegel, G. W. F., 60, 149, 212
Heidegger, Martin, 8, 66, 109, 130,
152–53
Hexam, Lizzie, in *Our Mutual
Friend*, 158
Hippolytus (Euripides), 30–31, 51
Hippolytus, in *Hippolytus*, 30–31,
33, 51
Hopkins, Gerard Manley, 161–62,
164–65
Hopkins, Samuel, 119–20
Husserl, Edmund, 66, 87–88,
92–93, 135–36, 159, 163, 183, 184

"Ideology and Ideological State Apparatuses (Notes Towards an Investigation)" (Althusser), 229n7
Illuminations (Benjamin), 179
"In the Cage" (James), 190
"Intentional Fallacy, The" (Wimsatt and Beardsley), 105–6

Jacob, in Genesis, 203–4
James, Henry, ix, 9–11, 17, 47, 190
James, William, 164, 166
Jefferson, Thomas, 113, 120, 121–23, 127
Jespersen, Otto, 52
Jesus, 30–31, 204, 209–12, 232n25
John, 209–11, 232n25
Jokes and Their Relation to the Unconscious (*Der Witz und Seine Beziehung zum Unbewussten*, Freud), 224n
Joseph, in Genesis, 204–5
Joseph, in the Gospels, 204
Joyce, James, 188, 197, 204, 230n11
Juive, La (Halévy), 205–7, 212–13
Julie (Rousseau), 151, 180

Kant, Immanuel, 25, 27, 129, 129–30, 132, 154
Kelly, Walt, 52
King Lear (Shakespeare), 8–9
Kittler, Friedrich, 156
Kleist, Heinrich von, 147
Kristeva, Julia, 179

Laban, in Genesis, 203–4
Leah, in Genesis, 203–4
Lear, King, in *King Lear*, 8
"Logical Status of Fictional Discourse, The" (Searle), 222n18
Lord Jim (Conrad), 179
Lot, in Genesis, 203, 232n25

Lot's wife, in Genesis, 203, 212

"Madness of the Day, The" (Blanchot), 125
Mallarmé, Stéphane, 123
Margel, Serge, 64
"Martinus Scriblerus peri bathous: Or the Art of Sinking in Poetry" (Pope), 221n
Marvell, Andrew, 2
Mary, 204
Mary Magdalen, 208–12
Mary Queen of Scots, 158–59
Matthew, 30–31
Meditations (Descartes), 97–98
Merchant of Venice, The (Shakespeare), 35
Middlemarch (Eliot), 10–11
"Mimique" (Mallarmé), 123

Nietzsche, Friedrich, 37, 66, 81, 86, 89, 112, 117, 118, 141–45, 175
Nixon, Richard, 43
Nourrit, Adolphe, 206–7

Odyssey, The (Homer), 230n8
"On Truth and Lie in an Extra-Moral Sense" ("Über Wahrheit und Lüge im aussermoralische Sinn," Nietzsche), 142–43
Orpheus, 196, 203
Othello (Shakespeare), 35, 48
Other Minds (Wisdom), 170
Our Mutual Friend (Dickens), 158
Oxford English Dictionary, 21

Palliser, Plantagenet, in *Can You Forgive Her?*, 1
Petit Robert, 100–1
Petrey, Sandy, 219n1
Phaedrus (Plato), 67, 106–7

Philosophical Investigations (Wittgenstein), 160, 165

Pickwick Papers (Dickens), 107

Pip, in *Great Expectations*, 18

Plato, 18–19, 37, 43, 67, 106–7

Pocket, Herbert, in *Great Expectations*, 18

Ponge, Francis, 123–24

Pope, Alexander, 221n

Poulet, Georges, 178

Proceedings of the Aristotlean Society, 170

Protagoras (Plato), 19

Proust, Marcel, ix, 109–10, 137, 138, 155–56, 161, 163, 169, 177–213, 229–30n8, 230–31n13, 231n17, 231n20, 232n24, 232n25; *À la recherche du temps perdu*, ix, 109–10, 155–56, 177–213, 214–15; "The Guermantes Way," 179–213; *Jean Santeuil*, 188; "Journées de lecture," 186, 192, 229–30n8; "La prisonnière," 177, 178. *See also À la recherche du temps perdu*, characters

Rachel (Elisa Félix, 1820–1858), French actress, 205, 231n20

Rachel, in Genesis, 203–5, 212

Rachel, in *La juive*, 205–7, 213

"Reiterating the Differences: A Reply to Derrida" (Searle), 68, 69–77

Remarks on the Philosophy of Psychology (Wittgenstein), 160

Rêveries (Rousseau), 147

Richard, Jean-Pierre, 179

Rickels, Laurence, 156, 187–88

Ronell, Avital, 156

Rousseau, Jean-Jacques, 52, 145–46, 151, 153, 180

Ruskin, John, 210

Scheherazade, in *Arabian Nights*, 198

Schlegel, Friedrich, 42, 147–48, 222n17

Scribe, Eugène, 205–7

Searle, John R., 22, 43, 66, 68, 69–77, 79–81, 86–88, 92, 93, 95, 96, 97–99, 100–3, 107, 108–111, 129, 131, 132, 133, 134, 140, 222n18, 222n19

Sévigné, Madame de, 182

Shakespeare, William, 25, 35, 40, 50, 171

Shattuck, Roger, 113, 115, 116

Shelley, Percy Bysshe, 147–49

Social Contract (Rousseau), 151, 153

Socrates, 4, 19, 106–7

"Sonnets of desolation, the" (Hopkins), 162

Speech Acts and Literary Theory (Petrey), 219

Speech Acts: An Essay in the Philosophy of Language (Searle), 222n19

"Spirit of Christianity and Its Fate, The" (Hegel), 211–12

Stendhal (Henri Beyle), 138

Stevens, Wallace, 104–5

Stossel, Scott, 220–21n1

Telephone Book, The (Ronell), 156

Tempest, The (Shakespeare), 35

Tess of the d'Urbervilles, in *Tess of the d'Urbervilles*, 79

Thomas Didymus, in John, 210–11

Through the Looking Glass (Carroll), 37

Tombeau du dieu artisan, Le (Margel), 64

Triumph of Life, The (Shelley), 147–49, 150, 153

Trollope, Anthony, 1, 47, 194

Ulysses (Joyce), 188, 197, 204, 230n11

Vavasor, Alice, in *Can You Forgive Her?*, 1
Vermeer, Jan, 177–78
View of Delft (Vermeer), 177–78
Voltaire, F. M. A. de, 25
Voraigne, Jacobus de, 211

Washington, George, 124
Wasteland, The (Eliot), 35
Weber, Samuel, 83, 91

Weller, Sam, in *Pickwick Papers*, 107
White, Nicholas, 158–59
Whitman, Walt, 25, 39, 40
Will to Power, The (*Der Wille zur Macht*, Nietzsche), 141–44
Wimsatt, W. K, Jr., 105–6
Wisdom, John, 170
Wittgenstein, Ludwig, ix, 137, 160–68, 169, 182
"Wreck of the Deutschland, The" (Hopkins), 162

M E R I D I A N

Crossing Aesthetics

J. Hillis Miller, *Speech Acts in Literature*

Maurice Blanchot, *Faux Pas*

Jean-Luc Nancy, *Being Singular Plural*

Maurice Blanchot / Jacques Derrida, *The Instant of My Death / Demeure: Fiction and Testimony*

Niklas Luhmann, *The Social System of Art*

Emmanual Levinas, *God, Death, and Time*

Ernst Bloch, *The Spirit of Utopia*

Giorgio Agamben, *Potentialities: Collected Essays*

Ellen S. Burt, *Poetry's Appeal: Nineteenth-Century French Lyric and the Political Space*

Jacques Derrida, *Adieu to Emmanuel Levinas*

Werner Hamacher, *Premises: Essays on Philosophy and Literature from Kant to Celan*

Aris Fioretos, *The Gray Book*

Deborah Esch, *In the Event: Reading Journalism, Reading Theory*

Winfried Menninghaus, *In Praise of Nonsense: Kant and Bluebeard*

Giorgio Agamben, *The Man Without Content*

Giorgio Agamben, *The End of the Poem: Studies in Poetics*

Theodor W. Adorno, *Sound Figures*

Louis Marin, *Sublime Poussin*

Philippe Lacoue-Labarthe, *Poetry as Experience*

Jacques Derrida, *Resistances of Psychoanalysis*

Ernst Bloch, *Literary Essays*

Marc Froment-Meurice, *That Is to Say: Heidegger's Poetics*

Francis Ponge, *Soap*

Phillipe Lacoue-Labarthe, *Typography: Mimesis, Philosophy, Politics*

Giorgio Agamben, *Homo Sacer: Sovereign Power and Bare Life*

Emmanuel Levinas, *Of God Who Comes to Mind*

Bernard Stiegler, *Technics and Time, 1: The Fault of Epimetheus*

Werner Hamacher, *pleroma—Reading in Hegel*

Serge Leclaire, *Psychoanalyzing*

Serge Leclaire, *A Child Is Being Killed*

Sigmund Freud, *Writings on Art and Literature*

Cornelius Castoriadis, *World in Fragments: Writings on Politics, Society, Psychoanalysis, and the Imagination*

Thomas Keenan, *Fables of Responsibility: Aberrations and Predicaments in Ethics and Politics*

Emmanuel Levinas, *Proper Names*

Alexander García Düttmann, *At Odds with AIDS: Thinking and Talking About a Virus*

Maurice Blanchot, *Friendship*

Jean-Luc Nancy, *The Muses*

Massimo Cacciari, *Posthumous People: Vienna at the Turning Point*

David E. Wellbery, *The Specular Moment: Goethe's Early Lyric and the Beginnings of Romanticism*

Edmond Jabès, *The Little Book of Unsuspected Subversion*

Hans-Jost Frey, *Studies in Poetic Discourse: Mallarmé, Baudelaire, Rimbaud, Hölderlin*

Pierre Bourdieu, *The Rules of Art: Genesis and Structure of the Literary Field*

Nicolas Abraham, *Rhythms: On the Work, Translation, and Psychoanalysis*

Jacques Derrida, *On the Name*

David Wills, *Prosthesis*

Maurice Blanchot, *The Work of Fire*

Jacques Derrida, *Points ... : Interviews, 1974–1994*

J. Hillis Miller, *Topographies*

Philippe Lacoue-Labarthe, *Musica Ficta (Figures of Wagner)*

Jacques Derrida, *Aporias*

Emmanuel Levinas, *Outside the Subject*

Jean-François Lyotard, *Lessons on the Analytic Sublime*

Peter Fenves, *"Chatter": Language and History in Kierkegaard*

Jean-Luc Nancy, *The Experience of Freedom*

Jean-Joseph Goux, *Oedipus, Philosopher*

Haun Saussy, *The Problem of a Chinese Aesthetic*

Jean-Luc Nancy, *The Birth to Presence*